Law and Philosophy Library

Volume 141

The Law and Philosophy Library, which has been in existence since 1985, aims to publish cutting edge works in the philosophy of law, and has a special history of publishing books that focus on legal reasoning and argumentation, including those that may involve somewhat formal methodologies. The series has published numerous important books on law and logic, law and artificial intelligence, law and language, and law and rhetoric. While continuing to stress these areas, the series has more recently expanded to include books on the intersection between law and the Continental philosophical tradition, consistent with the traditional openness of the series to books in the Continental jurisprudential tradition. The series is proud of the geographic diversity of its authors, and many have come from Latin America, Spain, Italy, the Netherlands, Germany, and Eastern Europe, as well, more obviously for an English-language series, from the United Kingdom, the United States, Australia and Canada.

Szymon Mazurkiewicz

Grounding Human Rights in Human Nature

Springer

Szymon Mazurkiewicz
Jagiellonian University
Krakow, Poland

ISSN 1572-4395 ISSN 2215-0315 (electronic)
Law and Philosophy Library
ISBN 978-3-031-30733-1 ISBN 978-3-031-30734-8 (eBook)
https://doi.org/10.1007/978-3-031-30734-8

This Springer imprint is published by the registered company Springer Nature Switzerland AG
The registered company address is: Gewerbestrasse 11, 6330 Cham, Switzerland

Contents

Chapter 1
Introduction

Why do we have human rights? This is a question that I try to answer in this book.[1] And as human rights are regarded to have foundations in human dignity I try to answer the question "why do we have human dignity" as well. I propose to take a look at these questions with the help of relevant natural sciences, especially evolutionary psychology and propose a naturalised view on the question on the foundations of human rights and human dignity. So, I claim that human rights and human dignity are grounded in human nature. But is what I propose a natural law theory? And how do I manage with the derivation of normative entities like human rights and human dignity from descriptive one like human nature (known as "is"-"ought" problem or Hume's Guillotine)? I think that making use of the relation of metaphysical grounding, widely discussed in the contemporary analytic metaphysics, can help with this problematics and shed light on how we can think about human rights and their foundations through lenses of very recent scientific and philosophical claims.

There can be many answers to the question of why (and how) human rights exist depending on the approach that one adopts. Many people, especially lawyers, would say that human rights hold in virtue of human dignity since such foundation is provided by numerous international and domestic legal documents. Other people might claim that human rights are simply primitive and independent of legal treaties.

[1] The author received funds within the financing of a doctoral scholarship from the National Science Centre, Poland for the Etiuda grant project "Explanation of human rights in light of contemporary analytic metaphysics", number 2019/32/T/HS5/00203.

The work is also a fruit of working on the Preludium grant project "Philosophy of human rights in light of contemporary analytic metaphysics" financed by the National Science Centre, Poland, number 2017/27/N/HS5/00856.

The book is based on my PhD thesis defended with distinction at the Jagiellonian University, Krakow. I would like to thank all the people who read the manuscript, especially my supervisor Adam Dyrda, auxiliary supervisor Wojciech Ciszewski and my first advisor Tomasz Gizbert-Studnicki—their help was enormous and I am very grateful for their time and advice, I also thank two reviewers of the dissertation—Marek Piechowiak and Pavel Ondrejek as well as an anonymous reviewer of the publisher manuscript.

S. Mazurkiewicz, *Grounding Human Rights in Human Nature*, Law and Philosophy Library 141, https://doi.org/10.1007/978-3-031-30734-8_1

Perhaps, for an ordinary man or a legal practitioner such answers are sufficient. However, a legal philosopher can pose further questions: "what actually human dignity is?", "what the foundation of human dignity is?" as well as what "in virtue of" means. Answers to such questions must be given by the philosophy of law or philosophy in general. The aim of this dissertation is to answer such questions. In due course, I will provide a new way of thinking about the foundations of human rights and explaining their existence.

This new approach to the philosophy of human rights is based on the contemporary analytic metaphysics. There are two broad conceptions within contemporary analytic metaphysics that I will utilise. First, I will treat entities researched by the philosophy of human rights (human rights, human dignity, human nature) not as concepts but as metaphysical entities and I will attempt to discover the metaphysical relations holding between them. This can be labelled as an exercise in this part of the analytic metaphysics that aims to explore and explain relations holding between different facts or entities. Let me here call this part of metaphysics "relational metaphysics". An important domain of this part of metaphysics is called "theory of grounding", yet I do not focus in this work only on the relation of grounding. Note that in this work I will not engage in the wholehearted, full-fledged metaphysical inquiry, but rather I will restrict myself to its part, developed mostly in the last two or three decades, that is occupied with the explanatory relations between various entities (relational metaphysics). Second, my aim is to naturalise the question on the foundations of human rights. This naturalisation will involve an attempt to discover natural facts (descriptive facts discovered by natural, empirical sciences) that may constitute the foundations of human rights. The project of naturalisation, as understood here, most generally aims to seek for relevant natural facts in philosophical inquiry and to base philosophical conceptions on them rather than on armchair conceptual investigations. To sum up, my inquiry into the foundations of human rights will be based on two broad theoretical conceptions: relational metaphysics and naturalisation project.

Contemporary philosophy of human rights almost entirely engages ethical methods of answering the question of the foundations of human rights. Moreover, the main focus of the analysis are concepts like "human rights" or "human dignity". Therefore, the justification of human rights takes a form of providing a warrant for the premises that themselves justify a conclusion about (the concepts of) "human rights" or "human dignity". However, the core of theoretical inquiry on the foundations of human rights is not merely a semantic analysis of these premises, but rather a more comprehensive inquiry into the real foundations of human rights understood as entities, and not only as concepts. This is why the "metaphysical turn" is needed in the philosophy of human rights.

Moreover, I believe that many contemporary ways of justification of human rights involve significant problems. One can mention, for instance, Christian, especially Catholic thought wherein every human possesses human rights due to human dignity, which in the most general terms is to be characterised as an inherent worth or value of every human being (since every human being is created as an image of God (*Imago Dei*). In the contemporary Anglo-Saxon philosophy, there is also a highly influential approach that is based on the Kantian notion of human dignity and analytic, descriptive notion of a person. According to this contemporary analytic-Kantian approach, human rights protect our personhood, which is defined as normative autonomy; thus we have human rights thanks to our normative agency.[2] However, if one does not believe in God, reference to human being as *Imago Dei* is implausible. If one does not support the western liberal point of view, but rather a more collective account of social life, human rights understood as the necessary protection of normative autonomy become unconvincing. And since human rights are considered universal, their justification must be universally accepted as well. My approach based on natural facts and metaphysical relations is designed to avoid these kinds of problems: it is supposed to be as much universally acceptable and independent of one's world-view as possible.

My argumentative strategy is as follows. My main aim is to apply contemporary analytic metaphysics to the explanation of the foundations of human rights. I will assume that the foundation of human rights is constituted by, quite uncontroversially, human dignity, as it is ascertained by many international and domestic legal documents. Then, I will argue that human dignity is rooted in human nature conceived in terms of evolutionary biology and evolutionary psychology. I will take advantage of the analytic philosophical project of naturalisation in order to establish the fundament of human dignity, which is a *normative* entity. My belief is that human dignity has foundations in human nature conceived of as a natural, descriptive fact. I think that there is a relation of ontological dependence between human rights and human dignity as well as between human dignity and human nature. I wish to find the most precise and adequate metaphysical relation expressing these ontological dependencies. Thus, in due course, I will test the relations of reduction, supervenience and metaphysical grounding, and eventually argue that that the ontological dependence is best understood in terms of metaphysical grounding.

There are several reasons to undertake such a method of theorising about the foundations of human rights. First, the contemporary philosophy of human rights rarely applies investigations from other fields. A notable exception is the part of the philosophy of human rights that widely refers to considerations of ethics and political philosophy.[3] In particular, contemporary philosophy of human rights often makes use of:

– the Kantian notion of human dignity—its application in contemporary analytic ethics and political philosophy leads to the concept of normative autonomy or normative agency;
– the analytic notion of "person"; to a less extent Christian thoughts on human dignity and Christian personalism;

[2] Griffin (2008), p. 33.

[3] Griffin (2008) and Nussbaum (2000, 2006, 2011).

- general conceptual frameworks characteristic of and developed within most normative disciplines, like the Hofheldian analysis of the deontic relations between various types of legal rights.

One part of the current philosophy of human rights, the so-called political approach,[4] takes advantage of the ideas developed in theories of international relations and international politics. Marek Piechowiak employs the conceptual framework of classical philosophy in his attempt to establish a solid fundament for human rights.[5] However, to my best knowledge, other main works on the foundations of human rights do not refer to other disciplines, except ethics and political philosophy.[6] Such a lack of reference to other fields of knowledge makes the contemporary philosophy of human rights quite a parochial discipline. By a parochial discipline I mean a field closed to knowledge from other disciplines and conducted on the basis of its own methods, which are not strongly related to methods of other, general or more fundamental disciplines. Imagine for instance a scenario where the empirical sciences discover that our basic, innate, evolutionary shaped structure of thinking and behaving is pessimistic or evil from the moral point of view. What would be then the sense of protecting such morally wrong humans by invoking human rights? The justification of human rights could, of course, be developed from many other perspectives. However, the knowledge about human basic, innate structure of thinking and behaving being pessimistic or evil still would be highly relevant for such other inquiries on the foundations of human rights. One cannot ignore the nature of the subject while discussing the rights (and respectively obligations) the subject is supposed to have.

The requirement of escaping parochialism, which is characteristic of major parts of the contemporary philosophy of human rights leads to the second reason for undertaking the approach proposed in this work. The parochial character of the ongoing enterprise is especially striking when the current developments of analytic metaphysics are juxtaposed and compared. Contemporary analytic metaphysics has developed useful tools for thinking about the structure of the world that can be highly useful for the philosophy of human rights: the naturalisation project and the relational metaphysics. As for naturalisation: if the basic furniture of the world consists of natural facts, then either all other spheres, like mental or normative, are reduced to natural facts (ontological naturalism), or all philosophical inquiry should start from relevant natural facts (methodological naturalism).[7] The same must apply to the philosophy of human rights. The dominant approach to the philosophy of human rights is in fact called the "naturalistic approach" but, as I will demonstrate, it has nothing to do with naturalism in its general philosophical meaning. As for relational metaphysics (theory of grounding): if any higher level facts hold in virtue of lower

[4] Rawls (1999), Pogge (2002), Beitz (2009) and Raz (2010, 2015).

[5] Piechowiak (1999, 2019).

[6] Griffin (2008), Tasioulas (2011, 2013, 2015), Nussbaum (2000, 2006, 2011), cf. Gardner (2008).

[7] Leiter and Etchemendy (2017), Nolan (2017) and Papineau (2020).

level facts, and the facts on the lower level explain the existence of the facts on the higher level, and, additionally, human rights and human dignity are real entities (not fictional ones, for example), then the analogous relation applies to them: human rights and human dignity must possess a certain kind of a natural, descriptive fundament (metaphysical characteristics) as well. Moreover, any serious conceptual study of human rights must define the relation between human rights and their foundations in a clear and precise way. Regretfully, the contemporary philosophy of human rights is unable to present the actual relation between human rights and their foundation, no matter what is regarded as this foundation by various theorists. By taking into account the naturalisation project altogether with the relational metaphysics and applying it to considerations on metaethical dimension we reach the following conditional result. If normative entities are so-and-so due to certain underlying natural facts, the same must apply to normative entities like human rights and human dignity.

This consideration leads us immediately to the third reason for seeking for a new approach to the foundations of human rights. The current rapid development of empirical science (i.a. neuroscience, evolutionary biology, evolutionary psychology) provides very interesting and scientifically founded claims concerning the basics of human functioning that are relevant for the inquiry on why we have human rights and on what makes us have (human) dignity. However, the contemporary way of philosophising about human rights is of an extremely rationalist character, which I understand as reliance on conceptual analysis of concepts and ideas that are arbitrarily and thoroughly detached from empirical findings.[8] Philosophers of human rights debate mostly about the necessary conditions for having human rights, by means of exercising conceptual analyses of a rather traditional (i.a. decompositional) kind, and in such a way they try to find the foundations of human rights.[9] There is hardly any place for empirical investigation, even though it may prove useful in seeking the fundament of human rights. Empirically oriented ways of thinking possess one significant advantage over a purely conceptual, rationalist mode of research, namely, they are scientifically legitimate and have clear conditions of falsification. Therefore, I believe that the application of certain results of evolutionary psychology supplemented by adopting the evolutionary way of thinking about human nature, will help justify the claim that human nature (defined in terms of evolutionary psychology) constitutes the foundation of human dignity. I will argue that the relation between human rights, human dignity and human nature is best understood as the relation of metaphysical grounding. Furthermore, due to the transitive character of the relation of metaphysical grounding, ultimately, human nature constitutes the foundation of human rights. The reference to human nature, as defined in terms of empirical science, will amount to the aforementioned naturalisation of the philosophy of human rights.

[8] Rosen (2012, 2013), p. 146; Hill (2013), p. 314.

[9] One notable exception is John Mikhail's work (2012).

Fourth, some major approaches in the philosophy of human rights, like James Griffin's approach,[10] reveal significant discrepancies between the content and scope of human rights discussed in light of certain philosophical assumptions, and the content and scope of human rights perceived according to the international and domestic human rights law. Of course, human rights described in legal documents can be subjected to philosophical critique and revealed not be the human rights as perceived from the philosophical, moral perspective. However, if some central human rights from legal perspective are claimed not to be genuine human rights under one's philosophical notion, I believe that it means that one's theory of human rights is falsified, rather than that these rights are proved not to be human rights. I believe that the burden of justification lies on the one who argues that a given human right ascertained by international law is not actually a human right from the "true", moral perspective. In my view, strong arguments must be provided in order to justify this claim. My approach does not involve such problems as it is referring to the legal understanding of human rights. An important reason for focusing on such legal understanding is the following. It is often claimed that the current (moral) theory of human rights leads to the inflation of human rights: simply every moral, political or social right or claim is labelled as a "human right".[11] Somewhat paradoxically, such inflation leads further to the erosion of the firm philosophical grounds of human rights and the social belief in them. This problem holds due to the imprecise tools of demarcation applied to distinguish between what is and what is not a human right. I think that starting from human rights as understood in international law will help to address this problem.

Fifth, the serious objection to the contemporary dominant way of justifying human rights and, in its stronger form, to human rights themselves is the objection of Western ethnocentrism.[12] The objection of Western ethnocentrism is that human rights are connected mainly with Western world-view. Other cultures may not and, as a matter of fact, quite often do not share the values that ground acceptance for human rights in Western world. For adherents of this objection, human rights are analysed and justified in terms of western values like normative agency, which are not commonly shared among different cultures all over the world.[13] The weak version of the Western ethnocentrism objection holds that the contemporary philosophical way of thinking about human rights assumes or implies a highly individualistic, or even atomistic, notion of the human being which is not shared world-wide. This is visible especially in case of Eastern cultures that put much more emphasis on collective values like social harmony. In turn, the strong version of the objection claims that human rights are the product of Western societies and as such, are not universal.[14] Some thinkers even regard human rights as just another example

[10]Griffin (2008).

[11]Cruft et al. (2015); Tasioulas (2015); Buchanan (2015), p. 245; Luban (2015), p. 264.

[12]Griffin (2008) and Cruft et al. (2015).

[13]American Anthropological Association (1947).

[14]cf. Donnelly (1984); Shestack (1998) who discuss this objection without adhering to it.

of western imperialism, this time in a politically-moral sphere.[15] I believe that my approach will provide additional arguments against the objection of Western ethnocentrism. Instead of making use of concepts based on individualistic notion of person, I will refer to the scientifically founded conception of human nature. It will turn out that the proposed concept of human nature, defined by reference to certain results of evolutionary psychology, is highly consistent with more collective views on human beings and human society, which, in turn, are shared by many non-Western cultures, especially Asian cultures.

To conclude, the reference to evolutionary science squares well with the business of explaining or justifying human rights by means of contemporary analytic metaphysics, for it helps to identify the basic metaphysical relata. I must also confess that my account has been encouraged by philosophers like John Mihkail and Stephen P. Marks who deeply regret the lack of use of scientific knowledge in the exploration of the foundations of human rights. They underlie that the late eighteenth century Enlightenment movement of human rights, which introduced the first grounds for the strong social belief in human rights, firmly applied the empirical sciences of that time. This movement developed the idea of human rights in tight connection with other fields of knowledge. Unfortunately, the contemporary method of doing philosophy of human rights is far from taking into account the relevant scientific knowledge of today's natural sciences, despite the significant development of natural sciences that occurred since the late eighteenth century.[16]

Even though the concept of human rights has a history dating back to the late eighteenth century[17] the revival of human rights occurred in 1948 (Universal Declaration of Human Rights, henceforth UDHR), it is often claimed that contemporary theoretical thought on human rights has been developing since not earlier than 1970s. Indeed, it was in 1970s when the political movement of human rights emerged.[18] Therefore, the philosophy of human rights seems to be a relatively young discipline. As it is often the case with youngsters, manifold discursive (research) procedures have to be conducted in order to clarify the debated issues and to explain the existence of human rights in a universally acceptable way.

One shall note also the difference between justification and explanation. Whether this work contributes to both or only to one of them in the described content will be examined in Sect. 7.1. Here, I will restrict myself to a few remarks. Justification

---

[15] Howard (1993, 1995).

[16] Mikhail (2012) and Marks (2013).

[17] Virginia Declaration of Rights (1776); Declaration of Human the Rights of Man and of the Citizen (1789). One can argue that modern human rights are a secularised version of middle ages and early modern natural rights, or try to find concepts corresponding with our notion of human rights and human dignity in even earlier thought (Piechowiak 1999). However, it is only in the late eighteenth century and especially after World War 2 when the concept of human rights gain so much public attention, and, most importantly, legal recognition. Incidentally, the disappearance of the concept of human rights in the nineteenth and early twentieth century is intriguing. It lies however beyond the scope of this work.

[18] Moyn (2010) and Eckel and Moyn (2014).

consists of providing reasons why a given entity is of a certain moral (or otherwise normative) characteristic.[19] In turn, explanation involves answering why something exists. For instance, we may justify the fact that X torturing Y is wrong by giving certain reasons, e.g. that torture violates someone's autonomy or that it causes pain. In turn, the explanation of why it happened will consist of trying to understand why this act of torture occurred (like the fact that X believed Y had a piece of important information or that X found causing pain to be enjoyable). It seems that explanation has more to do with causality and related notions, while justification is associated rather with a rational, non-empirical inquiry. However, consider the explanation of something that is of a positive characteristic (or simply is good), e.g. the explanation of human rights. I believe that the explanation of the existence of human rights simultaneously involves the justification of them. If I claim that human rights exist because of human dignity that we all possess (explanation), it means that the fact that we all have human dignity is the reason for us having human rights (justification). Therefore, anticipating the examination of those concepts in Sect. 7.1, I will use both concepts interchangeably.

There are two main hypotheses of my project. The first one is that the basis of human dignity, which is the foundation of human rights, is constituted by human nature understood in terms of evolutionary psychology. The second one refers to the determination of the exact character of the explanatory or justificatory relations holding between human rights, human dignity and human nature. This second hypothesis is that these relations cannot be qualified as reduction due to the impossibility of reducing human rights to human dignity and human dignity to human nature. Furthermore, even though the relation of supervenience technically holds between debated entities, it is not sufficient to properly express and explain the ontological dependence between human rights, human dignity and human nature. Thus, I claim that the explanatory or justificatory relation holding between human rights, human dignity and human nature has the form of metaphysical grounding, a particular relation of metaphysical explanation that expresses and explains ontological dependence.

It is not the aim of this work to provide a comprehensive critique of the current theories of human rights or to claim that my proposal is the best account in the philosophy of human rights. This work is rather a metaphysical exercise in the field of jurisprudence, more specifically in the philosophy of human rights, aiming to present the possible consequences of accepting certain metaphysical views for the question on the foundations of human rights. However, I believe that my claims are sound and illuminative with respect to the question of the foundations of human rights.

Chapter 2 provides a critical description of contemporary approaches in the philosophy of human rights. In Chap. 3, I give a detailed clarification of what I mean by human rights, human dignity and human nature. Chapter 4 presents the relevant ideas of contemporary analytic metaphysics and directly leads to the

[19] cf. Alvarez (2017).

subsequent chapter, where I investigate whether the relation between human rights, human dignity and human nature has the form of supervenience (Chap. 5) or metaphysical grounding (Chap. 6). Lastly, Chap. 7 addresses problems, possible objections and consequences of my approach and achieved results. The last section of this chapter encompasses the final summary in the form of the main argument of this dissertation presented step by step.

1.1 Methodology

The main method applied in this work is philosophical analysis. By philosophical analysis I mostly mean conceptual analysis. I will also sometimes use modal analysis that aims to discover modalities (possibilities, necessities, etc.); while doing so I will be especially interested in modalities concerning relations holding between different entities existing in the domain of human rights. The discussion of the explanatory relation of metaphysical grounding would require using another form of philosophical analysis: the explanatory method revealing the structure of reality which I call "relational metaphysics".[20]

This is a work within the field of philosophy of law, so it in most general terms analyses legal and legally related phenomena. As in every legal philosophy work, certain theoretical premises must be assumed. My first assumption is that any analysis requires a departure point.[21] I start from widely believed truisms about human rights that I reconstruct on the basis of the legal understanding of human rights. By the legal understanding of human rights or the legal notion of human rights I mean the understanding of human rights that is present in international and domestic human rights law. Therefore, I will try to explore deeper grounds of human rights as they are conceived in the folk notion of human rights and in law. The first theoretical step is thus to unpack the folk beliefs about human rights.

My second assumption is that the foundation of human rights is constituted by human dignity since such fundament is provided by international and domestic human rights law and that human dignity have certain features (properties using more philosophical language) that legal text ascribes to it.[22] I believe that legal text

[20] I could not find in the literature any single term to grasp this method of thinking so I propose this term. The debate on metaphysical grounding and the form of explanation has been going right now from around 10–15 years and many conceptions are not yet fully expressed. In the narrow sense it might be called "theory of grounding", but my research is not limited only to the application of the relations of metaphysical grounding, so I prefer not to use the term "theory of grounding" as it could be misleading.

[21] I share this assumption with many influential works in the field of jurisprudence or general philosophy (see e.g. Hart 1994; Shapiro 2011; Lewis 1972; Jackson 1998). See remarks below.

[22] There are some philosophers of human rights who argue against regarding human dignity as the foundation of human rights due to its unclarity, for example Sangiovanni (2017) claims that the basis of human rights is best understood in terms of a moral rights no to be treated as inferior, which

needs to be treated seriously, i.a. because they are normativised reflections of widely shared beliefs and intuitions. As I will present below, legal text is in my view the best tool to reconstruct truisms about human rights, which can serve as the starting point for further philosophical inquiry. Of course, these assumptions do not mean that the concept of human rights cannot be analysed in order to reveal its underlying structure, resolve conceptual problems, etc., to which I will turn in Sect. 3.1. The second assumption is limited just to the claim that human dignity is the foundation of human rights.

These assumptions have a significant methodological advantage—there exist clear criteria for the verification and falsification of the results of my account. These criteria of verification and falsification comprise of whether my explanation of human rights is consistent with human rights as understood by human rights law, and whether my theoretical approach provides their explanation.

The most crucial aspect is to provide an explanation of the manifold properties of human rights as ascribed to human dignity by international and domestic human rights law: equality, inalienability, being innate,[23] as well as universality, indivisibility, interdependence and being interrelated.[24] As for human dignity, the most crucial aspect is analogous. It consists of providing explanations for the key properties of human dignity: universality, being inherent, inalienability, equality and inviolability.[25] I follow here Marek Piechowiak's notion of the criteria of a proper philosophical theory of human rights, namely: to provide justification for the properties that human rights, as well as their foundation, have according to human rights law.[26]

Looking from the perspective of the current methodology of inquiry within analytic philosophy, philosophical inquiry starts from intuitions.[27] It is difficult to address what intuitions are in separation of addressing what role they serve.[28] Let me propose first that intuitions are beliefs that are considered to be obvious.[29] Intuitions are the basis for further philosophical inquiry that, among others, clarifies, explains and draws conclusions from them. More specifically, what I mean by intuitions are

---

is explained by rejection of cruelty. Sangiovanni's work is important in thinking about foundations of human rights in ethical way. Nonetheless, I hope my project of looking at this issue from metaphysical perspective is able to maintain human dignity, having clear meaning, as the basis of human rights.

[23] Universal Declaration of Human Rights (1948), Preamble, art. 1.

[24] Vienna Declaration and Programme of Action (1993), par. 5.

[25] Universal Declaration of Human Rights (1948), Preamble, art. 1; Basic Law for the Federal Republic of Germany (1949), art. 1.

[26] Piechowiak (1999), pp. 19–29, 110–113.

[27] There is also another approach, developing since the beginning of this century, called experimental philosophy, which aims to conduct experiments and then debate its results rather then begin inquiry from intuitions.

[28] Prust (2019).

[29] Prust (2019).

propositional platitudes that are widely accepted in society.[30] Under this conception, we are not concerned by intuitions of individuals, including particular philosophers. Rather, intuitions must be shared and accepted in society, although of course it is not required that they are realised by society or by its particular members. A similar concept to the concept of intuition, is the concept of truism. Truisms are "widely accepted utterances, formulated in colloquial language, which are considered to be true in usual circumstances".[31] They form a kind of common knowledge of a society, yet, of course, similarly, they do not have to be realised by the whole society or by every individual. As the concept of truism is more technical and less vague than intuition, in further parts of the work I will make use of the concept of truism. The direct conceptualisation of making use of intuitions or truism is a rather recent development of studies on the methodology of analytic philosophy, but of course philosophers of any time relied on intuitions.

The concept of truism has been already explicitly adopted in the philosophy of law. Scott Shapiro clearly states that he tries to illuminate truism about law and develop a theory that explains what law is.[32] Starting from truisms about law is promising also for one significant reason. Since law exists as a social artefact, it depends in its existence on beliefs, platitudes and actions of society. This is the reason for the legal philosophy claim that a global error on what law is cannot occur—as law exists as a social artefact, we cannot collectively fail to account what law is (of course, certain individuals, including officials can be in error as for law).[33] Truisms about law express these beliefs, platitudes, etc., so by illuminating them, one explains what law is. Of course, it does not mean that there are no contradictions between truisms—if there are, a theory must either demonstrate that on a theoretical level such contradictions do not hold, or reject some truisms as not representing the truth about law.[34] Shapiro presents the following list of truisms about law:

> "All legal systems have judges," "Courts interpret the law," "One of the functions of courts is to resolve disputes," "Every legal system has institutions for changing the law"; "Some laws are rules," "Some laws impose obligations," "Laws can apply to those who created them," "Laws are always members of legal systems"; Legal authority is conferred by legal rules," "Legal authorities have the power to obligate even when their judgments are wrong," "In every legal system, some person or institution has supreme authority to make certain laws"); "Simply knowing that the law requires one to act in a certain way does not motivate one to act in that way," "It is possible to obey the law even though one does not think that one is morally obligated to do so," "One can be a legal official even though one is alienated from one's job"; "There are right answers to some legal questions," "Courts sometimes make mistakes when interpreting the law," "Some people know more about the law than others".[35]

[30] Dyrda (2017), p. 145.

[31] Dyrda (2017), p. 176.

[32] Shapiro (2011).

[33] Gizbert-Studnicki et al. (2016), pp. 193–194.

[34] Gizbert-Studnicki et al. (2016) and Dyrda (2017).

[35] Shapiro (2011), p. 15.

As we see, truisms are obvious statements that we are most often not aware of. However, once one can see them expressed, their obviousness is apparent.

In my exercise in looking on the issue of foundations of human rights from the perspective of analytic metaphysics I also would like to begin from truisms about human rights and their foundations. I believe that some of such truisms, probably the most central to the question on the foundations of human rights, are already expressed in various legal documents on human rights. This is why I follow what is stated in legal documents about human rights as these documents express truism about human rights. Of course, these truisms hold only if one accepts that human rights exist. I do not reject the idea that there are certain members of society, or that there are some societies that do not believe in the existence of human rights. As I wrote earlier, I assume the existence of human rights. Let me write down such truisms (of course I do not claim that these are the only truisms about human rights):

1. Every human has equal human rights.
2. Human rights are a kind of moral rights.
3. Human rights are to protect human existence.
4. Human rights are universal.
5. Human rights do not depend on will or beliefs of people.
6. We have human rights due to having human dignity.
7. Every human being has equal human dignity.
8. Human dignity is a worth of human.
9. Human rights exist independently of legal enactment.
10. Human rights require legal enactment and protection.

Obviously, these truisms require analysis, clarification of their meaning, and presenting further philosophical claims. Similarly, the concepts of the properties of human rights and human dignity that are found both in the truisms and in legal documents (universality, equality, being inherent, etc.) can be analysed and their meaning may differ from the *prima facie* common or legal meaning. For example, being innate does not necessarily lead to a natural law theory, even though any claim about the foundations of human rights must be consistent with the claim that human rights are innate. Furthermore, claiming that every human being has human rights due to an epistemologically *a priori* political structure is in my view consistent with the innate character of human rights. Nonetheless, if a theory claims that human rights are possessed on the basis of a social or political convention of western societies, it would be inconsistent with the innateness of human rights. Consequently, such a theory would be an incorrect theory of human rights. Therefore, as already mentioned, I believe that the apparent discrepancies between the philosophical approach to human rights and the legal understanding of human rights should be solved in favour of legally conceived human rights when a philosophical theory of human rights is inconsistent with the core properties of human rights. A theory that does not explain the basic properties of human rights (or even undermines them) should be rejected. Consequently, the concepts of properties of human rights and human dignity can be analysed in order to uncover their proper meaning unless their philosophical analyses violate the core of those properties. The analysis of the concepts of these properties will be provided at the end of this work where I will test my account and determine if my approach fulfils the above-mentioned criteria. However, some views on the meaning of the concepts of properties of human rights and human dignity will be presented in the entire work, e.g. the section on human dignity (Sect. 3.2) will include an analysis on in what sense human dignity is inviolable.

I would like to address a possible objection against basing on truisms in the inquiry on the foundations of human rights. Someone may argue that human rights do not depend on what we think about them, they are objective and universal rights that are irrelated to collective views about them. As a result, by starting from truisms about human rights one is able to provide a notion of what people think about human rights, but never about what human rights actually are. In other words, by employing truisms one could provide a theory of a social understanding of human rights (i.e. a folk theory of human rights), but not a theory of "real" human rights. Human rights do not exist merely as social artefacts (contrary to law), so while in general philosophy of law there is a place for truisms, in the philosophy of human rights there is not. I believe that such an objection is incorrect. First, truisms are just a starting point, no one says that the notion of human rights must be fully compatible with them. In other words, a theory of human rights does not have to be reduced to what people think about human rights. Second, every philosophical inquiry must start from something. If someone remains hesitant about basing one's theory on truisms, one can rely on her own intuitions (unless one follows experimental philosophy and conducts experiments). But personal intuitions are much more vulnerable to be inadequate or incorrect than widely accepted truisms. Third, let me notice that truisms I presented above imply an independent existence of human rights, namely the existence that does not depend on someone's will or enactment by positive law (truisms no. 5 and 9). Thus, right in the truisms there is revealed the belief about the independent existence of human rights. Fourth, I expressed the truisms on the basis of what is said about human rights and their foundations in international and domestic human rights law, which encompass our basic views on human rights and formulate it in a written form. An alternative strategy in philosophical work on human rights could be to base simply on what is said in the international and domestic documents on human rights. However, I believe it would be equivalent to my version of the truisms strategy as I wrote down truisms on the basis of international and domestic documents on human rights. Lastly, the commonly shared intuitions or truisms are widely used as the starting point in ethical theories, also these ethical theories that do not claim that morality exists only as a social construct (Jackson 1998). For these reasons, it should be clear that although I start from truisms about human rights, I will not fall to writing about just a folk notion of human rights, but instead I will be able to say something about human rights and their foundations.

I often refer to the distinction descriptive vs normative. I do it for sentences, concepts, entities and facts. I follow the notion according to which it is the language that is used determines sentences, concepts, entities, and facts to be either descriptive or normative (one alternative notion is that it is a reason-giving function that makes a sentence normative). A sentence is descriptive if (1) it uses solely descriptive terms, i.e. terms that do not represent judgments, evaluations, etc.[36] and (2) it does not make use of deontic operators, e.g. *should*, or the sentence cannot be transformed to encompass such operators. To the contrary, a sentence is normative if (1) it makes use of terms that represent judgments, evaluations, etc. or (2) it makes use of deontic operators, e.g. *should*, or the sentence can be transformed to encompass such operators. For instance, the sentence "snow is white" is descriptive, while the sentence "human dignity is an inherent worth of every human being" is normative as it contains terms "dignity" and "worth". The sentence "every human being has human rights" is normative, for just as "right" it is a normative term. Moreover, one could claim that it actually could or should be transformed into the sentence "every human being *should* have human rights".

I understand the distinction between descriptive and normative concepts, entities and facts analogically. A concept is normative if it ascribes a normative property (to an object), which is a property that is described by making use of a normative sentence ass defined above. In turn, a concept is descriptive if it does not ascribe any normative properties. An entity is normative if its description makes use of a normative sentence, and an entity is descriptive if its description does not make use of any normative sentence. A fact is normative if its description makes use of a normative sentence, and a fact is descriptive if its description does not make use of any normative sentence. Therefore, the concept of human dignity is a normative one if it ascribes an *inherent worth* to every human being. An entity like the human right to free of charge elementary education (it will be further analysed what I mean by human rights as entities) is normative, since its description says it is a *right* to X. The fact that every human being possesses human rights (it will be further analysed why I regard it as fact) is a normative fact because by describing this fact we make use of a normative sentence.

We can think of two possible ways of researching the metaphysical foundations of human rights. Under the first one, the fundament of human rights is already known and we search for the relation between this fundament and human rights. Thus, the relata are known and on their basis, the proper relation is searched for by testing various possible relations and finding the proper one. Under the second, what is known is the relation between human rights and their fundament, and on that basis the entity that constitutes this fundament is searched for. In other words, what is known is one of the relata, i.e. human rights and the relation, while what is sought is another relata that is the foundation of human rights. The same applies as for the foundations of human dignity. My account follows the first strategy. I assume that the foundation of human rights is human dignity and aim to find the relation holding between human rights and human nature. Next, I argue that human dignity must hold in virtue of something more fundamental about human, which I call "human nature". Therefore, I am looking for the relation that holds between human dignity and

[36]It is debatable whether terms like "courage" or "honesty" are normative or descriptive, however this problematics is not related to this work.

human nature. However, the results of this research have consequences similar to the second strategy and lead to a slightly different account: if no proper relation between human rights and human dignity, or between human dignity and human nature, is found, it makes highly probable the claim that human dignity is not the foundation of human rights, or respectively, that human nature is not the foundation of human dignity.

References

Alvarez M (2017) Reasons for action: justification, motivation, explanation. The Stanford Encyclopedia of Philosophy (Winter 2017 Edition). https://plato.stanford.edu/archives/win2017/entries/reasons-just-vs-expl/

American Anthropological Association (1947) Statement on human rights. Am Anthropol 48:539–543

Beitz C (2009) The idea of human rights. OUP, Oxford

Buchanan A (2015) Why international legal human rights. In: Cruft R, Renzo M, Liao SM (eds) Philosophical foundations of human rights. OUP, Oxford, pp 244–262

Cruft R, Liao SM, Renzo M (2015) Philosophical foundations of human rights: an overview. In: Cruft R, Liao SM, Renzo M (eds) Philosophical foundations of human rights. OUP, Oxford, pp 1–44

Donnelly J (1984) Cultural relativism and universal human rights. Human Rights Q 6:400–419

Dyrda A (2017) Spory Teoretyczne w Prawoznawstwie. Wydawnictwo Naukowe Scholar, Warszawa

Eckel J, Moyn S (eds) (2014) The breakthrough: human rights in the 1970s. University of Pennsylvania Press

Gardner J (2008) Simply in virtue of being human: the whos and whys of human rights. J Ethics Soc Philos 2:1–22

Gizbert-Studnicki T, Dyrda A, Grabowski A (2016) Metodologiczne Dychotomie: krytyka pozytywistycznych teorii prawa. Wolters Kluwer, Warszawa

Griffin J (2008) On human rights. Oxford University Press, Oxford

Hart HLA (1994) The concept of law. Oxford University Press, Oxford

Hill T (2013) In defence of human dignity: comments on Kant and Rosen. In: McCrdudden C (ed) Understanding human dignity. OUP, Oxford, pp 312–326

Howard R (1993) Cultural absolutism and the nostalgia for community. Human Rights Q 15:315–338

Howard R (1995) Human rights and the search for community. J Peace Res 32:1–8

Jackson F (1998) From metaphysics to ethics: a defence of conceptual analysis. Clarendon Press, Oxford

Leiter B, Etchemendy M (2017) Naturalism in legal philosophy. In: The Stanford Encyclopedia of Philosophy (Summer 2017 Edition). https://plato.stanford.edu/archives/sum2017/entries/lawphil-naturalism/

Lewis D (1972) Psychophysical and theoretical identifications. Aust J Philos 50:249–258

Luban D (2015) Human rights pragmatism and human dignity. In: Cruft R, Liao SM, Renzo M (eds) Philosophical foundations of human rights. OUP, Oxford, pp 263–278

Marks S (2013) On human nature and human rights. In: Hanschel D Mensch und Recht: Liber amicorum Eibe Riedel. Duncker and Humblot, Berlin, pp 101–116

Mikhail J (2012) Moral grammar and human rights: some reflections on cognitive science and enlightenment rationalism. In: Goodman R, Jinks D, Woods AK (eds) Understanding social action, promoting human rights. OUP, Oxford, pp 160–202

Moyn S (2010) The last Utopia: human rights in history. Harvard University Press, Cambridge

Nolan D (2017) Methodological naturalism in metaethics. In: McPherson T, Plunkett D (eds) The Routledge handbook of metaethics. Talyor and Francis, New York, pp 659–673

Nussbaum M (2000) Women and human development: the capabilities approach. Cambridge University Press, Cambridge

Nussbaum M (2006) Frontiers of justice: disability, nationality, species membership. The Belknap Press Harvard University Press, Cambridge

Nussbaum M (2011) Creating capabilities, the human development approach. The Belknap Press of Harvard University Press, Cambridge/London

Papineau D (2020) Naturalism. The Stanford Encyclopedia of Philosophy (Summer 2020 Edition). https://plato.stanford.edu/archives/sum2020/entries/naturalism/

Piechowiak M (1999) Filozofia Praw Człowieka. Prawa Człowieka w świetle ich Międzynarodowej Ochrony. Towarzystwo Naukowe KUL, Lublin

Piechowiak M (2019) Plato's conception of justice and the question of human dignity. Peter Lang, Berlin

Pogge T (2002) World poverty and human rights: cosmopolitan responsibilities and reforms. Polity Press, Cambridge

Prust J (2019) Intuition. The Stanford Encyclopedia of Philosophy (Summer 2019 Edition). https://plato.stanford.edu/archives/sum2019/entries/intuition/

Rawls J (1999) The laws of people. Harvard University Press, Cambridge

Raz J (2010) Human rights without foundations. In: Besson S Tasioulas J (eds) The philosophy of international law. OUP, pp 321–338

Raz J (2015) Human rights in the emerging world order life. In: Cruft R, Liao SM, Renzo M (eds) Philosophical foundations of human rights. OUP, Oxford, pp 217-236

Rosen M (2012) Dignity: its history and meaning. Harvard University Press, Boston

Rosen M (2013) Dignity: the case against. In: McCrdudden C (ed) Understanding human dignity. OUP, Oxford, pp143–154

Sangiovanni A (2017) Humanity without dignity: moral equality, respect and human rights. Harvard University Press, Harvard

Shapiro S (2011) Legality. Harvard University Press, Cambridge

Shestack J (1998) The philosophical foundations of human rights human rights. Quarterly 20:201–234

Tasioulas J (2011) On the nature of human rights. In: Ernst G, Heilinger JC (eds) The philosophy of human rights: contemporary controversies. De Gruyter, Berlin, pp 17–59

Tasioulas J (2013) Human dignity and the foundations of human rights. In: McCrdudden C (ed) Understanding human dignity. OUP, Oxford, pp 291–312

Tasioulas J (2015) On the foundations of human rights. In: Cruft R, Liao SM, Renzo M (eds) Philosophical foundations of human rights. OUP, Oxford, pp 45–70

Chapter 2
Contemporary Approaches in the Philosophy of Human Rights

In this chapter I will present major contemporary approaches in the philosophy of human rights. I will also briefly provide their assessment and critique.

The core of the philosophy of human rights consists of providing an answer to the question: "what is the foundation of human rights". International and domestic legal documents concerning human rights give interesting claims on the fundament of human rights. International Covenant on Civil and Political Rights (1966) claims in its Preamble that:

> Recognizing that these rights [human rights – S.M.] derive from the inherent dignity of the human person.[1]

The Polish Constitution says:

> The inherent and inalienable dignity of the person shall constitute a source of freedoms and rights of persons and citizens.[2]

Interestingly, such formulations of dependence between human rights and human dignity are absent in the first, post-war legal documents on human rights. Universal Declaration of Human Rights (1948) places human rights and human dignity on the same level and does not state a dependence relation between the former and the latter:

> Whereas recognition of the inherent dignity and of the equal and inalienable rights of all members of the human family is the foundation of freedom, justice and peace in the world.
>
> All human beings are born free and equal in dignity and rights.[3]

A similar statement is found in the German Basic Law:

> (1) Human dignity shall be inviolable. To respect and protect it shall be the duty of all state authority.

[1] International Covenant on Civil and Political Rights (1966).

[2] Constitution of the Republic of Poland (1997), art. 30.

[3] Universal Declaration of Human Rights (1948), Preamble, art. 1.

S. Mazurkiewicz, *Grounding Human Rights in Human Nature*, Law and Philosophy Library 141, https://doi.org/10.1007/978-3-031-30734-8_2

(2) The German people therefore acknowledge inviolable and inalienable human rights as the basis of every community, of peace and of justice in the world.[4]

It seems that the recognition of a dependency relation between human rights and human dignity developed over time. After the strong establishing of legal recognition of human rights and the need of their protection after the Second World War, some time elapsed before it was explicitly recognised in legal documents that human dignity is the foundation of human rights.

However, no legal document answers the question what the foundation of human dignity is and what human dignity actually is. The probable reason behind that state of affairs is that there was a deep disagreement between the drafters of the legal acts on this issue. Jacques Maritain, who had a significant impact on the drafting process (although did not have a formal position in the drafting committee), said: "Yes, we agree about the rights but on condition no one asks us why".[5] The justification of human rights was left to purely philosophical inquiry. Therefore, some philosophers of human rights, like Martha Nussbaum or David Miller prefer not to bother about human dignity as an "intermediate" in the justification of human rights and seek the ultimate fundament of human rights.[6] Some authors, like James Griffin, thoroughly analyse human dignity in order to give its best account.[7] Other philosophers follow the claim implicit in the international law that human dignity is the foundation of human rights and provide the best theoretical[8] or philosophical[9] conceptions that justify human dignity.

The main distinction within the contemporary philosophy of human rights is the distinction between the naturalistic (also called: classical, orthodox) approach and the political approach. Tasioulas characterises the naturalistic approach by the following statement: "Human rights are moral rights possessed by all human beings simply in virtue of their humanity".[10] For Griffin a human right is "a right that we have simply in virtue of being human".[11] Under the naturalistic approach, every human possesses human rights, a subgroup of general moral rights, just because of the fact that one is human. However, what concepts of "humanity" or "being human" actually mean is discussed among proponents of the naturalistic approach. Different entities are proposed as referents of these concepts. Let me call the claim that something is the foundation of human rights the "foundational claim".

In turn, the political approach puts much more emphasis on the political role that human rights play in the contemporary world, especially in international law and

[4]German Basic Law (1949, art. 1).

[5]UNESCO (1948), p. I. This resembles an incomplete theorised agreement in terms of Cass Sunstein (2017).

[6]Nussbaum (2000, 2006, 2011) and Miller (2007, 2012).

[7]Griffin (2008).

[8]Tasioulas (2015).

[9]Piechowiak (1999, 2019).

[10]Tasioulas (2011), p. 26.

[11]Griffin (2008), p. 2.

international relations. Proponents of the political approach reject philosophical inquiry into the foundations of human rights and focus on an essentially (as they claim) political role of human rights.[12] This political role of human rights consists of being the test of the legitimacy of political authority; a violation of basic human rights justifies international intervention.[13] The political approach is a more practice-based approach as it is focused on the practice of human rights in the contemporary international law and international relations.

In the next sections I will describe major positions within the naturalistic approach. Then, I will describe the main tenets of the political approach, since there are few differences among its proponents. Obviously, it is hardly possible to refer to every philosophical work on human rights. My criteria for choosing the theories to be presented here are: (1) their philosophical recognition (i.e. being regarded as a prominent approach by major figures in the philosophy of human rights and being cited in the relevant literature), and (2) the quality of philosophical insight (i.e. providing a broad and deeply philosophical, comprehensive, and consistent conception on the foundations of human rights that can be labelled as "theory"). I also refer to philosophical approaches to the foundations of human rights rather than notions that refer to legal or institutional background—this is of course very important for the practical dimension of human rights but if human rights are human rights, they do not depend in their existence on any legal or institutional framework. Thus, to find their foundations one must look deeper than only at legal text, institutions that emerge upon it or Western post-war social practices.

My aim is not to provide a broad, comprehensive summary of any of these approaches as they are easily accessible and I believe there is no point in repeating other works. Instead, I focus on the most crucial elements of these approaches, especially on the elements that are relevant from the perspective of my proposal of analytic metaphysics looking at the foundations of human rights. This perspective includes seeking natural, scientific facts that may constitute such a foundation, as well as exploring the precise nature of the relation that holds between human rights and their supposed fundament. Thus, after each of the brief descriptions of one's approach, I will present the critique motivated by the reasons presented in the first chapter. My intention is neither to provide a comprehensive critique of each of these theories, nor to argue that my proposal is significantly better. My aims are rather modest. I try to present and discuss the problematic character of the relations holding between human rights and their foundations, as well as point out, quite striking, deficiency of references to empirical sciences and relevant natural facts in thinking about the basis of human rights.

[12] Rawls (1999), Pogge (2002), Beitz (2009) and Raz (2010, 2015).

[13] Rawls (1999), p. 90.

2.1 Alan Gewirth's Dialectically Necessary Approach

In contemporary thought the first one who presented a significant philosophical argument in favour of the naturalistic approach in thinking about human rights was Alan Gewirth (1981, 1982).[14] Gewirth's argument, which he calls "dialectically necessary approach", goes as follows:

> [it] is possible and indeed logically necessary to infer, from the fact that certain objects are the proximate necessary conditions of human action that all rational agents logically must hold or claim, at least implicitly, that they have rights to such objects.[15]

Gewirth argues that: (1) there are certain objects that are proximate necessary conditions of human action, (2) all rational agents must logically hold or claim them; therefore (3) all rational agents have rights to such objects. The objects that fulfil the proximate necessary conditions of human action are human rights. For Gewirth, the relation leading from (1) and (2) to (3) is the relation of logical entailment. Joseph Raz claims that this argument is logically flawed as it misconceives the relation between value and rights.[16] He argues:

> Gewirth, for example, thinks that since we all want and value having the proximate conditions of agency we must claim a right to have them. He ignores the possibility of believing that certain conditions are essential to our life, and even of striving to secure such conditions, without either claiming or having a right to them. Thus, he misconceives the relation between value and rights.[17]

Raz notices that an object may be essential for one's life and even an agent may strive for it, however no claim to have this object can be proposed. Therefore, the relation between the proximate necessary conditions of human action and rights to them is not the relation of logical necessity and Gewirth's argument fails. One can believe that the decisional autonomy is essential for her life, yet still do not claim any right to perform this decisional autonomy. In general, something may be valued, but it does not *ipso facto* have to be claimed even by an ideal rational agent.

Gewirth intends to justify human rights by the strongest available relation holding between premises and conclusion, namely logical necessity (by means of the deductive argument). In my view, his line of argumentation falls under Hume's Guillotine (*is-ought gap*).[18] From the factual assumptions that (1) there are certain objects that are proximate necessary conditions of human action (i.e. human rights) and that (2) all rational agents must logically hold or claim them, we do not logically necessarily infer that (3) all rational agents have rights to such objects (have human rights). The premises are of descriptive character—they describe facts about human agency (premise 1) and an idealisation of what a rational agent must hold or claim

---

[14] Gewirth (1981, 1982); cf. Raz (2010), p. 323.

[15] Gewirth (1981), p. 124.

[16] Raz (2010), p. 323.

[17] Raz (2010), p. 342.

[18] cf. Allen (1982).

(premise 2). These two descriptive premises are meant to logically entail that all rational agents have human rights and ought to be treated in a certain way. However, the conclusion is of normative character—it describes that humans have certain rights. As Hume argued in order to logically infer a normative conclusion, at least one premise must be of normative character.[19] In Gewirth's argument there is no normative premise, therefore his argument fails. Another simple possibility is that there is a hidden, enthymematic premise that is of normative character. In my view, such an enthymematic premise can be formulated as follows: (x) All rational agents should hold or claim the proximate necessary conditions of human action (i.e. human rights). If it's added to two clearly stated premises, the argument remains logically correct. Nonetheless, the enthymematic premise is not obvious. One can ask "why rational agents should hold or claim human rights" and the answer to this question actually refers to the justification of human rights. Thus, the justification of the enthymematic premise can only be done by providing arguments supporting the claim that we have human rights. As the claim that we have human rights is intended to be the conclusion of Gewirth's argument, by revealing the enthymematic premise his argument turns out to be self-referring and thus logically flawed. The conclusion that we have human rights cannot be established on the basis of a premise requiring the very justification of the claim that we have human rights. Another possibility is that the hidden premise is much more complicated, however Gewirth gives no reason to believe so, thus I omit such an option. As we see, Gewirth's argument is logically flawed both in its explicit form proposed by Gewirth, as well as in the form of an elliptical argument supplemented with a reconstructed implicit premise.

One should however notice that Hume's Guillotine cuts only logical relation between factual and normative– one could still argue for (3) on the basis of (1) and (2) by means of a weaker relation[20]—e.g. convincing explanation[21] or a sort of rational justification referring to instrumental or prudential connection between what are proximate necessary conditions of human action and human rights. Nonetheless, Gewirth's account of the relation as a relation of logical necessity remains flawed.

Gewirth's argument is interesting from the methodological point of view. He proposed a justification of human rights by a purely rational method, with no reference to empirical sphere. He deserves respect for an attempt to explicitly formulate the relation between human rights and their foundation. As it will turn out, it is not often among philosophers of human rights to clearly name the relation that is proposed to connect human rights and its fundament, whatever this fundament is.

[19] Hume (1739), p. 335.

[20] Putnam (2002). Hume's Guillotine cuts only a logical entailment between factual premises and a normative conclusion. Total separation between descriptive and normative spheres was not intended by Hume and, as Putnam argues (2002), the idea of such a radical separation is a child of logical positivism of early and mid-twentieth century.

[21] Witkowski (1975); Makowski (2011), p. 325.

2.2 James Griffin's Normative Agency Approach

The second major approach comes from James Griffin.[22] Griffin proposes to perceive human rights as protections of human normative agency or personhood.[23] He analyses these notions by means of conceptual analysis. According to Griffin, there are three components of being an agent: autonomy, minimum provision and liberty.[24] Autonomy is the lack of domination or control in choosing one's own path through life. Minimum provision involves a certain amount of education and information that enables the choice of a realistic path through life. Liberty amounts to others not forcibly stopping one from pursuing her conception of a worthwhile or good life.[25] These are substantive values of personhood that ground human rights. Griffin claims that there is also the second ground of human rights—practicalities, which amount to a set of empirical information about human nature and human societies, especially about the limitations of our understanding and motivation. Practicalities determine precisely concrete norms of human rights.[26]

So far so good. But who is a normative agent? Is it simply a human? For Griffin, a normative agent is someone who is capable of having a conception of a worthwhile life and being able to exercise it.[27] He explicitly states who is not a normative agent, and consequently who does not possess human rights:

> Human infants are not normative agents. Neither are human foetuses, nor the severely mentally handicapped, nor sufferers from advanced dementia.[28]

Such subjects do not have human rights, however it is not the case that they have no rights at all—they have moral rights, perhaps of very similar content to human rights, which nonetheless are not human rights. Since they have rights, others—normative agents have corresponding duties. Griffin's general motivation is to provide a well-established and precise criterion of labelling a right as a "human right".[29] He believes that we name too many rights as moral rights and we try to put too many moral considerations into the idea of human rights. This is the reason to narrow the scope of holders of human rights. However, this is the most criticised part of Griffin's approach. For instance, Tasioulas argues that Griffin's approach leads to the statement that torture is a human rights violation because and only because it violates one's normative agency.[30] He claims that there are other aspects that make

[22] Griffin (2008).

[23] Griffin (2008), p. 4; p. 33.

[24] Griffin (2008), p. 33.

[25] Griffin (2008), p. 33.

[26] Griffin (2008), p. 38.

[27] Griffin (2008), p. 47.

[28] Griffin (2008), p. 83.

[29] Griffin (2008), p. 14.

[30] Tasioulas (2013), p. 302.

torture a human rights violation beyond only undermining one's decision making capabilities, such as causing pain (2013, p. 303). Tasioulas concludes:

> By his (Griffin's – S.M.) reckoning, wantonly killing an infant or an Alzheimer's patient is murder, a wrong far graver than most human rights violations, even though in neither case is the killing a human rights violation.[31]

Massimo Renzo makes a similar objection. He claims that the reason not to torture a child or someone in the advanced stage of dementia is the respect we owe them *qua* human beings. He notices:

> The sort of disrespect for our common humanity that we are invoking when we blame the torturer is the same, whether his victim is a fully rational agent, a child or someone in the advanced stage of senile dementia.[32]

For Renzo, the moral blame of torturing a human is the same, irrespectively whether a victim is a normative agent under Griffin's account or not. If the moral wrong we intuitively ascribe is the same, the same is the violated right and consequently we should reject Griffin's approach.[33] Interestingly from the point of view of this work and my later analysis of metaphysical relations presented in Chaps. 5 and 6, Renzo's argument is based on the supervenience approach to ethics—if two acts are identical in natural properties, they are identical in moral properties. According to Renzo, Griffin differentiates two situations that are of the same moral characteristic, therefore his approach fails in general. Normative agency is the crucial issue in Griffin's justification of human rights. Let me present another objection to Griffin's view that among others, human infants, do not have human rights. But an infant grows and develops and one can ask when moral rights become human rights and an infant/child starts to possess human rights. If an age boundary is based on development, it can differ among individuals and on one day an infant/children does not possess human rights, while on another it will hold them. If an age boundary is to be given in general for everyone, it must be arbitrary and ignore individual differences, and consequently stand to the contrary to the fundamental condition of having normative agency.

Griffin proposes a method of assessing his approach. It is "by deciding whether it gives us human rights that fit into the best ethics overall".[34] According to Griffin, the best ethics overall is the ethics based on analytic notion of a person, dating back to Locke, wherein cognitive capabilities determine being a person. Griffin's concept of normative agency highly resembles the analytic concept of person, and it is, according to Griffin, what makes his approach fit into the best ethics overall. It may fit into it if someone accepts such a concept of person. Nonetheless, the problem is that it does not fit into the *legal* notion of human rights and probably also remains at odds with most shared intuitions about human rights (i.e. truisms). Consider a state

---

[31] Tasioulas (2013), p. 303.

[32] Renzo (2015), p. 574.

[33] Renzo (2015), p. 574.

[34] Griffin (2008), p. 4.

officer torturing young children or a group of state officials killing severely mentally handicapped people belonging to a national, ethnical, religious or racial group. Both situations are considered to be the crucial forms of legal human rights violations; the second qualifies even as a genocide[35]—probably the most serious violation of human rights we can imagine. However, none of them would constitute a violation of a human right under Griffin's approach. Under Griffin's approach, German Nazi Aktion T4—extermination of 275,000–300,000 mentally ill people in 1939–1945 in the scope where the murdered people were not normative agents, does not qualify as human rights violation. Surely, the philosophy of human rights should also criticise and assess the practice of human rights, which is of legal nature, and state when legal provisions go too far from the moral view of human rights. Philosophy of human rights has not only to justify the human rights described by the current state of international law (legal human rights), it has also to propose and secure new ones that depend on some changing conditions. Notwithstanding, the above mentioned cases of violations of legal human rights constitute the essential core of human rights violations from the legal perspective. Such violations occurring during the Second World War were the main reason to enact a series of universally binding legal documents that establish the protection of human rights such as Universal Declaration of Human Rights and International Covenant on Civil and Political Rights that are the fundament of the protection of human rights. If one's moral theory justifying human rights fails to recognise the kinds of atrocities mentioned above as violations of human rights, it is a highly implausible theory that does not fit into the core of the legal understanding of human rights (such moral theory probably also conflict with truisms about human rights, yet it should be noted that individual's intuitions, especially of philosophers who are used to conceptual categorisations, can significantly differ here).

Griffin seems to be one of the first among the major philosophers of human rights to recognise the objection of ethnocentrism.[36] In my view, two forms of this objection can be distinguished. The objection of ethnocentrism in the strong version consists of the claim that human rights in general are the product of western liberal, individualised political conceptions and should not be transmitted to other cultures that do not share such political and moral beliefs.[37] The weak form consists of a proposal that a plausible approach theorising human rights cannot refer only to western liberal values and western way of thinking but should be based on a world-wide acceptable, culture-independent arguments. In short, the strong version of the objection undermines human rights in general, while the weak one undermines only some approaches in the philosophy of human rights. Griffin believes that his approach is immune to this objection in both forms. He claims that the

[35] Convention on the Prevention and Punishment of the Crime of Genocide (1948), art. II.

[36] Griffin (2008), ch. 7; Griffin (2015).

[37] American Anthropological Association's Statement on Human Rights (1947), p. 542.

incompatibility between individually oriented western cultures and community-oriented eastern cultures is exaggerated.[38] He also states:

> But anyone who thinks seriously about the value of our status as normative agents and the benefits of living in a cohesive fraternal community will recognize that both are highly important. And they will recognize the same about both others' having to respect our individuality and our having duties of concern and care for others.[39]

He seems to argue that his account of normative agency as the foundation of human rights is acceptable irrespective of values shared in a culture as it can be justified by pure reason. To the contrary, I believe that Griffin's approach is actually the most vulnerable to the ethnocentrism objection in the weaker form among all major contemporary accounts of the philosophy of human rights. It is based on western, liberal assumptions that the most valuable aspect of human being, which is able to ground human rights, is normative agency with its values such as autonomy and liberty. Normative agency is meant as enabling choosing one's own path through life—it may be a path a society believes to be wrong. I doubt that such an attitude is common in non-western cultures. Raz argues that Griffin's emphasis on not being controlled or dominated in fact smuggles a particular ideal of a good life.[40] For Raz, such emphasis undermines Griffin's approach in general, but it is also a sound argument for the ethnocentric character of Griffin's notion.

Moving to the problem of the precise nature of the relation holding between human rights and their foundation, Griffin avoids the main problem of Gewirth's argument. Griffin does not claim that the relation between human rights and their fundament—normative agency and related values—is a logical one. He argues: "I claim no logical necessity for my proposal that we see human rights as protections of normative agency".[41] Further in his book, he provides a more detailed formulation of the relation he identifies between human rights and their foundation:

> When I speak here of the 'derivation' of the human right to autonomy, I do not mean an entailment. I mean only that a reasonable person who recognizes the prudential value of autonomy will also recognize the respect that it is due.[42]

He makes an example by referring to a specific human right, the right to autonomy, but this argument can be easily extended to human rights in general and shaped in the following form: "a reasonable person who recognises the prudential value of normative agency will also recognise a human right"'. The relation between human rights and normative agency is a prudential one—anyone who believes in the value of normative agency should also believe in the value of human rights. It is a weaker relation than logical entailment, although I think weakening the relation is not required in Griffin's approach for the very same reason it was required under

[38] Griffin (2008), p. 133.

[39] Griffin (2008), p. 133.

[40] Raz (2010), p. 324.

[41] Griffin (2008), p. 4.

[42] Griffin (2008), p. 135.

Gewirth's account—normative agency, unlike Gewirth's "proximate necessary conditions of human action", is a normative concept, thus a premise using it would be a normative premise. Therefore, a normative conclusion might be logically entailed in reasoning including such a premise. Griffin's relation between human rights and normative agency is an example of a weaker relation than logical entailment, which can be called rational justification or convincing explanation.[43] Such a sort of relation can hold between factual premises and normative conclusions, and does not fall under Hume's Guillotine. Under rational justification we agree on a conclusion on the basis of some premises, for instance for prudential reasons, yet these premises are not sufficient to logically entail the conclusion. On the other hand, applying such a relation, which is of a rather weak force, is vulnerable to the objection that there is no strong enough logical or metaphysical connection between normative agency and human rights. By logical connection I mean logical entailment (holding between true propositions). By metaphysical connection I mean a metaphysical relation, which is a relation holding between existing (metaphysical) entities and not between propositions. Griffin's argument is based on an assumed necessary human acceptance of normative agency, yet this acceptance is not as self-evident as Griffin assumes. Since there is no indication of any strong logical or metaphysical relation between (the propositions about) human rights and (the propositions about) its fundament, (any conclusions about) deeper metaphysical grounds of human rights are unlikely to emerge.

Griffin's approach is of highly ethical nature in terms of the method. He provides some arguments in favour of normative agency and its value, which for him seem to be self-evident, thus not requiring any further justification. If one wants to interpret his position in metaphysical or metaethical terms, that is, in a way oriented to investigate what kind of entity normative agency and human rights actually are, one would find no explicit clue in his work.

Griffin's approach to human rights involves many significant drawbacks. Most importantly, it stands in opposition to the core of the legal understanding of human rights, it falls into the objection of ethnocentrism, and last but not least, it fails to propose a strong justificatory relation for the foundations of human rights.

2.3 Martha Nussbaum's Capabilities Approach

Martha Nussbaum claims that human rights are justified by the reference to human capabilities which they protect.[44] For Nussbaum, invoking capabilities is the answer to the question "What is this person able to do and to be?".[45] Cruft, Renzo and Liao provide the precise characteristics of Nussbaum's notion of capabilities:

[43] Witkowski (1975); Makowski (2011), p. 325.

[44] Nussbaum (2000, 2006, 2011).

[45] Nussbaum (2011), p. 20.

> According to Nussbaum, capabilities are an individual's real opportunities to choose and to act to achieve certain functionings, and functionings are various states and activities that an individual can undertake.[46]

Capabilities are freedoms, but they are not simply "natural" abilities of every human being, but also freedoms interdependent of the environment around human being.[47] They do not belong to anything that could be labelled as "human nature" but exist rather somewhere between the human and the external world. Nussbaum claims that her approach "focuses on the protection of the areas of freedom so central that their removal makes a life not worthy of human dignity".[48] She provides the following list of central capabilities: "life; bodily health; bodily integrity; senses, imagination and thought; emotions; practical reason; affiliation; relations to other species; play; and control over one's environment".[49]

The basic Nussbaum's meaning of (human) dignity is the claim to be treated with respect.[50] Dignity is a sort of a formal property that demands certain ways of treatment. Capabilities and their protection are then what follows from dignity. Nussbaum claims: "The capabilities are not understood as instrumental to a life with human dignity: they are understood, instead, as ways of realising a life with human dignity".[51] There is a connection between capabilities and human dignity such that one's dignity gives grounds for one's having capabilities. Yet, capabilities are not just means to realise dignity in the meaning that they are without their own value, instead they are valuable on their own and not simply as some means. However, it is not simply that dignity is some prior entity or property that only later gives grounds for or entails capabilities. Nussbaum claims:

> Dignity is not defined prior to and independently of the capabilities, but in a way intertwined with them and their definition. [. . .]The guiding notion therefore is not that of dignity itself, as if that could be separated from capabilities to live a life, but, rather, that of a life with, or worthy of, human dignity, where that life is constituted, at least in part, by having the capabilities on the list.[52]

The relation between dignity and capabilities is more nuanced—dignity and capabilities are interconnected in such a way that they cannot be taken separately. One the one hand, dignity requires having capabilities. On the other hand, life with human dignity or life worthy of human dignity have roots in enjoying capabilities. As we see, the relation between these two concepts or entities, whatever one wants to regard

[46]Cruft et al. (2015), p. 15.

[47]Nussbaum (2011), p. 11.

[48]Nussbaum (2011), p. 31.

[49]Nussbaum (2011), pp. 33–34.

[50]I put the term dignity in brackets as Nussbaum sometimes makes use of the term dignity, rather than human dignity. Moreover, she explicitly extends her capability approach to animals and considers whether they have animal dignity (2011, ch. 6).

[51]Nussbaum (2006), p. 161.

[52]Nussbaum (2006), p. 162.

them, is not very clear in terms of which one and in what precise way is the basis of the other one.

This interconnection, especially the part where human dignity is a consequence of having capabilities, is the reason of critical reading of Nussbaum's approach. First, notice that Nussbaum in the above citation, but also in other parts and works, often speaks not about dignity itself, but about living life with, or worthy of, human dignity.[53] If one can live life with human dignity, it seems that one can also live life without human dignity.[54] Capabilities are then means to achieve this level of life—life with human dignity. When one is able to live a worthy life due to enjoying central capabilities, (human) dignity emerges. Dignity is therefore understood rather as a product of a worthy life than an innate value that is the foundation of human rights irrespective of any circumstances. A consequence of this notion of dignity is that removal of any of the central capabilities makes life not worthy of human dignity, even if it is a removal of the capability to play or to have a relation to other species. Did slaves or peasants who had to work almost all the time have a life unworthy of human dignity?[55] Does a modern person who lives in a big city, never spends time in nature, and has no relation with animals and pets, have a life unworthy of human dignity? Nussbaum's approach leads to an affirmative answer to this question, which seems highly implausible. And the claim that those two categories of persons, slaves/peasants and modern big city people, have no human dignity contradicts the core idea lying behind the *legal* understanding of human rights and socially believed truisms about human rights, namely that every human possesses human dignity, regardless of any factual constraints. I believe that a person whose human rights are violated still possesses human dignity, whereas under Nussbaum's approach a person whose central capabilities are violated ceases to possess human dignity. However, I believe that another reading of Nussbaum on the relation between capabilities and human dignity is possible. Notice that she makes use of the term "dignity", rather than "human dignity". It is possible that by dignity she does not mean the human dignity that is considered to be the foundation of human rights.[56] Perhaps, by dignity she means a worth that emerges when one lives a good life and enjoys capabilities. Then, indeed, someone deprived of capabilities does not possess dignity—for instance a slave working 16 hours per day in a mine lives a life without dignity. But it is a different kind of dignity than the dignity that is the fundament of human rights according to legal documents. Consequently, a person deprived of capabilities lives a life without dignity (understood as a worth of living a good life with capabilities), but still possesses human dignity that is the foundation of human rights. I will address the extreme unclarity of the concept of human dignity in Sect. 3.2.

---

[53] Nussbaum (2011).

[54] cf. Nussbaum (2011), p. 33 where she speaks about having a life that is not worth living.

[55] Cruft et al. (2015), p. 16.

[56] Notice that in her work on religious intolerance (2012) she makes use and analyses the concept of human dignity in its meaning starting from international legal documents on human rights.

Nussbaum's approach raises a similar problem as Griffin's account: the problem concerning children as right holders. Liao notices:

> [c]apabilities also cannot adequately explain many children's rights because many children's rights are concerned with functionings rather than capabilities. For example, children have rights to health care, education, name, nationality, to be protected from economic exploitation, and so on. These rights are best understood as rights to certain functionings rather than rights to certain capabilities.[57]

Since for Nussbaum capabilities are real opportunities that are not simply innate natural abilities, it is clear that children do not have such capabilities at all. Nussbaum is aware of it and unlike Griffin, she does not deprive children of human rights; rather she argues that in case of children the foundation of human rights is formed not by capabilities themselves but by functionings that "are important for helping children to develop adult capabilities".[58] It seems that in case of children she regards the foundation of human rights in the potentiality of having capabilities in the future. Thus, capabilities can be developed. Liao finds such a line of argumentation rather implausible due to its incoherence[59] and argues that capabilities cannot justify status rights (like the right to equal protection or the right to a fair trial):

> Capabilities do not seem particularly well suited to explain these rights, because if they (capabilities – S.M.) were able to explain these rights, it would imply that one can sometimes choose not to exercise these rights, since capabilities are concerned with our real opportunities to choose. But it does not seem that one can sometimes choose whether or not to exercise these rights.[60]

Capabilities as real opportunities dependent on the will of their holder cannot be the foundation of rights that are independent of one's choice. On the other hand, it may be claimed that the status procedural rights are not human rights, but rather they are the necessary conditions of protecting human rights. One has the right to life, the basis of which consists of the central opportunity to be able to live to the end of human life of normal length.[61] Status rights simply enable this and other human rights to be exercised.

The capabilities approach is free of two problems emerging in Griffin's normative agency approach. First, Nussbaum's approach defies the ethnocentrism objection. The concept of capabilities is not a western concept, it seems to be easily accepted among any culture.[62] Second, Nussbaum does not explicitly exclude young children from the set of right holders of human rights. Nonetheless, the second part of her formulation of the central capability to life as "not dying prematurely, or before

---

[57] Liao (2015), p. 92.

[58] Nussbaum (2006), p. 172.

[59] Liao (2015), p. 93; Cruft et al. (2015), p. 15.

[60] Liao (2015), p. 92.

[61] Nussbaum (2011), p. 32.

[62] cf. Sen (1999, 2005) who makes use of this concept in economics and has been the leading figure in the so-called development economics.

one's life is so reduced as to be worth living"[63] raises concerns about whether people with dementia and similar diseases can enjoy capabilities and, consequently, have human rights.

The most significant problem of her approach (under the first interpretation of the relation between human dignity and capabilities) is that someone who does not enjoy even one central capability, does not possess human dignity. This statement questions the legal understanding of human rights. Moreover, the nature of the relation between capabilities and human rights remains unexplained (perhaps it is rational justification similar to proposed by Griffin?). In turn, under the second interpretation of the relation between human dignity and capabilities, the concept of human dignity is very unclear.

Notwithstanding, capabilities, unlike normative agency, belong rather to the factual sphere. This may lead to serious concerns from the point of view of Hume's Guillotine related to the character of the justificatory relation holding between premises describing capabilities and conclusions describing human rights. Capabilities are very interesting entities, I will analyse what they may be in the metaphysical sense in Sect. 3.3, especially I will analyse if they can be considered as constituting "human nature", despite Nussbaum's implicit rejection of understanding them in such a way.

2.4 David Miller's and Massimo Renzo's Human Needs Approach

David Miller and Massimo Renzo claim that human needs, or more precisely, basic human needs, constitute the foundation of human rights.[64] Human rights protect basic human needs, which are the conditions of minimally decent life, by providing the opportunity to satisfy these needs.[65] The aim of this approach is to overcome the problem emerging in the context of other approaches, namely the problem of a too large scope of human rights. The reference to concepts such as good life[66] or capabilities (broadly understood as in Nussbaum's approach) that are supposed to justify human rights, leads to an extremely broad scope of human rights. Proponents of the basic needs approach criticise this; for them human rights, especially legally understood human rights, are meant to protect every human against the most severe violations of human functioning only.

Therefore, the level of human life protected by human rights is restricted to "decent human life".[67] Under the basic human needs approach human rights are

[63] Nussbaum (2011), p. 32.

[64] Miller (2007, 2012) and Renzo (2015).

[65] Miller (2007, 2012); Cruft et al. (2015), p. 14.

[66] Griffin (2008).

[67] Renzo (2015), p. 579.

not meant to enable everyone to achieve a level of "flourishing life" in Aristotelian terms.[68] The level of human well-being that human rights protect is therefore lowered just to an average level of human functioning. All in all, human rights are *rights*—if we accept that the level of human functioning protected by human rights is the level of "flourishing life", we conclude that persons could legally claim means enabling a quite high standard of life. One might even sue the government for enabling the flourishing of one's life.

There are three objections against an approach referring to the stand of flourishing life. First, it has extremely costly consequences, especially visible in case of poorer countries that could not provide everyone with such a high standard of life. Second, it is actually against the legal practice of human rights in which human rights protect human functioning against severe violations (the right to life, the right not to be tortured, etc.). Third, the meaningful reference to flourishing life must assume certain political doctrines, which are inherently controversial. The basic needs approach overcomes these objections by stating that human rights protect decent human life. Nonetheless, one may claim—in analogy to the criticism of the capabilities approach—that the human needs approach cannot explain the idea of status rights.[69] However, it can be responded that these rights are necessary conditions for the protection of human rights, analogically as it was responded in the above section on the capabilities approach.

Basic human needs belong to the factual sphere, as a sentence stating that X is a basic human need is formulated without using normative, evaluative or prescriptive language It is unclear how such statements could actually justify human rights, which are supposed to be normative in their character. Miller openly formulates his problem:

> I cannot explain why needs can ground obligations (human rights – S.M.) whereas other interests, however strong, do not; that is a fundamental intuition that I take for granted here.[70]

His humbleness and open admittance of this difficulty, quite rare in the philosophical world, demonstrates difficulties that the philosophy of human rights deals with while proposing a clear and precise relation justifying or explaining human rights, simultaneously sharing a vivid intuition that it has to be a strong enough relation. I hope my further adoption of analytic metaphysics will solve this fundamental problem. Despite the fact that Miller does not know how human needs explain or justify human rights, it seems clear that human needs are "descriptive entities", i.e. ones that can be described without reference to evaluative or normative terms, whereas human rights are "normative" (for it is impossible to describe them without references to normative terms). Falling under Hume's Guillotine is therefore obvious, since in a formulated argument the sentences describing human needs serve as premises and

[68] Renzo (2015), p. 579.

[69] Cruft et al. (2015), p. 15.

[70] Miller (2012), p. 422.

they are meant to entail the sentences describing human rights.[71] In my view, the basic human needs approach is best understood from the internal and theoretic point of view as the claim that there exists a particular relation of rational justification between needs and rights: human rights are simply the best means of protecting basic human needs; these rights must be accepted if one believes in securing basic human needs. However, as it was just stated in the previous sections, looking from the philosophical perspective, this relation is a weak relation that cannot provide a necessary justification of human rights by reference to human needs. It is at best a pragmatic relation that holds only if the necessity of protecting basic human needs is accepted or presumed.

I find Miller's remark to be a key point demonstrating and developing certain fundamental intuitions of the foundations of human rights: first, that there is a sort of justificatory or explanatory relation that holds between human rights and their fundament; and second, that this fundament can consist of some factual entities like e.g. human needs; or under Nussbaum's approach, capabilities that share some similar properties with human needs.[72] Further parts of this work will explore those two intuitive statements in detail.

2.5 Marek Piechowiak's Classical Philosophy Approach

Marek Piechowiak, the most prominent Polish philosopher of human rights, seeks the foundations of human rights in classical philosophy).[73] After identifying the features (properties) of human rights—universality, inalienability, equality, etc.—and their ground—human dignity with its features (properties) as well[74] he intends to discover philosophical theories that are the most consistent with so characterised human rights and therefore, can best serve as the justification of human rights. Unlike Griffin, Piechowiak does not want to develop his theory of justification of human rights starting from extra human rights issues, like some ethical theory, and then try to fit human rights into this ethical theory. Rather, he prefers to begin with human rights themselves as they are conceived by international human.[75] He argues that such theories can be found in classical philosophy. So, while Griffin intends to give an approach fitting into the best ethics overall, Piechowiak shares a very similar aim, but he believes that it is not the best ethics overall but the best philosophical theory that is the most consistent with the legal notion of human rights.

In his first proposal Piechowiak analyses both Plato's and Aristotle's philosophy and finds there concepts and frameworks that can properly play a role in the

[71] Hapla (2018).

[72] Hapla (2018), pp. 10–12.

[73] Piechowiak (1999, 2019).

[74] Piechowiak (1999), pp. 79–85, 110–117.

[75] Piechowiak (1999), p. 19.

justification of human rights, like notions of freedom, equality or theories of justice.[76] He argues that personalism, which develops Aquinas' notion of human dignity, as best suited for being the ground for recognition of human rights. It was Aquinas who was the first one to directly use the notion of human dignity in the meaning close to the one of the modern philosophy of human rights. According to Piechowiak's reading of Aquinas, someone is a person if one possesses human dignity, contrary to the modern claim that someone has human dignity due to being person.[77]

The second Piechowiak's book concerning the philosophy of human rights focuses on Plato's philosophy.[78] It provides an interpretation of Plato's political philosophy, found especially in Plato's *Republic*. Piechowiak rejects Popper-like views that Plato created grounds for totalitarian ideologies. To the contrary, Piechowiak argues that Plato's political views can be even labelled as liberal in modern terms. As far as the issue of the foundations of human dignity is concerned, Piechowiak reads Plato's reflections on inner unity that constitutes being as considerations on the foundations of the existence of beings.[79] Piechowiak analyses the Demiurge's speech in the *Timaeus* (41a-b) and highlights the fragment about "being-well-fitted-together" or "being beautifully harmonised", which are characteristics of every being created by the Demiurge (including human souls). These conditions of being do indicate the perfection of existence and they are the foundations of the same properties that nowadays are recognised to be essential for dignity, or so Piechowiak argues. Under the classical notion, human is a person in virtue of possessing dignity underlying its existence. In comparison, the modern analytic notion of the individual, often used in contemporary Anglo-Saxon philosophy of human rights, has the opposite meaning: one (a human) has dignity because one is a person. And since being a person is understood as having certain cognitive functions, some human beings (e.g., humans in a coma) are not persons. As a result, they do not possess human dignity. According to classical philosophy, one always has dignity, as it is based on the very foundation of being, and not on mutable properties (i.e., the actual "content" of a being). As long as a human exists, this foundation can never cease to exist. The consequences of these two approaches to dignity are highly divergent. Interestingly, it is a rather classical notion of human dignity that is compatible with the legal understanding of human rights.

Piechowiak finds recognition of human dignity as early as in Plato's philosophy. The original unity (of existence) of a human soul is independent of any moral behaviour and is the reason for the Demiurge's love, which results in everlasting life. This unity creates for a human (soul) the basis for being an aim in itself.

---

[76] Piechowiak (1999), pp. 226–264.

[77] Piechowiak (1999), p. 273.

[78] The description of Piechowiak's second work (2019) is based on a part of my review of Marek Piechowiak's work (Mazurkiewicz 2020); similar, yet much shorter piece of work was also published (Mazurkiewicz 2019).

[79] Piechowiak (2019), pp. 41–42.

Consequently, it involves the prohibition of purely instrumental treatment. According to contemporary views, these are the essential consequences of the recognition of human dignity. The recognition of human dignity in Plato's work is of utmost importance when discussing the universality of human rights, which are derived from the dignity inherent in human beings. Contemporary philosophy of human rights dates back the historical recognitions of human dignity to the Enlightenment, the early modern theory of natural law, the thinkers of the Renaissance, scholastic natural law, and Cicero's *dignitas*.[80] In fact, Piechowiak argues, we are able to date the recognition of human dignity, albeit without direct conceptualisation but with its essential properties, back to Plato's philosophy.[81] Piechowiak believes that dating back the recognition of human dignity to Plato gives another plausible argument in favour of the recognition of truly universal nature of human dignity and human rights that derive from human dignity. If the notion of human dignity can be found as early as in Plato's thought, one of the very first philosophers, then the philosophical recognition of the universal human dignity is much earlier than many thought and by far it's not true that the concept of human dignity has been discussed only in modern times. Consequently, as human dignity is the basis of human rights, the recognition of the foundations of human rights can be found right in the most early philosophy.

In my view, Piechowiak's approach is the best proposal among all naturalistic propositions in the philosophy of human rights due to its consistency with the notion of human rights formulated on international human rights law and deep insight into the properties and foundations of legal human rights. Piechowiak recognises fully the universal character of human rights without excluding any category of people from possessing human rights. His notion of human dignity is highly sophisticated and its deeply inquired ontological basis results in far-reaching ethical consequences. Such an account of human dignity is able to explain the strong, normative characteristic of human dignity in international and domestic law, as well as the ability of human dignity to constitute the foundation of human rights. Piechowiak's philosophical theory of human rights is the most consistent with the legal understanding of human rights from other discussed theories.

Notwithstanding, one may pose external objections to Piechowiak's account. If one does not accept ontological background of his theory, she will unlikely accept his justification of human rights. This ontological background consists of classical metaphysics, Aquinas' in his first work and Plato's in the second.[82] If one does not believe in God as conceived by Aquinas and his Aristotelian framework, or if one does not accept Plato's notions, such as Platonic Ideas, which are an inseparable part of classical philosophy, she will find Piechowiak's approach unconvincing. It can be

---

[80] Griffin (2008) and Waldron (2012, 2015).

[81] The recognition of the fact that human existence is an aim in itself is of course incompatible with the totalitarian subordination of human good to the good of the state and is another argument for rejecting Popperian reading of Plato's political views.

[82] Piechowiak (1999, 2019).

especially true for people coming from non-Western cultures that do not track their civilisational fundaments to ancient Greek philosophy.

Piechowiak, especially in his first major work,[83] often used Polish term "ugruntowanie" (English: grounding) to name the relation between human rights and their foundations. Although he does not propose further analysis of this relation, his intuition to name it as "grounding" is inspiring. It appears that the way he uses this term indicates a strong relation holding between metaphysical states of affairs, and not merely between concepts or propositions. In fact, Piechowiak's relation seems to be very similar to the relation of metaphysical grounding. I will develop this idea in Chap. 6.

2.6 Political Approach

The crucial thesis of the naturalistic (classical, orthodox) approach is that human beings have human rights simply in virtue of being human. The political approach argues against this thesis.[84] However, the strength of the alternative accounts varies. Since the political approach is a cohesive approach with minor differences between its adherents, I will present it as a whole. Tasioulas presents two general objections formulated by the political approach against the naturalistic one, which serve as two defining features of the political approach itself.[85] The first objection is that the naturalistic approach ignores the essential political character of human rights. This political character of human rights is ascertained by the role that they play in contemporary international law and international relations. This political role has two dimensions: legitimisation of state's authority and reversely, legitimisation of international intervention. John Rawls puts it in the following way:

> Human rights are a class of rights that play a special role in a reasonable Law of Peoples: they restrict the justifying reasons for war and its conduct, and they specify limits to a regime's internal autonomy.[86]

The second objection is that human rights need a specific kind of justification in the form of Rawlsian public reason in order to avoid the objection of parochialism, or even Western ethnocentrism.[87] Tasioulas distinguishes two versions of the political approach. Under the first one, human rights are a sub-set of the general class of universal moral rights distinguished by the political role such rights perform.[88] In turn, the second version does not presuppose universal moral rights as the underlying

[83] Piechowiak (1999).

[84] Rawls (1999), Pogge (2002), Beitz (2009) and Raz (2010, 2015).

[85] Tasioulas (2011), p. 44.

[86] Rawls (1999), p. 79.

[87] Tasioulas (2011), p. 44.

[88] Tasioulas (2011), pp. 44–45.

level for human rights and argues that human rights are best understood in political terms, especially in terms of international law and international relations. Tasioulas calls the first version *sub-set* approach and the second version *sui generis* approach.[89] The first version of the political approach argues against the naturalistic approach mainly by claiming that human rights have an essential political role, which is ignored by the naturalistic approach, without rejecting the idea that human rights are universal moral rights. In turn, the second version is agnostic, or even sceptical, about human rights as universal moral rights.[90] Tasioulas regards Raz's and Rawls's accounts as belonging to the *sub-set* version and Beitz's to the *sui generis* version.[91]

For Raz, who is a proponent of the sub-set approach,[92] the main argument against the naturalistic approach is that it does not take into account the practice of human rights, which is a practice existing mainly within the context of international law. This practice consists in dealing with issues like state responsibility for human rights violations and international intervention or legitimacy of a state government, and not with normative agency or other moral concepts helping to justify human rights under the naturalistic approach.[93] It results in shortening the list of human rights. This is because human rights are only these rights that while being violated justify international intervention, and while being preserved give grounds for the legitimacy of state authority. These are the rights that the government must protect in order to be morally and politically justified. The political justification of state authority is understood as the most general legitimacy of state authority, and not as the justification of particular state actions. Of course, even a legitimised state can occasionally violate human rights, yet a state without moral authority is highly likely to do it systemically, and only severe violations of human rights remove state authority and justify an intervention according to the proponents of the political approach. Rawls for instance gives the following list of human rights:

> The right to life (to the means of subsistence and security); to liberty (to freedom from slavery, serfdom, and forced occupation, and to a sufficient measure of liberty of conscience to ensure freedom of religion and thought); to property (personal property); and to formal equality as expressed by the rules of natural justice (that is, that similar cases be treated similarly).[94]

Consequently, these are the rights the violation of which justifies international intervention. Under the political approach there is no list for other human rights, including those enumerated in the Universal Declaration of Human Rights and other international law documents on human rights. Still, the political approach is able to justify the fundamental human rights—the right to life, liberty in various aspects and

[89] Tasioulas (2011), pp. 44–45.

[90] Tasioulas (2011), p. 45.

[91] Tasioulas (2011), p. 54.

[92] Raz (2010), p. 334.

[93] Raz (2010), p. 327.

[94] Rawls (1999), p. 65.

formal equality. Surely, no international intervention would be performed in a country violating the right to paid holidays.[95] The political approach narrows the list of human rights, but without excluding any fundamental human right. There are, however, other significant objections against the political approach. The main one is that human rights under the political approach are simply not universal. The objection is directed especially against the *sui generis* version of this approach. Under this version, human rights are not a real class of universal moral rights or it is irrelevant whether they are. Therefore, the concept of human rights is actually not a concept of human rights that can be found in legal documents and that seems to be accepted by contemporary people accept. Under the *sui generis* version of the political approach human rights are merely principles of the contemporary international law that provide limitations of state sovereignty that exist only since the end of the Second World War, or even later when the theoretical views on states' sovereignty restrictions were introduced into the practice of international relations. There is nothing universal in human rights conceived in such a way—they are just norms of contemporary international law, contingent from the moral point of view. According to this version of the political approach human rights are not simply human rights (if the concept of human rights is built upon truisms about human rights and the legal notion of human rights)—they are not universal moral rights we have simply because we are humans, but rather norms of the contemporary international law.

For this reason this version of the political approach is not especially popular. Among the major philosophers of human rights it is probably only Charles Beitz who can be understood as a proponent of the *sui generis* political approach, as he claims:

> We understand international human rights better by considering them sui generis rather than as instantiations of one or another received idea [i.e. universal moral rights – S.M.]. Human rights are the constitutive norms of a global practice whose aim is to protect individuals against threats to their most important interests arising from the acts and omissions of their governments (including failures to regulate the conduct of other agents).[96]

He explicitly rejects the understanding of human rights as a sub-class of moral rights and finds them to be the constitutive norms of the practice of protecting people against violations of the most basic interest. This practice is performed on the level of international politics, which comprises of international relations along with an important role of international law governing proper international relations.

In turn, both Rawls and Raz can be characterised as proponents of the *sub-set* version of the political approach. For them, there exist universal moral rights, and human rights constitute a sub-set of them. However, the essential characteristic of human rights includes their political role in determining the legitimacy of the state authority, as well as the legitimacy of international intervention in certain circumstances.

---

[95] Universal Declaration of Human Rights (1948), art. 24.

[96] Beitz (2009), p. 197.

The naturalistic approach rejects the claim that the political role of human rights is an element of their essential characteristics. According to the naturalistic approach it is just a contingent property of contemporary international law and international relations. There are other aspects of human rights that are essential, perhaps mostly related to their universal character. If anything, the political role of human rights might be dependent on these fundamental, essential features, but not the other way around. Human rights by far involve political consequences, most probably highly similar or even the same to what the proponents of the political approach propose: legitimisation of political authority in case of preserving human rights and justification of international intervention in case of their severe violations. It is highly likely that such is the current practice of international relations (rather not of international law as there are strict limitations of using force and without authorisation by the UN Security Council an intervention is rather illegal, I refer to this problem in a few pages). But the legitimisation of political authority and justification of international intervention are consequences of the universal character of human rights, not any essential features of human rights *per se*.

I believe that the view that the political role is essential for human rights is flawed. We should ask the question what "essential" actually means. Intuitively, essential property is a property that makes an entity to be exactly *this* entity. In analytic philosophy, for a long time essential properties were simply considered as necessary properties.[97] Let me follow the view that necessary properties are properties that an entity possesses in every possible world.[98] A possible world is a technical term, popularised by David Lewis[99] referring to any consistent situation a world could be.[100] For instance, there is a possible world where Donald Trump won the 2020 U.S. election (it could have happened) and there is a possible world where Sun does not exist (we can imagine such a world). However, there is no possible world where 2+2 equals 5 or where a bachelor is not an unmarried man (they are unconceivable as a world could not be like this). As such, the semantics of possible worlds is often used in the modal analysis and determining of various possibilities, necessities, etc. Coming back to the issue of necessary properties, if a property is possessed by an entity across every possible world, it means that this is a necessary property of this entity as we cannot imagine a possible world where the entity does not possess this property. It is often claimed that since necessary properties are possessed by an entity in every possible world, they make this entity to be exactly *this* entity and are therefore its essential properties as well (modal understanding of essence).[101]

[97] cf. Fine (1994); Robertson and Atkins (2018).

[98] Kment (2017). I believe that there is no need to enter here into the analytic philosophy debate on possible worlds (for a detailed study see e.g. Menzel 2017). Let me just notice that although philosophical interpretation of what possible worlds are vary, they can and rather tend to be understood on a purely semantic level. Following this view, they have nothing to do with what may resemble "parallel universes".

[99] Lewis (1973).

[100] Menzel (2017).

[101] Robertson and Atkins (2018).

However, Kit Fine noticed that there are properties that are necessary but not essential.[102] It is a necessary property of Socrates that he is a sole member of a unit set {Socrates}, but it is counterintuitive that the fact that he is a sole member of a unit set {Socrates} makes him Socrates.[103] Therefore, a necessary property is not always simultaneously an essential property (non-modal understanding of essence). For Fine, in order to find an essential property one needs to look into the necessary properties and find those properties that make an entity *this* entity.

Irrespective of whether we accept Fine's view or not, I claim that the political role of human rights is not essential since it is not even necessary. Bearing in mind that human rights are universal moral rights (even if the universality of particular rights, like the right to nationality or to paid holidays[104] is understood as being related to the exact space and time within history), we see that the political role of human rights emerged quite recently. It happened after the Second World War and perhaps even later when the doctrine of humanitarian intervention started to be developed and practiced around 1970s. Before that time human rights rather had no internationally recognised political role.[105] Thus, there was a time when human rights existed (as universal moral rights) but they did not have the political role that the political approach ascribes. The political role of human rights, presumably manifested in providing the legitimacy of state power and the justification of intervention when human rights are violated (no matter if human rights in fact play such a role), can only be regarded as characteristic for the so-called liberal world order after the Second World War, and especially after the end of the Cold War. Before that time there was no practice in the international community of discussing whether, for instance, the monarch in country X violates human rights. Quite to the contrary, the world order was cemented rather by the divine legitimacy of monarchs that could not be overthrown by the lack of conformity with human rights.[106] Notice here that what the adherents of the political approach refer to is the practice of the international community, not thoughts of some individual scholars on how things should look like.

---

[102] Fine (1994).

[103] Fine (1994), p. 8.

[104] Universal Declaration of Human Rights (1948), art. 15, art. 25.

[105] One may argue that in the past human rights were used to frame arguments supporting the justness of a rebellion against tyrannical monarchs, so they had a political role. For instance, the French Revolution utilised the idea of human rights to fight against the tyrannical monarch. Nonetheless, there was no consensus in international law of that time concerning the role of these rights. Actually quite to the contrary, rebellion was seen as an illegal attack on king's eternal authority coming from God. Moreover, the conception of international intervention was not needed as war was a legal means in international relations. It should be stressed that the political approach ascribes the essential role of human rights to the international law and politics and not to the thought of scholars. Scholars or political philosophers developed some theories about the role of natural or human rights but these theories were not implemented into the law and practice of international relations.

[106] cf. the decisions of Vienna Congress in 1815 that established rules of international order up to the First World War.

What I mean is that fulfilling the political role by human rights is not a necessary feature of human rights. If it is not necessary, it is also not essential under the modal understanding of essence. As argued, it is not true that the political role makes human rights what they actually are. It might happen that human rights do not play the political role that is ascribed to them.

Let me address the difference between Rawls notion of the political approach and his later continuators.[107] It should be stressed that if we follow the claims of the current proponents of the political approach like Beitz and Raz we should search for an essential property on the level of *practice* of international law and international relations, not on the level of an ideally constructed, "proper" international law and relations as set up by the Rawls's proposal.[108] One cannot simply argue against the above line of argumentation by claiming that even if human rights did not play a political role on the real, practical level of international law and international relations of that time, they *should have done so*, as an essential part of the ideally *good* international law. However, the contemporary proponents of the political approach believe that human rights play an essential political role in the *practice* of international law and not in the ideally conceived international law. Someone might counterargue in such a way, but it would constitute a rather different approach in the philosophy of human rights than the currently discussed political approach. And if anyone wants to claim that essentiality relates to the *contemporary* international law and international relations, she has to explicitly deny that this political role is an essential property of human rights in general. If the political role of human rights arose only in the post-war period, when the current international order has been built, there is nothing essential in the political role of human rights. To conclude, the political role of human rights, perhaps indeed of significant importance in contemporary international law and international relations, is just a contingent property, relative to our times and circumstances.

There exists another objection to the political approach, which is based on positive law. I believe that the political approach overestimates the political role that human rights play in contemporary international law. More precisely, the political approach misunderstands the human rights role in relation to the conditions of justification of state's authority and, respectively, to legality of international intervention in a country that fails to realise the most basic human rights. The political approach refers in this role to what is known as humanitarian intervention in international law. The problem is that the legality of humanitarian intervention is highly controversial.[109] In fact, the UN Charter strictly prohibits using force against another country[110] with only two exceptions: self-defence[111] and authorisation from

[107] Rawls (1999), Beitz (2009) and Raz (2010).

[108] Rawls (1999).

[109] Zajadło (2005, 2010).

[110] UN Charter (1945), art. 2.4.

[111] UN Charter (1945), art. 51.

the Security Council.[112] A humanitarian intervention is using force against another country and in fact most of them happen without an authorisation of the Security Council (e.g. in Yugoslavia in 1999 or in Libya in 2011). Furthermore, humanitarian interventions are not conducted always when basic human rights are violated in a given country. If it were so, we would have had interventions to stop the Rwandan genocide, Syrian civil war, and North Korean regime. It means that there is no possibility of identifying a *practice* of human rights in the current system of international law and affairs. Such a practice does not exist, humanitarian interventions happen too rarely to constitute any meaningful practice. And those that are actually performed, are often conducted illegally—without the authorisation of the Security Council.[113] There is also no possibility of framing an argument for an alternative basis of legality of humanitarian intervention, as e.g. an international custom. International customs require evidence of a general practice accepted as law.[114] In others words, in order to prove that there exists an international custom, there must be evidence for an existing practice and for the common opinion on the legality of a given practice. No such thing can be proven. The doctrine of Responsibility to Protect, going further than humanitarian intervention by establishing an obligation to intervene in the most violent scenarios of violating human rights is only mentioned in one U.N. document and can be at most regarded as soft law.[115] Of course, humanitarian intervention can be legitimate from a moral point of view, but it is not legitimacy on legal grounds.[116] Moreover, the idea of humanitarian intervention can be cynically used in international politics by a hegemonic power to justify wars conducted for purely political goals. In such cases, human rights and the need of humanitarian intervention play the role of a moral argument presented to the public, while the real justification of an armed conflict is of a totally different kind. U.S. war in Iraq started in 2003 seems to be an example of such actions. If human rights are to be protected and promoted, they cannot be used in a way that can disperse or even undermine the public commitment to them.

Jeremy Waldron presents a different argument against the political approach, which is worth mentioning.[117] He notices that in order to justify a humanitarian intervention (on the moral level, for, as I noticed above, without the authorisation of

---

[112] UN Charter (1945), art. 42–44.

[113] Danish Institute of International Affairs (1999), p. 94.

[114] Statute of International Court of Justice (1945), art. 38.1(b).

[115] UN World Summit Outcome Document (2005), par. 138–140.

[116] There is however one version of the political approach that is immune to this argument. This is Rawlsian realistic utopia (1999) where Rawls aims to find the best fundamental rules for a fair international order. Rawls does not build his theory on currently existing international order, consequently his notion of the role of human rights neither refers to contemporary international law nor international relations. Rather it refers to an ideal of just international law or international relations. Thus, my analysis of contemporary international law has nothing to do with his theory. On the other hand, adherents of the political approach after Rawls speak rather of existing, current international law and international politics.

[117] Waldron (2013).

the UN Security Council the conducting of intervention is illegal) the violations of human rights must have a systemic character.[118] In other words, even a very severe violation of rights of an individual (e.g. torturing) does not justify a humanitarian intervention.[119] And since what justifies a humanitarian intervention is the violation of human rights, it turns out that a violation of rights on a non-systemic scale is not a violation of human rights at all. Consequently, the right not to be tortured becomes a human right only if it is violated on a systemic scale. Furthermore, the key idea that human rights are related to individual human beings in order to protect them seems to break up. I adhere to Waldron's argument. Human rights should play the justificatory role with regard to the (moral) legitimisation of actions of political authorities—this is an idea underlying the political approach that I by far accept. However, the relation between human rights and the legitimacy of actions conducted by a political authority, and resp. the justification of conducting humanitarian intervention, is not as straightforward as the proponents of the political approach believe when they claim that it is the essence of human rights to legitimise the actions of a given political authority and justify humanitarian intervention.

To conclude, the political approach in the *sui generis* version[120] is unacceptable as it finds the basis of human rights solely in the contemporary international law and politics which are agnostic as to whether human rights are actually universal moral rights. Universality is an essential property of human rights in their legal understanding (resp. according to the folk intuitions about human rights), so if one's theory cannot explain it, or implies that human rights are not universal, it is simply a wrong theory of human rights. The sub-class versions of the political approach[121] is free of that objection, however, it, as a thoroughly political approach, is wrong concerning the essentiality of the political role of human rights.

Due to all above reasons, I believe that the naturalistic approach, which is free of the discussed problems, grasps better the foundations of human rights. Human rights indeed play a political role in the contemporary world, including international law, but this role is not as strong as advocates of the political approach claim. The basic working hypothesis of my work is that the naturalistic approach is right, and I aim to find some deeper metaphysical foundation(s) for human rights and human dignity. So, even if the presented critique of the political approach missed the point, in what comes I would still follow the naturalistic (classical, orthodox) path of searching for the grounds of human rights.

---

[118] Waldron (2013), p. 10, p. 12; cf. Rawls (1999), p. 38; Beitz (2009), pp. 105–106.

[119] Waldron (2013), p. 10, p. 12.

[120] Pogge (2002) and Beitz (2009).

[121] Rawls (1999) and Raz (2010).

2.7 Towards Contemporary Analytic Metaphysics

I believe that the main claim of the naturalistic approach, which is that "human rights are moral rights possessed by all humans simply in virtue of their humanity or being human"[122] is correct. It represents our basic intuition that we have human rights due to something, in some sense, more fundamental about us. It is something that we all share that makes us have human rights. On the other hand, each of the above presented particular conceptions, trying to present thoroughly what this claim means in detail, encounters significant problems. Gewirth fails to establish the relation of logical entailment between human rights and their foundation. Griffin does not regard certain basic sorts of violations of human rights from the legal point of view as violations of human rights (as he conceives them). His theory also does not respond to the objection of Western ethnocentrism. The justification of human rights it provides is convincing only if one accepts the conception of normative agency. Griffin also proposes a justificatory relation between human rights and their fundament that is too weak. Nussbaum struggles with the justification of status right, so she must justify children's human rights only by reference to the potentiality of their having capabilities in the future. She also does not propose any view on the nature of relation between human rights and capabilities. The "human needs" account is a victim of Hume's Guillotine. In my view, Piechowiak's theory fits the best with the legal understanding of human rights, but it is based on philosophical assumptions that may not be acceptable for everyone, especially with respect to the objection of Western ethnocentrism. I also believe that we should be able to find a plausible philosophical basis for human rights in contemporary philosophy, which seems to be closer to the way of thinking of a contemporary man, even if classical philosophy does not. Eventually, the political approach overestimates the role that human rights actually play in contemporary international law.

Three difficulties, common to the above-mentioned theories, are especially significant in my view. First, the justificatory or explanatory relation between human rights and their foundations, whatever these foundations are, remains unidentified. Second, the "is"-"ought" gap is a serious challenge to identify the grounds for human rights. Third, the theories analysed above do not refer to any scientific facts that can be relevant to the philosophical issue under discussion. In the naturalistic approach the whole method of discussing the foundations of human rights consists of a purely rational, armchair way of philosophising with no reference to the natural world. There are of course references to legal facts, as well as, especially within the political approach, to institutional facts about the international law, international relations, and the practice of human rights in international institutions. Yet, the contemporary philosophers of human rights do not encompass any studies on natural facts that may be, and as I argue, are relevant for the justification of human rights. The lack of references to scientifically researched natural facts is especially striking, because empirical sciences in the last decades have witnessed an enormous growth of

[122] Griffin (2008), p. 2; Tasioulas (2011), p. 27.

scientifically proved knowledge about humans, which in my view is relevant to the debated issue of the foundations of human rights. To mention just a few disciplines: neuroscience, cognitive studies, moral psychology, and evolutionary psychology. The rationalistic methodology of philosophising about human rights, characterised by the complete and systematic absence of empirically based inquiry has been already criticised i.a. by Rosen.[123]

These difficulties can be regarded as a consequence of a sort of parochialism of the philosophy of human rights which does not make use of tools developed by other disciplines. By far, the philosophy of human rights has been open to ethics and political philosophy, it also has taken advantage of some general issues like theories of rights. However, with few exceptions[124] the findings of other disciplines are rarely applied in the philosophy of human rights. As I think, the reference to analytic metaphysics may provide us with useful tools for resolving the three difficulties listed above.

I will refer to natural facts relevant to the question of foundations of human rights, within the framework constituted by the analytic philosophy project of naturalisation (sometimes referred to as "naturalism").[125] I will present the naturalisation project in detail in Sect. 4.1. Naturalisation generally either aims to reduce entities that used to be researched by philosophical methods to some natural facts (ontological naturalism), or begin philosophical investigations by gaining scientific knowledge and develop one's philosophical theory on its basis (and in accordance with it), without however reducing debated entities to natural facts (methodological naturalism). Interestingly, it turns out that what is referred to in the philosophy of human rights as the naturalistic approach has nothing to do with naturalism as understood in philosophy. Under the naturalistic approach to human rights neither human rights are reduced to natural facts, nor relevant natural facts are invoked in order to develop one's theory.[126] This terminological confusion is evidence for the parochialism of the philosophy of human rights. The label of the main approach has nothing in common with the well-established philosophical meaning of the term.

The project of naturalisation is the first conception I will use. The second one is the contemporary relational metaphysics (theory of grounding). It researches dependence relations between objects, which illuminates why some objects (or their properties) hold due to the (presumed existence) of other objects (properties). It will help clarify and possibly solve the first and the second difficulty I formulated above, namely the lack of clear knowledge of the relation between human rights and their foundations, as well as the "is"-"ought" problem.

In general jurisprudence (general philosophy of law) both the project of naturalisation and the relational metaphysics have been applied. In the last decade or two, the project of naturalisation has been developed in order to find deeper,

[123] Rosen (2013).

[124] Piechowiak (1999, 2019) and Mikhail (2012).

[125] Leiter and Etchemendy (2017) and Papineau (2020).

[126] With a minor but notable exception of Mikhail (2012).

natural, scientifically discovered, foundations of law.[127] Similarly, analytic metaphysics has been introduced in order to clarify the relation between law and its foundations, both in naturalistic conceptions[128] and in non-empirically oriented ones that aim to discover the actual relation of the determination of legal facts by social facts.[129] Both kinds of studies gave new, significant insights into the philosophy of law. I believe that introducing these tools of analytic metaphysics into the philosophy of human rights will also provoke new, interesting ways of reflection on the foundations of human rights.

I said that I found the main claim of the naturalistic approach to human rights correct. It holds that "human rights are moral rights possessed by all humans simply in virtue of their humanity or being human".[130] My account can be understood as a metaphysical reading of this claim motivated by the naturalisation project and relational metaphysics.

Notice that concepts like "being human" in Griffin's version or "being human" in Tasioulas's refer to something that makes us humans. It can be simply labelled as "human nature". There are thousands of thousands of pages on human nature from philosophical perspective, but this term is used also in empirical sciences that try to discover and define what constitutes human nature by means of scientific, experimental methods. The reference to such discoveries in philosophising on the foundation of human rights would amount to the methodological naturalisation of the philosophy of human rights. In turn, if human rights could have been reduced to scientifically, experimentally discovered human nature, it would mean that ontological naturalisation in the philosophy of human rights is possible.

Next, let me relate to the phrase "in virtue of", which occurs in the main claim of the naturalistic approach. It denotes a dependence relation between human rights and their fundament, which is "being human"/"humanity". I will refer to this "being human"/"humanity" on the following pages simply as human nature. This sort of dependence is referred to by analytic metaphysics as ontological dependence.[131] Ontological dependence is a general concept, meaning that a certain entity depends in its existence on (the existence of) another entity.[132] Contemporary analytic metaphysics introduced a few concrete relations that can express and explain general ontological dependence. Those relations will be tested with respect to whether they hold between human rights and their fundament.

However, I will not take the straight and easy path, and focus on the direct relation of dependence between human rights and human nature. Things seem to be more

---

[127] To mention just a few: Leiter (2007), Pardo and Patterson (2013), Załuski (2009a, b, 2018), Brożek (2012, 2017a, b, 2020) and Brożek et al. (2017).

[128] Załuski (2009a, b) and Brożek (2012, 2017c).

[129] Plunkett (2012), Gizbert-Studnicki (2015, 2016, 2021) and Chilovi and Pavlakos (2019).

[130] Griffin (2008), p. 2; Tasioulas (2011), p. 27.

[131] For certain reasons, the concept that is commonly used in metaphysical debates is ontological dependence, rather than metaphysical dependence. I will stick to this terminology.

[132] Tahko and Lowe (2016).

complicated and the relations "in between"—more complex. Thus, I will identify "human dignity" in between, for it seems pretty clear for any reader of international documents on human rights that under the legal notion of human rights it is human dignity that is the *closest* foundation of human rights. Then, I will analyse whether human nature constitutes the foundation of human dignity. Ultimately, as a consequence, it will be indirectly analysed whether human nature is the foundation of human rights. Specifically, I will claim that the fundament of human dignity, (being the foundation of human rights), is human nature understood in terms of evolutionary psychology. I will square this thesis with arguments for the view that the relations between human rights, human dignity and human nature have a form of metaphysical grounding.

But before discussing this, I will explain to which entities I refer to by using such concepts as "human rights", "human dignity", and "human nature". Since I propose a metaphysical reading of the issue of foundations of human rights, they will be understood as entities. One may be confused why I speak about human rights, or human dignity, as "entities" but this objection will be also directly answered. I use the term "entity" in the broadest possible way: an entity denotes something that exists—everything what exists (or at least is presumed to exist) can be named "entity". If I wish to find the foundations of human rights and human dignity in the natural sphere (*via* thoroughly analysed relations between human rights, human dignity and human nature) it must first be clearly explained what these entities are.

References

Allen P (1982) A critique of Gewirth's "Is-Ought". Deriv Ethics 92:211–226

American Anthropological Association (1947) Statement on human rights. Am Anthropol 48:539–543

Beitz C (2009) The idea of human rights. OUP, Oxford

Brożek B (2012) Normatywność Prawa. Warszawa, Wolters Kluwer

Brożek B (2017a) On the naturalisation of law. Polish Law Rev 3:13–33

Brożek B (2017b) Neuroscience and the ontology of law. Polish Law Rev 3:90–105

Brożek B (2017c) Law, normativity and supervenience. In: Brożek B, Rotolo A, Stelmach J (eds) Supervenience and normativity. Springer, Dordrecht, pp 123–138

Brożek B (2020) The legal mind. a new introduction to legal epistemology. CUP, Cambridge

Brożek B, Stelmach J, Kurek B (eds) (2017) The province of Jurisprudence naturalized. Wolters Kluwer, Warsaw

Chilovi S, Pavlakos G (2019) Law-determination as grounding: a common grounding framework for jurisprudence. Legal Theory 25:53–76

Cruft R, Liao SM, Renzo M (2015) Philosophical foundations of human rights: an overview. In: Cruft R, Liao SM, Renzo M (eds) Philosophical foundations of human rights. OUP, Oxford, pp 1–44

Danish Institute of International Affairs (1999) Humanitarian intervention: legal and political aspects. Copenhagen

Fine K (1994) Essence and modality. Philos Perspect 8:1–16

Gewirth A (1981) The basis and content of human rights. Nomos 23:119–147

Gewirth A (1982) Human rights: essays on justification and application. University of Chicago Press, Chicago

Gizbert-Studnicki T (2015) Metafizyka Pozytywizmu Prawniczego. Principia 61:19–40

Gizbert-Studnicki T (2016) The social sources thesis, metaphysics and metaphilosophy. In: Banaś P, Dyrda A, Gizbert Studnicki T (eds) Metaphilosophy of law. Hart Publishing, Oxford, pp 121–146

Gizbert-Studnicki T (2021) Social facts and legal facts: Perils of Hume's Guillotine. In: Spaak T, Mindus P (eds) The Cambridge companion to legal positivism. Cambridge University Press, Cambridge, pp 419–442

Griffin J (2008) On human rights. Oxford University Press, Oxford

Griffin J (2015) The relativity and ethnocentricity of human rights. In: Cruft R, Liao SM, Renzo M (eds) Philosophical foundations of human rights. OUP, Oxford, pp 555–569

Hapla M (2018) Theory of needs as justification of human rights: current approaches and problems of uncertainty and normativeness. Age Human Rights J 10:1–21

Hume D (1739) A treatise of human nature. John Noon, London

Kment B (2017) Varieties of modality. In: The Stanford Encyclopedia of Philosophy (Spring2017 Edition). https://plato.stanford.edu/archives/spr2017/entries/modality-varieties/

Leiter B (2007) Naturalizing jurisprudence: Essays on American legal realism and naturalism in legal philosophy. OUP, Oxford

Leiter B, Etchemendy M (2017) Naturalism in legal philosophy. In: The Stanford Encyclopedia of Philosophy (Summer 2017 Edition). https://plato.stanford.edu/archives/sum2017/entries/lawphil-naturalism/

Lewis D (1973) Counterfactuals. Blackwell Publishers, Harvard University Press, Oxford/Cambridge

Liao SM (2015) Human rights as fundamental conditions for a goof life. In: Cruft R, Liao SM, Renzo M (eds) Philosophical foundations of human rights. OUP, Oxford, pp 79–100

Makowski P (2011) Gilotyna Hume'a Przegląd Filozoficzny. Nowa Seria 76:317–334

Mazurkiewicz S (2019) Review of Marek Piechowiak Plato's conception of justice and the question of human dignity Sophia. Int J Philos Tradit 59:177–179

Mazurkiewicz S (2020) Marek Piechowiak's Plato's conception of justice and the question of human dignity (2019). Archiv für Rechts- und Sozialphilosophie 106:471–481

Menzel C (2017) Possible worlds. The Stanford Encyclopedia of Philosophy (Winter 2017 Edition). https://plato.stanford.edu/archives/win2017/entries/possible-worlds/

Mikhail J (2012) Moral grammar and human rights: some reflections on cognitive science and enlightenment rationalism. In: Goodman R, Jinks D, Woods AK (eds) Understanding social action, promoting human rights. OUP, Oxford, pp 160–202

Miller D (2007) National responsibility and global justice. OUP, Oxford

Miller D (2012) Grounding human rights. Crit Rev Int Soc Polit Philos 15:407–427

Nussbaum M (2000) Women and human development: the capabilities approach. Cambridge University Press, Cambridge

Nussbaum M (2006) Frontiers of justice: disability, nationality, species membership. The Belknap Press Harvard University Press, Cambridge

Nussbaum M (2011) Creating capabilities, the human development approach. The Belknap Press of Harvard University Press, Cambridge/London

Papineau D (2020) Naturalism. The Stanford Encyclopedia of Philosophy (Summer 2020 Edition). https://plato.stanford.edu/archives/sum2020/entries/naturalism/

Pardo M, Patterson D (2013) Minds brains and law. The conceptual foundations of law and neuroscience. Oxford, OUP

Piechowiak M (1999) Filozofia Praw Człowieka. Prawa Człowieka w świetle ich Międzynarodowej Ochrony. Towarzystwo Naukowe KUL, Lublin

Piechowiak M (2019) Plato's conception of justice and the question of human dignity. Peter Lang, Berlin

Plunkett D (2012) A positivist route for explaining how. Facts Make Law Legal Theory 18:139–207

Pogge T (2002) World poverty and human rights: cosmopolitan responsibilities and reforms. Polity Press, Cambridge

Putnam H (2002) The collapse of fact/value dichotomy and other essays. Harvard University Press, Harvard-London

Rawls J (1999) The laws of people. Harvard University Press, Cambridge

Raz J (2010) Human rights without foundations. In: Besson S Tasioulas J (eds) The philosophy of international law. OUP, pp 321–338

Raz J (2015) Human rights in the emerging world order life. In: Cruft R, Liao SM, Renzo M (eds) Philosophical foundations of human rights. OUP, Oxford, pp 217-236

Renzo M (2015) Human needs, human rights. In: Cruft R, Liao SM, Renzo M (eds) Philosophical foundations of human rights. OUP, Oxford, pp 570–587

Robertson T, Atkins P (2018) Essential vs. Accidental Properties. The Stanford Encyclopedia of Philosophy (Spring 2018 Edition). https://plato.stanford.edu/archives/spr2018/entries/essential-accidental/

Rosen M (2013) Dignity: the case against. In: McCrdudden C (ed) Understanding human dignity. OUP, Oxford, pp143–154

Sen A (1999) Development and freedom. Oxford University Press, New York

Sen A (2005) Human rights and capabilities. J Human Dev 6:151–166

Tahko T, Lowe J (2016) Ontological Dependence. The Stanford Encyclopedia of Philosophy (Winter 2016 Edition). https://plato.stanford.edu/archives/win2016/entries/dependence-ontological/

Tasioulas J (2011) On the nature of human rights. In: Ernst G, Heilinger JC (eds) The philosophy of human rights: contemporary controversies. De Gruyter, Berlin, pp 17–59

Tasioulas J (2013) Human dignity and the foundations of human rights. In: McCrdudden C (ed) Understanding human dignity. OUP, Oxford, pp 291–312

Tasioulas J (2015) On the foundations of human rights. In: Cruft R, Liao SM, Renzo M (eds) Philosophical foundations of human rights. OUP, Oxford, pp 45–70

Waldron J (2012) Dignity, rank and rights. OUP, Oxford

Waldron J (2013) Human rights: a critique of the Raz/Rawls approach NYU School of law. Public Law Res Pap 13:1–22

Waldron J (2015) Is dignity foundation of human rights? In: Cruft R, Liao SM, Renzo M (eds) Philosophical foundations of human rights. OUP, Oxford, pp 117–137

Witkowski K (1975) The "is-ought" gap: deduction or justification? Philos Phenomenol Res 36: 233–245

Zajadło J (2005) Dylematy Humanitarnej Interwencji: Historia, Etyka, Polityka, Prawo. Gdańsk, Arche

Zajadło J (2010) Humanitarian intervention: threat to international order, moral imperative or customary norm in statu nascendi? In: Zajadło J, Sykuna S, Widłak T (eds) Humanitarian interventions. reflection of the Special Workshop at the 23rd IVR World Congress. Wydawnictwo Uniwersytetu Gdańskiego: Gdańsk, pp 15–34

Załuski W (2009a) Evolutionary theory and legal philosophy. Edward Elgar, Cheltenham

Załuski W (2009b) Ewolucyjna Filozofia Prawa. Wolters Kluwer, Warszawa

Załuski W (2018) Law and evil. The evolutionary perspective. Edward Elgar, Cheltenham

Chapter 3
Entities in Philosophy of Human Rights

3.1 Human Rights

Human rights are rights. They are moral rights that necessarily claim to be recognised as legal rights. In fact, often they are recognised by law. My presentation of what human rights are will be based on how they are understood by the philosophy of human rights as well as by law, especially with respect to their properties. The scopes of concepts "moral rights" and "human rights" are, however, not equivalent.[1] Human rights are moral rights possessed simply in virtue of being human.[2] This statement is primarily the statement of the foundations of human rights, but it also affects human rights themselves. The lack of equivalence between moral rights and human rights implies that not every moral right is a human right. There are moral rights that have foundations other than the human status of their holder. For instance, we have moral rights that are rooted in formal justice, e.g. persons in similar situations should be treated in a similar way. Some moral rights hold due to the considerations of distributive justice. Others come due to the structure of the political community. Nickel puts it in the following way

> Not every question of social justice or wise governance is a human rights issue. For example, a country could have too much income inequality or inadequate provision for higher education without violating any human rights.[3]

Therefore, not every violation of morality constitutes a violation of a human right. Yet, every human right is of course a moral right. There is a prevailing tendency in the contemporary usage of the concept human rights to consider every issue about justice in terms of human rights.[4] From time to time various theorists propose new

[1] Wellman (2010), p. 21.

[2] Griffin (2008), p. 2; Tasioulas (2011), p. 26.

[3] Nickel (2019), Chap. 3.

[4] Cranston (1973), Wellman (1999), Orend (2002) and Griffin (2008, 2011).

S. Mazurkiewicz, *Grounding Human Rights in Human Nature*, Law and Philosophy Library 141, https://doi.org/10.1007/978-3-031-30734-8_3

human rights, for example, Pan American Health Organisation and WHO stated that the right to sexual pleasure is a human right[5] and, as Raz noticed, there are proposed the human rights to globalisation and to the lack of boring work, transparency and coexistence with nature.[6] However, many philosophers of human rights oppose this tendency.[7] This opposition is meant to be a tool stopping an over-expanding usage of human rights leading to inflation of the content of this concept. As a result, this inflation may undermine the whole project of human rights. If every violation of social justice becomes a violation of human rights, the concept of human rights violations, once so powerful in ascribing responsibility and holding accountable of international troublemakers, becomes more and more diluted. If we qualify the inequality of income to the same category as crimes against humanity, the latter may lose its special status. Griffin develops his account in order to respond to this particular problem. The aim of Griffin's theory is to provide the direct criteria for determining whether something is a human right.[8] However, his answer to the effect that infants, foetuses, handicapped, and people suffering from dementia, are excluded, is incompatible with the legal notion of human rights (and arguably also with truisms about human rights), because all these categories of people have human rights from the legal perspective.[9] Other human rights philosophers opt for applying the label "human rights" only to the rights that protect "decent level of human well-being"[10] or "minimally good life" rather than "good life" or "flourishing life".[11] Under the first, minimalist conception, one does not have the human right to education beyond some basic scope, even if she should have such opportunities on the basis of considerations of justice in a particular society. Under the second, maximalist conception, every moral right leading to a good or flourishing life is a human right. These problems with determining the scope of human rights trigger objections even against human rights that are explicitly recognised by law. Art. 24 of UDHR says that:

> Everyone has the right to rest and leisure, including reasonable limitation of working hours and periodic holidays with pay.[12]

Some may wonder whether such a right is actually a human right.[13] First, how can being a human be a foundation of the right to rest and leisure, including payable periodic holidays? Second, does this right enable a decent level of life or rather

[5]Pan American Health Organisation and WHO (2000).

[6]Raz (2010), p. 322; Pendelton (1999); Alston (1984).

[7]Tasioulas (2015).

[8]Griffin (2008), pp. 14–18; Griffin (2011), pp. 3–16.

[9]It is most discussable in case of foetuses, but ethical debates on abortion are out of scope of the aim of this work.

[10]Miller (2007, 2012) and Renzo (2015).

[11]Griffin (2008) and Nussbaum (2000).

[12]Universal Declaration of Human Rights (1948), art. 24.

[13]Cruft et al. (2015), p. 24; Liao (2015), p. 80.

something beyond this scope? The view that it is a human right leads us to the conclusion that for the most part of human history this right was violated.[14] It is only in the late nineteenth and early twentieth century when the limitation of working hours appeared with payable periodic holidays coming even later. I rather adhere to claims that human rights protect only a decent level of human life. Moreover, I believe that international documents on human rights, like Universal Declaration of Human Rights or European Convention of Human Rights drafted and established after the atrocities of the Second World War meant rather a decent level of well-being. They were not meant to provide everyone with a flourishing life, but rather to stop further genocides.

Therefore, in my view, human rights are moral rights that protect a decent level of human life. As a result, not everything called human right in the public discourse, or promoted as human right is actually a human right in the above-mentioned sense. Some countries may include in their list of rights, labelled as "human rights", rights that do not merely protect a decent level of human life but refer to a certain higher standard (e.g. flourishing life); the same applies to rights that are moral rights that exist not merely in virtue of "humanity" of the right holders human like most rights concerning social justice. Those rights are not truly human rights and they should be better named "basic rights" of "constitutional rights" since they are mostly enlisted in states' constitutions.

Wellman argues that the fact that human rights belong to the category of rights does not determine that they are only claim-rights in Hohfeldian terms as Shue) and Donnelly seem to claim.[15] Wellman provides a very illustrative presentation of different types of rights in Hohfeldian terms:

> X has a legal claim against Y that Y do act A if and only if Y has a legal duty to X to do A. X has a legal liberty in face of Y to do A if and only if X has a no-claim against X that X not do A. X has a legal power over Y to bring about some legal consequence C for Y if and only if Y has a legal liability in face of X that Y bring about this legal consequence C. And X has a legal immunity against Y's bringing about some legal consequence C for X if and only if Y has a legal disability in face of X to bring about this legal consequence.[16]

He argues that in fact human rights belong to every category of rights, although it is true that the core of human rights has a form of claim-rights like the right to life or the right to not to be tortured. I have the right not to be killed against everyone since anyone has a duty not to kill me. All positive liberties forming the second generation of human rights have a form of claim-rights. Human right to liberty is a liberty-right whereas right to enter into agreements is a power right. A right against a state that might enact laws violating human rights is in turn immunity-right.[17] As we see, human rights belong to very different formal categories of rights under Hohfeldian analysis of rights, and not only to right-claims as it might appear *prima facie*. Human

[14] Cruft (2015), p. 108.

[15] Wellman (2010), p. 23; Shue (1996), pp. 14–15; Donnelly (2003), p. 8.

[16] Wellman (2010), pp. 17–18.

[17] Wellman (2010), p. 23.

rights possess very distinctive properties.[18] They are equal, inviolable and inalienable.[19] Equality means that every human possesses the same human rights, being inviolable means that there must never be violated (rather than they cannot be violated, we all know that unfortunately they happen to be violated), and inalienability means that no one can trade her human rights or have them limited. Other properties such as universality, indivisibility or interdependence are derived from these properties or found by analysis of the concept of human rights.[20] Universality means that they are universal across time and space, indivisibility and interdependence mean that human rights are equal in importance and cannot be divided or separated. If human rights are to be moral rights possessed by every human simply due to being human they must be equal and universal. It is also often claimed that human rights are innate, as we can read in UDHR—"All human beings are born free and equal in dignity and rights"[21]—it means that we already have them right from the beginning and there are not enacted in the form of positive law.

The universality of human rights triggers certain difficulties. The problem of the pre-late nineteenth century right to rest, leisure, and paid holidays is a notable example. Similarly, one may object to the whole idea of human rights by asking if there was a human right to free, elementary education in the Neolithic period. One promising strategy of overcoming difficulties of this kind, often adopted in the philosophy of human rights, is to claim that particular rights are dependent on a given time, space and location. Particular human rights are relative to specific problems that are dealt with at particular times and places, along with respective goods that can help solving those problems. In fact they are instantiations of universal human rights.[22] Griffin argues that there are three basic and abstract human rights: the right to autonomy, the right to liberty and the right to welfare. All other particular human rights, like the right to privacy, are derived from those basic human rights under specific circumstances and are formulated in the language of time, place and actual concerns.[23]

I generally adhere to this position, with a very minor change in formulation: I believe it is better to talk about the "right to security" instead of the "right to welfare" or the "right to minimum provision".[24] I believe that the right to security includes the whole Griffin's right to welfare but security is a more basic term that suits better the notion of the most general and universal rights. The term "welfare" has too many connotations with the political and social theory of welfare state and may be quite misleading. By security I mean the basic level of goods that are necessary to live. Griffin defines autonomy in the following way: "a capacity to recognize

---

[18] Hohfeld (1913).

[19] Universal Declaration of Human Rights (1948), Preamble; German Basic Law (1949), art. 1(2).

[20] Vienna Declaration (1993).

[21] Universal Declaration of Human Rights (1948), art. 1.

[22] Tasioulas (2011), p. 33.

[23] Griffin (2008), p. 50.

[24] Griffin also makes use of the second term, cf. Griffin (2008), p. 50.

good-making features of human life, both prudential and moral, which can lead to the appropriate motivation and action".[25] Therefore, the right to autonomy is the right to have such a capacity. In turn, according to Griffin "liberty guarantees not the realization of one's conception of a worthwhile life, but only its *pursuit*."[26] The right to liberty is thus the right to the pursuit of one's conception of a worthwhile life. So, while autonomy relates to one's own moral judgments, liberty relates to being able to strive for one's goals. Under such a view, universal moral human rights boil down to the three most general rights: the right to autonomy, the right to liberty and the right to security.

All other particular, concrete, specific rights are instantiations of these universal human rights and related to time and space. More precisely, being "relative" to time and space means that some contingent environmental and social facts occur that together with universal and more abstract rights to autonomy, to liberty or to security give rise to particular, specific human rights. For instance, the human right to basic healthcare could not emerge before healthcare started to exist. The human right to a fair trial in modern understanding did not exist until the emergence of the modern state with its coercive powers, yet hunter-gatherers seem to have had a basic right to be sentenced impartially by members of their tribe. The right to free of charge elementary education becomes an instantiation of the right to liberty only when the development of society rises to the level when the traditional form of passing knowledge, necessary to the proper level of life, is insufficient. Such a characteristic solves the problem of the art. 24 of UDHR right to rest, leisure and paid holidays. Only when a capitalistic, massive form of industrial employment emerged, this right appeared as an instantiation of the right to liberty.

Concerning the space relativity of human rights, following such a solution, in some regions in the modern world (Canada, Scandinavia) humans do not have the human right to clean water since there simply is enough clean water for everyone. What would be the point of having a moral right to something that everyone has unlimited access to? Do we have the human right to oxygen? I believe that we do not have such a right, since oxygen is fully available. Having the right to oxygen does not protect the decent level of human functioning. Thus, there is no human right to oxygen. The same goes for the human right to clean water in regions where no shortages of clean water occur. On the other hand, in regions with water shortages, there is such a right. Other specific rights, including lists found in UDHR, other international human rights law and democratic states' constitutions are instantiations of those human rights in our contemporary times. In fact, after other changes in the world occur, we may witness new instantiations of human rights, like presumably rights concerning privacy in the Internet-based world. It can be said that in some sense particular human rights respond to the human needs. However, they do not respond to all human needs but only those that ensure a decent level of life. Moreover, and this is the difference with the human needs approach, some more

[25] Griffin (2008), p. 157.

[26] Griffin (2008), p. 160.

abstract human rights, as normative entities, are necessary to form particular human rights. Therefore, to avoid terminological confusion, I will call those contingent facts that trigger the concrete realisation of the abstract human rights "environmental and social facts". Nonetheless, particular human rights are also universal, however, their universality is related to some concrete time and spice, while abstract human rights are universal no matter of time and space.

The distinction on universal and particular human rights doesn't match with the distinction on moral and legal human rights—it is not that universal human rights are moral rights and particular human rights are legal rights. I consider human rights as primarily moral rights—in the sense that they belong to moral sphere. If they are included in a legal text and positivised, they become also legal human rights—they are clearly mentioned in a legal text and this text can be referred to while claiming certain things. But it doesn't mean that they loose their moral status and that their foundations is only of legal matter. To the contrary, on moral or metaphysical level, their foundations is of an extra-legal character. As I intent to discuss the foundations of human rights, while speaking about human rights I mean moral human rights. If, however, moral human rights are incorporated into a legally binding text, they are also legal human rights and this distinction is only conceptual. It may be discussed whether practically only particular human rights (so rights like the right to nationality, freedom of press, etc.) are included in legal documents. Nonetheless, UDHR includes the right to liberty and the right to security (art. 3), so it seems that both universal and particular human rights can be included in legal texts.

One might object to the distinction of universal and particular human rights claiming that e.g. the right to life or the right not to be tortured are universal rights not instantiated by any contingent facts. Yet, I believe that there are such facts that instantiate those human rights. Only when people started acting violently against one another, these rights emerged as the realisation of the right to security (and perhaps also the right to liberty). Imagine a hunter-gatherer group of early modern humans 200.000 years ago. If there is no violence in their social life, the right to life and the right not to be tortured are pointless. Now, consider a despotic city-state where its habitants have the right to life and the right not to be tortured, and that is due to the social structure of the despotic city-state. Assume that in the contemporary world we have the human right to clear air as it is necessary for a decent level of life. Did those hunter-gatherers have this right? In my view, they did not since in their time and space there was only clear, unpolluted air, unlike today. Perhaps, in the future there will be discussed the human right to oxygen, however now we do not possess this right—there is plenty of oxygen in the atmosphere and such a right would be pointless. Coming back to potentially controversial for some placing the human rights as the right to life and the right not to be tortured in this category: without violence in human social life there is no point in having those rights just as there is no point in claiming that we have now the right to oxygen, despite the fact that oxygen is necessary for our life.

As I think, such an approach enables us to solve the problem of universality of human rights. In particular, it enables the recognition of newly emerging human rights without rejecting the crucial claim that human rights are universal.

Universality in the very strongest sense—spaceless and timeless (across all time and space)—is attached to the most fundamental, abstract (in terms of dispositions that can be formulated) human rights.

One should also not forget that the idea of human rights as universal moral rights assumes strong moral objectivism[27] and moral development in learning moral truths. The fact that for so many years we did not recognise the right against slavery does not mean that in the former historical conditions humans could be held in slavery. Rather, we have understood the moral wrongness of slavery at all times and comprehended that the moral beliefs of previous generations were wrong. In fact, social recognition of other instantiations of human rights, like recognition of full gender equality, children's rights, etc. can be regarded as an example of such a moral development. Human rights, both universal, as well as particular, hold independently on their social recognition.

3.1.1 Human Rights as Entities and Moral Facts

Human rights belong to a normative sphere. Propositions about human rights usually tell us what to do and give us reasons for actions. The question arises whether such propositions are truth apt. This question pertains to metaethics, and in particular is a part of the dispute between cognitivism (characterised by the claim that normative propositions, including moral propositions are truth apt) and noncognitivism or expressivism (which is characterised by the opposite claim). It is beyond the scope of this work to enter into the details of this dispute.[28] I will adopt the cognitivists stance, and I will assume that propositions about human rights are truth apt. I have in mind such propositions as "all humans possess the human right X"—if we take human rights and human rights law seriously, such propositions must have truth value. A proposition is true due to some fact, which is called "truthmaker".[29] The

---

[27] It is very interesting whether the idea of human rights is coherent only with moral realism. However, this issue lies beyond the scope of this work as my aim is to present the approach to human rights in metaphysical terms, rather than in metaethical ones.

[28] In turn, moral realism is the view there exist (certain) mind-independent moral facts. I believe that the idea of human rights as inherent, inborn (art. 1 UDHR), and not established by positive legislation, is most simply accounted for from the perspective of moral realism ("realism about human rights"). Simplicity, consistency, and intuitiveness are major theoretical virtues of this position. Obviously, there are also alternative accounts. The most significant alternative is the view exploiting the conceptual possibility of thinking about human rights as mind-dependent, rational creations, like other, moral and social norms. However, in my view, such a philosophical position would deal with significant problems related to legal understanding of human rights, as it has been expressed in international and domestic human rights law. The discussion on metaethics is of course connected to metaphysics yet the aim of this work is to focus on metaphysical foundations of human rights so I decide not to discuss further the issue of moral realism and human rights besides this short comment.

[29] Mulligan et al. (1984).

proposition that snow is white is true due to the fact that snow is white. If the proposition of the form referred to above is true, the fact that all humans possess the human right to X must obtain. This presupposes that the human right to X exists.

From the point of view of contemporary analytic metaphysics, we can think of both ahistorical, universal human rights and their historical, particular instantiations as moral facts. One should not be confused by the usage of the term "fact" in relation to human rights.

We enter here into the difficult and controversial area of metaphysics. The notion of "fact" is far from being clear and is not used in a unified way. Two main approaches can be distinguished. Under the first one, facts are just true propositions.[30] This approach seems to be based on the confusion between the object level and the linguistic level. Propositions are representational, so they refer to something that is different than the proposition itself. Facts are not representational. Facts are what makes a proposition true or false.

Under the second approach facts are obtaining states of affairs.[31] There are states of affairs that do not obtain, like the one that Pegasus exists. Therefore, it is not the fact that Pegasus exists. Yet, there are states of affairs that obtain, like that Warsaw is the capital of Poland. Thus, it is the fact that Warsaw is the capital of Poland. Similarly, if there is an obtaining state of affairs that all humans have the human right X, it means that there is a fact that every human has the human right X.

Such conception of fact is broad in the sense that it includes various sorts of facts. In particular, it includes empirical facts (for example: a horse has four legs), mental facts (X suffers pain), conceptual facts (for example: square has four angles) and normative facts (for example: parents should care about their children). All those facts are obtaining state of affairs. Normative facts are facts about normative properties and relations in which they stand,[32] while for instance legal facts are facts about the actual content of the law. Since moral facts are normative facts, moral facts are simply facts about moral properties and their relations. Moral facts can be simply understood as facts about the actual content of morality. It is a legal fact that in Poland one needs to be above 18 years old to buy alcohol. It is a moral fact that one is entitled to free, elementary education. There is a moral fact that every human has the right to liberty. This discussion suggests that human rights exist as a sort of entities. Such entities are of course able to be possessed by their holders. Notice also that when we talk about human rights from the perspective of the foundations of human rights, we focus not on the statements such as "X should be done", but rather on statements like "every human being has the right to X".[33] Both are normative statements, yet the second one is related to rights that are possessed. If we think

[30] Mulligan and Correia (2017).

[31] Mulligan and Correia (2017).

[32] cf. Rosen (2017), p. 135.

[33] Of course, I do not mean that other categorisations related to human rights are wrong. For instance, norms, including legal norms, can make use of human rights in stating an obliged, prohibited or allowed matter. This is however outside the aim of this work.

about these rights not as concepts, existing in our minds, but as more independent beings, we can call them "entities". Consequently, the debate on the foundations of human rights can be presented as the debate on why and how there exist certain (moral) entities. As we see, it does not have to be only an ethical debate, it can also be considered as a metaphysical debate and the usage of terms like "entities" (or even "facts" following the current analytic language convention) is justified.

To sum up: the way I use the words "fact" and "entity" is a neutral way, characteristic of the contemporary analytic philosophy. However, I am personally not entirely convinced whether the broadening of the usage of the term "fact" fits our intuitive understanding. It is important to notice that the set of referents of the concept of fact in contemporary analytic philosophy is not limited to empirical, natural facts. I follow this philosophical *façon de parler* in order to make my discussion consistent with the philosophical debate that I refer to.[34] A fact is any obtaining state of affairs (or in other words everything "what is the case that") and an entity is anything that exists. Thus, it is a fact that every human has the human right X, provided that it is actually the case. The human right X is an entity, provided that it exists.

To conclude, human rights are universal moral rights to live life on a decent level. I understand the decent level just as do the proponents of the basic human needs approach: it is the level of average human functioning. This notion stands in opposition to the notion of flourishing life that human rights should supposedly protect. There are fully universal human rights, such as—in my proposal—the right to autonomy, the right to liberty and the right to security, which are further instantiated by particular rights related to specific historical conditions. Those particular historically-related human rights can change over time but they are universal in relation to specific time and space, meaning that every human being in the same location in terms of space and time has the same human rights. Our moral development enables us to recognise the rights that were possessed by their holders, even though they were not recognised in their times.

[34] The current analytic philosophy usage of the term "fact" does not presuppose that these facts are facts like natural, physical facts. In ethical debate, the earlier discussions on the existence of moral facts have been transformed into the discussion on whether they are mind-independent moral facts. However, this new terminology and the constant usage of "facts" can be confusing for those who are not accustomed to it. For this reason, even though speaking of human rights as moral facts is correct under the current terminological usage, I will often refer to human rights as "entities". An entity is an object that exists. The concept of entity has also strong metaphysical connotations, just like the concept of fact, but I believe it will be much easier to intuitively accept for those who are not accustomed to the current analytic philosophy usage of "fact".

3.2 Human Dignity

The term "human dignity" is a very ambiguous term and it is often highly unclear what it denotes and what human dignity actually is.[35] Most generally, human dignity can be characterised as an inherent worth of every human possessed only due to being human.[36] Some authors emphasise that human dignity involves the prohibition of solely instrumental treatment of human beings.[37] In international legal documents on human rights, as well as in many contemporary constitutions, human dignity is regarded as the foundation of human rights. With regard to its properties, human dignity is inherent, innate, equal, inviolable and inalienable.[38] It means that every human being has human dignity only due to being human (an inherent property) and that every human being has human dignity from the very beginning of being human. It also means that there is no need to establish human dignity by means of positive law. At best, legal documents can refer to human dignity, but there is no legal definition of "human dignity", for it is not a legal concept (the concept of human dignity is analysed in legal terms, but as I argue in the next paragraphs, such analyses are conducted to meet the aims of purely legal interpretation and are not very useful in analysing what human dignity as the foundation of human rights *per se* is). Positive law can of course, and should, refer to human dignity, but it is not the case that human dignity exists because of such positive law enactments. Human dignity, like Cartesian reason, is equally distributed between all men. We all have the same human dignity, no matter any personal traits. It is inviolable, which will be analysed in detail above. Let me claim that inviolability means that human dignity can never be undone and destroyed. Human dignity is inalienable, which means that no one can waive it or have human dignity limited. The usage of the term "human dignity" is extremely ambiguous, yet it is possible to clarify what this term means. Human dignity is an inherent worth of every human being and has the properties mentioned above.

It is extremely difficult to say anything else about human dignity itself without moving to the debate on the foundations of human dignity, which will be discussed later. Similarly, the discussion on human dignity can very rapidly move into the debate on its moral or legal consequences—this is what is the case in most legal works on human dignity. That is why I rarely refer to works on human dignity conducted in the legal sciences or to the views on human dignity presented in the rulings of constitutional courts. As I will present, they very often confuse human dignity as the foundation of human rights and human dignity as one of human rights or the core of a given right. Here, the main argument against the firm normative force of human dignity, seen in the contemporary debates, can be mentioned: human dignity tends to be interpreted as one prefers in order to enhance one's persuasive

[35] Lee and George (2008).

[36] Tasioulas (2011), p. 17; Tasioulas (2013), p. 292.

[37] Piechowiak (1999).

[38] Universal Declaration of Human Rights (1948); German Basic Law (1949).

force. As such, human dignity is regarded to have merely a rhetorical meaning and its content is invented by a given institution, for instance a court, once it wants to justify its claims in the most strong moral way. Christopher McCdrudden in his analysis of the legal interpretation of human dignity gives many examples of such claims.[39] To cite just some of them: the Preamble to the Convention for the Suppression of Unlawful Acts against the Safety of Maritime Navigation (1988) claims: "world-wide escalation of acts of terrorism in all its forms, which endanger or take innocent human lives, jeopardize fundamental freedoms and seriously impair the dignity of human beings";[40] Arab Chart on Human Rights claims that "All forms of racism, Zionism and foreign occupation and domination constitute an impediment to human dignity [. . .]";[41] The Supreme Court of Israel, in the case concerning censorship of film due to degrading scenes, ruled that artistic value must be weighted with the obligation to protect human dignity.[42] But, do these actions actually violate human dignity or it is simply more morally persuasive to say so? More importantly, is the concept of human dignity used in the above documents the same concept as human dignity that is the inviolable foundation of human rights?

Piechowiak distinguishes twelve different meanings of the word "dignity" that should not be confused with dignity that is the foundation of human rights.[43] The other most important meanings of the word "dignity" are: dignity based on cognitive functions of a developed person, dignity as moral perfection of a person, dignity as reputation or good name, dignity as a golden mean between arrogance and servility in attitude towards others, dignity in terms of conditions (especially extremely tough) of life and dignity of an office or a social role.[44] Some of these meanings are more likely to be confused with dignity that is the basis of human rights. If one conceives dignity as conditions of someone's life, such as living in extremely tough conditions (like suffering a disease causing constant and great pain), one can be led to the statement that such a life is a life without dignity. Consequently, if someone lives without dignity, whereas human rights are derived from dignity, one would cease to possess human rights. If dignity is based on being a person in Lockean meaning of "person", a human with dementia would have no dignity. As a result, she would not have human rights. Griffin's and Nussbaum's (although for Nussbaum dignity is less important in her theory) approaches are based on such a notion of dignity. As it has been said, Griffin explicitly excludes people with dementia and

---

[39] McCrudden (2008).

[40] Convention for the Suppression of Unlawful Acts against the Safety of Maritime Navigation (1988), Preamble.

[41] Arab Chart on Human Rights (2004), art. 2(3).

[42] Station Film Co. v. Public Council for Film Censorship (1994).

[43] Piechowiak (2011), pp. 5–6.

[44] Piechowiak (2011), pp. 5–6. Other meanings of 'dignity' distinguished by Piechowiak, in my opinion, less vulnerable to be confused with dignity as foundations of human rights, are: dignity based on one's feeling of her dignity, dignity of appearance and behavior resulting from dignity of an office or a social role, dignity ascribed not only to humans but also to animals and specific to Polish language, dignity as one's surname.

those in coma from the category of human rights bearers, because they do not possess normative agency, which for Griffin is the proper understanding of human dignity. I oppose such a view as it cannot explain the existence of many key human rights and stands to the contrary to the essential practice of human rights law.[45] Griffin's failure can be analysed in terms of confusing two different types of dignity—the one which is the foundation of human rights with the one that derives from the cognitive functions of a person.

Dignity understood in terms of conditions of life serves as the departure point for many misinterpretations and misconceptions, thus leading to misunderstandings between those who believe in the inherent worth of every human life and those who believe that human life can become unworthy of living. The first group takes euthanasia to be always wrong as it violates inherent worth of every person and violates the internal dignity of person, wherein the second group recognises that it may happen that life becomes such a suffering that there would be no value in living it. It is not the aim of this book to settle such moral dilemmas, however, it is important to keep in mind the manifold important consequences of the particular applications of the concept of dignity (as utilised by different approaches).

In context of the issue of justification of human rights there is one further possible notable confusion with respect to the term "dignity". If human dignity is the foundation of human rights, how the "right to dignity" can ever be violated (as sometimes is claimed)? For instance, in Explanations Relating to the Charter of Fundamental Rights of the European Union, which is meant as a tool helpful in interpreting provisions of the Charter of Fundamental Rights, we read: "The dignity of the human person is not only a fundamental right in itself but constitutes the real basis of fundamental rights".[46] But how something inviolable can be simultaneously a right, which by definition can be violated? To give other examples: South African Constitutional Tribunal stated: "dignity is not only a value fundamental to our Constitution, it is a justiciable and enforceable right that must be respected and protected".[47] South African Constitutional Tribunal regards human dignity both as a right and as a value that is the basis of other rights. The Polish Constitutional Tribunal, provided following arguments:

> These situations lead to depriving the individual right to privacy. It can also, under some conditions, lead to the violation of human dignity. [. . .] In the assessment of Constitutional Tribunal, there occurs a close relation between the threat for human dignity, constituting the basis of individual's constitutional liberties and rights, and all actions invading individual's privacy.[48]

It seems that Polish Constitutional Tribunal equates dignity as the foundation of rights and dignity as a specific right. Krystian Complak believes that in trying to

[45] For advanced arguments see Sect. 2.4.

[46] Explanations Relating to the Charter of Fundamental Rights (2007), Title I.

[47] *Dawood v. Minister of Home Affairs* (2000), 5 Law Reports of the Commonwealth 147, 2000 (3) SA 936 (CC), para. 35.

[48] Verdict of 23.06.2009, K. 54/2007; (my translation).

understand Tribunal's line of argumentation, "it might be said that dignity is a qualified version of privacy.[49] However, how dignity can be violated while it simultaneously constitutes a foundation of all rights and is said to be inviolable? If one's dignity can be violated, it is conceivable that sometimes it may be violated to such an extent that we all could agree that it was destroyed. And once human dignity is destroyed, the basis of human rights disappears. With no basis for human rights, human rights themselves seems to vanish as well. However, this consequence seems to be absurd and thus unacceptable. Possessing the right to dignity can be regarded as a positive thing at a first glance, for there is always something positive in having a right. But after a deeper examination, if the object of this right is the same dignity that is the inviolable basis of all rights, the right to dignity turns out to be pointless. If I already possess inherent and inviolable human dignity, what is the point in having the right to it? Let us assume that simply being human is the foundation of human rights, not human dignity. Is every human's right to be human meaningful in any sense? If someone is a human being, as long as one lives one cannot renounce being human. One may, however, have a right to be treated like a human being, and this different option seems to be meaningful. But the object of the right alters from being a human to being treated like a human. Perhaps this is what both Constitutional Tribunals wanted to say: that everyone has a right to be treated with dignity. But dignity in this meaning denotes a peculiar form of respect of someone's autonomy rather than an inherent worth that is the source of human rights.[50] This respect becomes abbreviated to the claim of having the "right to dignity" that provides a peculiar difficulty in understanding the proper meaning of the term "dignity".

Let me also present a potential perfidious line of argumentation. Assume that the inviolability of human dignity means that it *should not* be violated. We know that human dignity is the foundation of human rights. Imagine a Nazi criminal from a concentration camp defending oneself by claiming that he had destroyed human dignity of his victims, what consequently led to the situation where the victims ceased to have human dignity. His terrible crimes led to the destruction of human dignity of the concentration camp prisoners. As a consequence, since victims qua human beings have human rights due to having human dignity, they cease to have human rights at the moment when their human dignity is destroyed. Here the paradoxical result arises: it seems that no human rights were violated, for there are no such rights after severe violations of human dignity, even to the extent that, as we can claim, human dignity was destroyed. We reach a horrible and by far unwanted conclusion that if someone's human dignity is destroyed, she ceases to have human rights. Of course, there is something wrong in such a line of argumentation. What is wrong is the first assumption stating that the requirement of the inviolability of human dignity means that that human dignity *should* not be violated. Instead, the

---

[49] Complak (2014), art. 30; (my translation).

[50] Obviously unless one believes that the proper meaning of the concept of dignity is having autonomy or normative agency, as Kantian or neo-Kantian reading, e.g. Griffin's, would propose.

inviolability of human dignity means that it can simply never be violated, no matter what happens. Inviolability of human dignity holds on modal, not deontic level.

However, I believe that distinguishing human dignity as the fundament of human rights, along with the right to demand that others respect one's dignity, does not solve the problem. If human dignity is inviolable, what is the point of having a right to respect something inviolable? I think that this inviolability should not be understood in the weak, deontic, form as a claim that human dignity *should not* be violated, rather in the modal form that it *cannot* be violated. I believe that what human rights law, both international and domestic, claims is not a rhetorical phrase about the prohibition of violating human dignity, but rather a firm statement defending a strong value of every human being, such that one's dignity can never be violated. Therefore, it seems proper to thoroughly distinguish between human dignity as the foundation of human rights and the right to human dignity (that can be respected or violated). The object of this right is dignity in a different meaning. This meaning is also somewhat unclear, for it can denote either a respect to one's autonomy, the central part of the right to privacy (the core of one's private life where state cannot have any access), or the most central aspect of other specific human rights (the core or the "essence" of the most important rights). Further clarification of this issue lies outside the aim of this work.[51] What I want to emphasise here is that human dignity, understood as the basis of human rights, is not the content of the right to human dignity or the right to have one's human dignity fully respected. Rather, human dignity is the foundation of human rights. It is inviolable—nothing can violate or undo human dignity. Let contrast it with some rights or goods (interests, benefits) that follow from human dignity. Health as a good can be violated and even destroyed, whereas human dignity as its foundation can never be violated.

As we see, what human dignity actually means is unclear and vulnerable to many confusions. The right to dignity is something different than dignity as the source of human rights. In the following parts of this work by human dignity I mean human dignity as inherent worth of every human that is the foundation of human rights. There are two broad traditions of thinking about human dignity in such a meaning. It is not my aim to reconstruct them fully but rather to present the core of argument and focus on problems that each of the positions involves in the context of justification of human rights.

[51] Perhaps it would be better to use a different term instead of "dignity" as the content of this specific rights, e.g. "respect" in order to avoid confusion with human dignity as the foundation of human rights.

3.2.1 Classical and Christian Approach to Human Dignity

The first major approach is the classical approach, along with its Christian continuation. The two approaches are connected as Christian philosophy is highly influenced by classical philosophy. The relation is not the same in the different direction: one can endorse classical approach to human dignity without claims of Christian philosophy of theology. Under the classical approach human dignity is understood as an inner unity and perfection of existence that holds due to the very foundation of being.[52] Human dignity is the basis for being a person. A human being is a person because of possessing dignity underlying her existence.[53] This notion forms the philosophical basis of the Christian approach to human dignity. In Christian thought every human possesses inalienable and inherent dignity by virtue of being created as an image of God.[54] Every human possesses the inherent resemblance to God (is *Imago Dei*) and is unconditionally loved by God.[55] That makes every human dignified. While it is a plausible justification of human dignity for those who believe in God, Tasioulas notices that the reference to God's love in the justification of human dignity, especially in Wolterstroff's account, raises serious and unexpected difficulties. If God's love is based on some qualities (properties) possessed by human beings, why not to identify human dignity directly in these qualities? On the other hand, it is claimed that if God's love is independent on any humans' qualities, it seems to be arbitrary.[56] Moreover, following this approach, irrespective of the above-mentioned problem, our significant moral duties towards other people derive from their resemblance to God and ultimately consist of respecting God himself, as Tasioulas.[57] But therefore human beings happen to be remote from human rights,[58] for human rights are justified by reference to other things than the sole human beings that they are supposed to protect. Human dignity happens to be one thing, which is the inherent human worth possessed due to God's love or God's resemblance, and human rights turn out to be other, namely universal moral rights that protect every human. Another theological argument for human dignity is Christ's incarnation and salvation—if God became human to redeem human, being human (i.e. human nature) has enormous worth. But although human dignity has a very strong justification, the link from human dignity to human rights turns out to be too weak, or even inadequate, in relation to the presumed properties of human rights. How could one's resemblance to God justify a particular human right? It seems that human dignity belongs to a category of divine values or eternal moral truths, whereas human rights are real moral rights protecting the basic aspect of human functioning.

---

[52] Piechowiak (1999, 2019).

[53] Piechowiak (1999, 2019).

[54] Catechism of Catholic Church, para. 6 art 357.

[55] Wolterstorff (2008).

[56] Tasioulas (2013), p. 295.

[57] Tasioulas (2013), p. 295.

[58] Tasioulas (2013), p. 295.

On the one hand, it is true that human dignity conceived in such a way is adequate to explain the inherent worth of every human, but, on the other hand, it is also incapable of determining the exact scope and object of particular human rights. Tasioulas who is an adherent of regarding human dignity as the foundation of human rights, proposes, therefore, another object (or category of things/objects) to be the foundation of human rights along with human dignity, namely universal human interests.[59] Human dignity expresses general worth (value) and stands as the main reason to protect human beings, whereas universal human interests enable us to directly identify the scope of putative human rights. The Christian justification of human dignity is very strong and plausible provided strong theological assumptions are accepted. But the justification of human dignity and human rights must be universal, in the sense it is acceptable for every human being no matter of theological beliefs. For this reason, we must seek another foundations of human rights and human dignity for the justification of human rights even if one finds the Christian justification plausible on theological level.

Piechowiak's first book focuses on developing an approach justifying human rights under the classical and Christian understanding of human dignity.[60] He is an adherent of understanding human dignity in terms of classical philosophy developed up to modern Christian personalism. He believes that we cannot fully conceptualise human dignity. He understands human dignity as something underlying the fact that every human being is person that cannot be unambiguously defined.[61] This approach does not, however, underrate the importance of human dignity, as it provides the necessary link to human good, which also cannot be properly grasped by our concepts, yet remains a crucial element to be taken into consideration in an inquiry on human rights. Moreover, Piechowiak notices that even though the concept of human dignity is unclear and difficult to define, human rights are grounded in human dignity itself, rather than in the concept of human dignity.[62] Thus, there is no need to fully conceptualise the concept of human dignity: it is the reality itself—human dignity—that grounds human rights.[63] I will come back to this idea in further parts of my work. Interestingly, Piechowiak argues that the classical notion of human dignity provides every human with more freedom than the Kantian one.[64] According to the classical notion of "good" there is the objective indeterminacy of what is good. What is good, and especially what is the best to do in a particular case, is determined by an individual by free, but rational, choice between various interests. In turn, according to the Kantian notion moral laws are universal and there is no individual's freedom to choose.[65] Therefore, it is the classical, and not the Kantian, way of understanding

[59] Tasioulas (2013, 2015).

[60] Piechowiak (1999).

[61] Piechowiak (1999), pp. 86–88.

[62] Piechowiak (1999), p. 87.

[63] Piechowiak (1999), p. 87.

[64] Piechowiak (2011).

[65] Piechowiak (2011).

human dignity that is compatible with the contemporary notion of human rights, where individual's freedom plays such a significant role.

Despite this positive theoretical aspect of the classical notion of human dignity, it involves theoretical problems that have been already mentioned in Sect. 2.5. The Christian notion of human dignity is unacceptable for those who do not believe in Judeo-Christian God, along with the whole ethical system founded on that belief. In turn, the classical notion is based on philosophy adopting numerous strong metaphysical assumptions and must be taken into consideration altogether with the broad conceptual framework underlying classical thought. I am not an adversary of classical philosophy but for many it can be difficult to accept it. Therefore, I would like to propose an alternative approach to human dignity that might appear to be more intuitively acceptable for a modern man. Before that, however, let me present the Kantian notion of human dignity and its later development.

3.2.2 Kantian and Kantian-Analytic Approach to Human Dignity

The second major approach to human dignity is based on Kantian philosophy. One can point two main types of arguments to argue in favour of human dignity in Kant's thinking. The first type of argument in favour of human dignity lies in one of Kant's formulations of Categorical Imperative: "Act so that you use humanity, as much in your own person as in the person of every other, always at the same time as end and never merely as means."[66] Human is the one and only being to be treated as an end in himself. This gives every human an intrinsic value, which is called human dignity. The second Kant's type of argument for human dignity is that it is only human who is capable of establishing moral norms.[67] As moral norms are established purely by reason they must be established by humans as only humans are reasonable beings. That provides human beings with innate worth—human dignity. In sum, these two ways of argument together imply that "humanity" in Categorical Imperative means rationality, since it is rationality that constitutes human nature by differentiating humans from other beings.[68] Therefore, we have a moral duty to respect the rationality of others as it constitutes their nature and is the foundation of their human dignity.

The Kantian notion of human dignity is very often used in the contemporary analytic philosophy, including ethics, and ethically oriented accounts in philosophy of human rights. It can be even named a sub-class of Kantian approach or a neo-Kantian notion. However, in order to avoid confusions, I will refer to it as Kantian-analytic notion, since it is also based on the analytic notion of "person".

---

[66]Rachel (1986), p. 114; Kant (1785), G 4:429.

[67]Rachel (1986), p. 115.

[68]Rachel (1986), p. 115.

Under analytic (sometimes called "psychological") notion of "person", to be a person is to possess higher cognitive functions, to be rational, to have consciousness and to be able to feel pain and pleasure.[69] To compare, under substantive (sometimes named "ontological") notion of "person", possessing inherent human dignity makes someone a person.[70] Since according to the substantive notion dignity is understood in classical terms, every human being has dignity, and consequently is person. This is, however, rather a minor position in contemporary analytic philosophy, and generally in Anglo-Saxon thought. If we take together the analytic notion of person and Kantian account of human dignity, it can be claimed that those who possess higher cognitive functions are rational beings who are capable of establishing moral norms and rationally deciding about their own lives. These conditions enable them to be persons and to possess an inherent value that prohibits others from intruding into their scope of rationally exercised freedom. This inherent value is human dignity. The capability of establishing moral norms and choosing one's way of life is often called normative (or moral) agency (or autonomy). It is fiercely discussed in the contemporary Anglo-Saxon philosophy of human rights. Griffin is aware of the fact that both for international law and for many theorists of human rights it is human dignity that is considered to be their foundation. He believes that the proper justification of human rights should illuminate human rights in light of our best ethics overall. The core line of his argumentation consists in arguing for human rights on the basis that they serve our normative agency. By means of conceptual analysis he seems to argue that human dignity is a value being founded on normative agency, or even to claim that human dignity actually is reducible to a form of normative agency.[71] His notion of normative agency is fully based on the analytic notion of person—only those who are able to rationally choose are normative agents. Nussbaum's capabilities approach takes advantage of analytically conceived concept of person as well. Her capabilities form the foundations of human rights and they enable having a flourishing life. Capabilities can be regarded as properties of someone who is a person under the analytic conception of this concept.

The Kantian notion of normative autonomy focuses entirely on purely moral issues—that one is able to establish moral norms and obey moral duties. In turn, the contemporary concept of normative (or moral) agency (or autonomy) puts a strong emphasis on all aspects of human conduct without limiting itself only to the moral sphere. Normative agency refers to enabling everyone choosing one's conception of good or flourishing life.[72] Everyone has a moral duty to respect others' choices. These choices come from exercising one's normative agency, and since normative agency is either the foundation of human dignity or human dignity can be reduced to normative agency, this respect means the respect of others' human dignity. Under

---

[69] Załuski (2011), p. 84.

[70] Załuski (2011), p. 85; Piechowiak (1999, 2019).

[71] The second interpretation means that the concept of human dignity is reduced to the concept of normative agency; Griffin (2008), pp. 21, 45, 226.

[72] Griffin (2008) and Nussbaum (2000).

this approach, the above-analysed problematic issue of human dignity as a right can be understood as a right to have one's normative autonomy respected.

The contemporary notion of normative agency can be regarded as a development of Kantian views on human dignity, influenced also by analytic notion of person. The prohibition of purely instrumental treatment and the duty of respect to others are important consequences of this notion that has influenced the practice of human rights.[73] On the other hand, this contemporary Kantian-analytic notion has serious drawbacks. The main is that human dignity, conceived as a consequence of higher cognitive functions cannot be possessed by those who lack those functions, like people in coma, the people suffering from strong dementia, foetuses and even very young children. Perhaps, for an ethical theory it is proper to not regard them as persons, nonetheless, all of them have human rights according to the legal understanding of human rights.[74] Of course, philosophical inquiry on human rights is not limited only to the justification of the current list of human rights from international documents. Philosophy of human rights can also examine them and propose that some human rights from the legal point of view are actually not human rights from the moral point of view. Still, if a theory fails to justify the core of human rights, it simply seems to be wrong. Thus, a massive killing of people in coma would be considered as a core example of violation of human rights. However, for a proponent of the contemporary analytic conception of human dignity, it would not constitute a violation of human rights from the moral point of view as those who were killed did not possess human dignity. There is a strong contradiction between analytically conceived human dignity and human rights as understood by law and I believe this contradiction should be solved in favour of human rights legally understood.

The above-mentioned problem is a problem of internal nature—application of such a notion of human dignity leads to certain unacceptable conclusions from the point of view of the legal practice of human rights. There are, however, also significant problems of external nature concerning the whole method of inquiry that leads to such conceptualisation of human dignity. The first one is that it is based on a purely rational method of philosophical investigations, which seems not to be convincing nowadays.[75] T. Hill characterises this objection in the following way:

> That is [. . .] Kant's apparent attempt to ground human dignity on the premise that there is in each person an awesome 'transcendental kernel' of a noumenal we-know-not-what. The

[73] Duty to respect others' autonomy seems to be reflected by the right to privacy.

[74] I do not want to enter ethical debate but it seems that the claims about legitimisation of e.g. euthanasia are based not on the view that e.g. someone in coma is not a human or ceased to have human rights, but on considerations about her pain, her potential will what should happen with her in such a case, etc.

[75] However, this objection cannot go too far—Kant of course was interested in the success of natural, empirical sciences, think about his claims on analytic/synthetic and a priori/a posteriori judgments. What is here meant is that Kant took no advantage of empirical claims in direct argumentation in favour of human dignity and relied solely on rationalistic type of argumentation.

problem is that this would mean that Kant derives his ethical belief from unsupportable, non-empirical metaphysics.[76]

Kantian method is assessed negatively here. For Hill, as well for others,[77] Kant derives the existence of human dignity from the noumenal sphere that we have no access to. Consequently, there is no empirical background for the acceptance of the existence of human dignity. I found it a very sound objection, especially for a contemporary human who perceives the world rather from an empirical point of view. This way of perceiving reality is called the scientific world-view and is considered to be a dominant framework since the entrenching of the scientific revolution in the nineteenth century.[78] Under the scientific world-view, science has the only or the main role in explaining the world; non-empirical spheres of knowledge are also based, even though sometimes indirectly, on scientific facts. Positivism in the nineteenth century, logical positivism of Vienna Circle, then neo-positivism, along with certain branches of naturalistically oriented (neo)-pragmatism, are representations of this change in the perception of reality where strong emphasis is put on scientific findings in philosophical inquiry. Such "empiricistic" turn is characterised by the resignation from a traditional rationalist dependence of the inquiry on the so-called "first philosophy", as well as by the orientation towards epistemological issues of scientific methodology, being a departure point for any meaningful reflection about the world.

The project of naturalisation developed in the second half of twentieth century is also a reflection of the world-view in which science has its primary role in explaining reality. Therefore, Rosen's and Hill's objections to rationalistic method in the Kantian approach to human dignity can be extended into another way of criticism: irrespective of a purely philosophical assessment of the Kantian method, this method is very far from the way in which contemporary man perceives the world. Consequently, the Kantian approach is likely not to be convincing for contemporary humans, regardless of its purely philosophical plausibility or implausibility. And the justification of human dignity, which is the foundation of human rights, is crucial for contemporary worldly affairs, and thus needs a strong theoretical fundament fitting the current dominant human mindset. Therefore, there is a serious need for another method of inquiry into the existence of human dignity, much closer to the intellectual sensitivity characterising modern human beings, namely empirical, scientific method. The next chapters of this work will provide deeper insights into such approach of mine, proposed in order to explain and justify the existence of human dignity.

There are other interesting objections to the Kantian approach to human dignity. The most important of them are not closely related to my line of argumentation, yet they are worth mentioning. First, it is claimed that the Kantian notion of human dignity is inadequate for practical application in ethics as it either is too vague to

[76] Hill (2013), p. 314.

[77] Rosen (2012, 2013).

[78] cf. McNeill (1998).

decide anything or provides absolutistic conclusions.[79] Second, dignity under the Kantian notion can be used as a limitation of someone's autonomy by claiming that one cannot do what she decided to do as it violates her dignity.[80] It results in an illiberal and paternalistic determination of another's freedom on the basis of human dignity. Therefore, some argue, yet this discussion is developed in the bioethical domain, that the concept of human dignity is not useful and should be replaced by the concept of respect[81] or informed consent,[82] which are easier to understand and to apply. For them, we should only examine if an action was performed consensually with no inquiry on one's internal human dignity. Perhaps it is an adequate route in bioethics yet it rather operates on the grounds of the right to (respect) of one's dignity and not on the grounds of dignity as the inviolable (not being able to be violated) foundation of human rights.

To sum up, each of the two main approaches to human dignity involves major drawbacks: the classical notion implies strong metaphysical claims; the Christian account is a religious account and refers to the existence of God, but if one does not believe in God, there is no place for the *Imago Dei* view on the foundation of human dignity. And human dignity in order to be able to be the foundation of universal moral rights needs to have a basis acceptable for everyone. In turn, the Kantian notion of human dignity is developed in a highly nonempirical way of thinking. Moreover, its contemporary continuation that is highly influenced by the analytic notion of person, excludes some categories of people (people with dementia and even young children) from individuals having human dignity. This approach may be philosophically plausible for some, but it cannot serve as the justification of human dignity in a more legally oriented theory of human rights. The reason is that it cannot grasp the core examples of violations of legal human rights as violations of moral human rights. As for the classical and Kantian notions, one may wonder whether there could be proposed any more recent conceptions of human dignity. Of course, it may be the case that either classical philosophers or Kant (or their followers) grasped the ultimate structure of reality and their notions are perfectly adequate. It may, however, alternatively be the case that we simply lack an adequate insight into the

[79] Hill (2013), p. 314; Piechowiak (2011).

[80] Rosen (2013), pp. 149–151. The second objection has even its juridical basis. Manuel Wackenheim, suffering from dwarfism, voluntarily appeared in events when he was tossed by other people on short distances wearing protective gear. He received money for those events. The French Ministry of Inferior prohibited such events on the basis of the violation of human dignity. Manuel Wackenheim appealed and claimed that the prohibition restrained his autonomy but French administrative courts up to Conseil d'Etat upheld the ministerial decision. Manuel Wackenheim decided to file a complaint to the United Nations Human Rights Committee, mainly based on the violation of the right to non-discrimination and the right to liberty, but the Committee stated no violation of human rights (Manuel Wackenheim v France, Communication No 854/1999, U.N. Doc. CCPR/C/75/D/854/1999 (2002)).This case is considered by the critics of the Kantian approach to human dignity as an example of the situation when the claim that an activity violates someone's human dignity simultaneously violates her right to autonomy.

[81] Macklin (2003).

[82] Pinker (2008).

conception of human dignity that fits the contemporary world. It is possible that the emerging scepticism towards human dignity and human rights has foundations in the lack of a proper theoretical fundament that would be convincing for contemporary human.

Therefore, on the one hand, we witness an important role of human rights in domestic and international law along with a significant commitment to them in, at least, the Western world. Simultaneously, there are also major problems at the level of philosophical theory that could justify or explain the existence of human dignity, and further, of human rights. This is the reason why I propose a new view on the issue of the foundations of human rights and human dignity. Before that, let me briefly present the debate held by contemporary philosophers of human rights concerning what kind of object human dignity is.

3.2.3 What Kind of Metaphysical Entity Is Human Dignity?

Jeremy Waldron considers three kinds of entities for human dignity to possibly be as the foundation of human rights: (1) value, (2) status as an underlying idea, and (3) status containing a package of rights hardly distinguishable from human rights themselves.[83] Waldron regards human dignity to be status as an idea underlying human rights, while the majority of philosophers of human rights rather opt for it being a value.[84] The least promising account of human dignity is the status in the third meaning—status as a package of rights. Under this view, one has human dignity only if one has human rights, while human dignity contains the set of rights that one possesses.[85] Therefore, human dignity could actually be identical with human rights. Such a notion of human dignity falls into circularity, so it is unlikely to be a plausible account of what human dignity is. It explains the existence of human dignity by reference to human rights whereas simultaneously human rights are explained by reference to human dignity. For these reasons, Waldron opts for the claim that human dignity is status as an underlying idea justifying human rights. Waldron claims that human dignity is better understood as status than as value. For him, the main legal understanding of the term "status" refers to rights and duties that a subject possesses due to some special circumstances. It is simply easier to refer to this subject's position by a brief claim that she has this or another status, rather than by referring to all the rights and duties she holds. Bankruptcy or infancy are such statuses—instead of enlisting all rights and duties a bankrupt company possesses, like obligation to not enter into new contracts etc., it is easier to say that this company is bankrupt. Some may say that being bankrupt simply contains all rights and duties of a bankrupt entity—having status is nothing more than having some

[83] Waldron (2012, 2015), p. 133.

[84] Tasioulas (2013, 2015).

[85] Waldron (2015), p. 134.

rights and duties. Waldron, however, opposes this mainstream understanding of the term "status". For him, there is something more in ascribing a status to an object—it is that status comprises a set of rights rather than only contains them. In other words, status justifies a given possessed set of rights and makes sense of the fact that these rights are possessed due to some state of affairs. The status of infancy contains children's rights and obligations as well as justifies them due to e.g. their incapacity of making rational decisions. In case of human dignity understood as status, human dignity not only contains human rights. Human dignity is an idea underlying human rights that helps explain and unify human rights in one concept (Waldron 2015, p. 136). Human dignity understood as the special status is not only an abbreviation of all possessed human rights in one concept but something more beneath them.

Nonetheless, the prevailing view among philosophers of human rights is that human dignity is a value.[86] I adhere to this majoritarian position. It is disputable what a value actually is from the metaphysical point of view. Jaap Hage claims that values are abstractions of valuable things.[87] The realisation of values (compliance or violation) is ranged on a scale of many in-between possibilities where values themselves cannot conclusively determine the proper conduct. Two latter properties differentiate values from norms—norms can either be complied or violated without any in-between scenarios based on the formula of weight.[88] As a result, norms can conclusively determine the proper normative state of affairs. Perhaps, human dignity is considered as a value by the vast majority of philosophers of human rights, since it is generally easy to develop a justificatory link from values to norms that are to protect and practically realise these values. In the case of the justification of human rights, such a value is human dignity, while norms that protect and realise it are human rights. However, the route from human dignity, being a value, to human rights is not as easy as it may appear. Raz pointed out that there are things that are valuable, yet we do not have any right to them.[89] Love is a great example: love is both valuable and is an important value, however, I do not have a right to be loved—I cannot plausibly claim that someone should love me.[90] How can we know that the same does not apply to human dignity? These considerations make me think that something more must be added in the process of justifying human rights by reference to human dignity, understood as value, than a simple claim that human rights protect and realise the value of human dignity.

The characteristic of value as something that needs to be practically realised rises the problem mentioned a few pages above. On the one hand, human dignity is inviolable, on the other hand it requires to be realised and protected in practice by concrete norms. As it was said, the best solution of this ambiguity is to distinguish the innate and inviolable human dignity that is the foundation of human rights from

---

[86] Tasioulas (2013, 2015).

[87] Hage (2016), p. 41.

[88] Hage (2016).

[89] Raz (2010), pp. 324–325.

[90] Raz (2010), pp. 324–325.

other things covered by other concepts, referred to by the term "human dignity".[91] These other concepts include the idea that human dignity is a form of respect to someone's autonomy, which is by far a value—it can be realised by norms and cannot solely determine a desired normative state of affairs. However, this human dignity is different from the one which is the foundation of human rights. Human dignity that is the basis of human rights is an abstraction of a valuable being—human being. More precisely, human dignity is an abstraction of some inner humanity we value in every human. It is an inviolable value, yet it can and should be practically realised. The means of this realisation are human rights.

From the point of view of analytic metaphysics, an important insight is that human dignity is by far a normative entity, irrespective of whether we regard it as a value, including different views on values, or as status. By a normative entity I mean an entity that cannot be described by solely descriptive language. Since human dignity is an inherent *worth* of every human being, its description consists of normative language, and hence, human dignity is a normative entity. If one would prefer to follow the reason-giving view on normativity, human dignity is a normative entity because the fact of its presumed existence is reason giving—it gives certain reasons for action in relation to the way in which human beings should be treated. Under the first notion of fact, wherein facts are true propositions, true propositions concerning human dignity are facts. So, true propositions about human dignity, like the proposition that every human has human dignity or propositions about its properties are facts. Of course, facts about human dignity are normative, moral facts as human dignity belongs to normative, moral sphere. Under the second notion of fact, wherein facts are obtaining states of affairs, if it is the case that every human possess human dignity, it means that it is the fact that every human possesses human dignity. If this foundation is human dignity, as international and domestic documents claim, it is also possessed universally by every human. Human dignity exists independently of human will and recognition. And this independent existence by far qualifies as "obtaining" in the moral sphere. However, by "obtaining" I do not mean existing with no connection to other spheres, like a Platonic idea. I prefer the notion of facts as obtaining state of affairs than as true propositions, since it is closer to intuitive views on natural and metaphysical (i.e. concerning metaphysical relations) reality, and as such it does not involve the representational problem. So, every obtaining state of affairs related to or dependent upon the existence of human dignity, like that it is possessed by every human, like that it is inherent, universal, etc., is considered in this dissertation a fact. Also, human dignity is an entity, provided that it exists, which does not seem to be a significantly controversial idea. It turns out that from the metaphysical point of view, there is no big difference whether human dignity is status or value. Both of them can be classified as moral, normative facts.

To conclude, I understand human dignity as an inherent worth of every human being, equipped with properties described by international and domestic human

[91] Piechowiak (2011), pp. 5–6.

rights law. Human dignity is a value, but most importantly it is a normative, moral fact. This part of the work provided the analysis of what human dignity is and what kind of entity it is. These issues are very difficult to be separated from the question about the foundations of human dignity. I have already presented major theories on the foundations of human dignity: the classical notion with its Christian continuation, the Kantian notion, and the contemporary Kantian-analytic notion connecting the Kantian approach and the analytic conception of person. Each of them involves significant drawbacks.

Therefore, I would like to propose another foundation of human dignity. I believe that this foundation is constituted by descriptively understood human nature discovered by empirical methods of evolutionary psychology. But first, I will explain what I mean by "nature" and "human nature".

3.3 Human Nature

Generally and intuitively the concept of human nature denotes certain necessary or essential characteristic of every human.[92] It is sometimes explicitly used in the philosophy of human rights, although without being precisely conceptualised. Human nature, often without the direct usage of this term, is regarded as the fundament of human rights, even more profound than human dignity. Many philosophers of human rights formulate statements of the following form: "human rights are moral rights possessed by all humans simply in virtue of their humanity"[93] or "human rights are rights we have simply in virtue of being human".[94] These statements represent the key claim of the naturalistic approach to human rights. Tasioulas and Griffin by using terms "humanity" and "being human" seem to mean something that makes that humans are human. This is what "human nature" means. Nonetheless, the exact meaning of the concept of human nature remains unclear. In order to understand what human nature is, we should firstly examine what the concept "nature" means. After that, the concept of human nature will become much clearer—it will be simply nature of human beings.

Tomasz Gizbert-Studnicki, Adam Dyrda and Andrzej Grabowski distinguish three main understandings of "nature".[95] According to them, the nature of "X" can denote: (1) the set of necessary (or essential) properties of all X-es, (2) an ideal or pattern, which X-es can or should strive to and (3) a statistically dominant tendency

[92] My analysis of three notions of "nature" and "human nature" is based on my Polish language paper (Mazurkiewicz 2018).

[93] Tasioulas (2011), p. 27.

[94] Griffin (2008), p. 2.

[95] Gizbert-Studnicki et al. (2016), p. 43; cf. also Wróblewski (1970).

(or tendencies) characterising all X-es as a genre although not always characterising every individual X.[96]

In the general analytic philosophy, especially contemporary analytic metaphysics, the term "essence" is used more often than the term "nature". However, I believe they both denote the same object in reality, despite the different linguistic roots of each of the two terms. Generally, essence and nature mean something that makes an entity to be that entity that it actually is. Therefore, I will use terms "essence" and "nature" interchangeably, especially as for the first of the above-mentioned meanings of "nature". Moreover, I understand "essence" not individualistically (it would denote essence of a particular entity), but generically (it denotes an essence common to all entities being members of a set), since I do not aim to conceive an essence of a particular individual human, but rather the essence of human as a category of being.

3.3.1 Human Nature as a Set of Necessary/Essential Properties

Under the first notion of "nature", the nature of an entity X is constituted by a set of necessary or essential properties of X.[97] This is a descriptive account of human nature—it states what properties a human must possess to be human. The differentiation between necessary/essential properties refers to the discussion on the modal and non-modal understanding of essence in analytic philosophy, which was mentioned in Sect. 2.6. Let me here briefly explain it once more. Under the modal notion of essence, the essence of X is a set of necessary properties. More specifically, P is an essential property of X if and only if it is necessary that every X possess property P.[98] However, Fine noticed that necessary properties do not have to be essential properties.[99] Essential features are features that make a thing to be *that* thing. Therefore, under the non-modal notion of essence, essential properties are those properties that make an entity to be *that* entity. Essential properties are not simply necessary properties.

Applying these ideas to the question of human nature, for modal essentialists human nature will be constituted by necessary properties belonging to every human being. On the other hand, for modal non-essentialists human nature will be constituted by essential properties possessed by every human being, that is these properties that make human beings human. Modal tools cannot be employed in a non-modal approach; rather, a type of rational justification needs to be adopted.

Many historical examples of conceptions of human nature were based on the notion that essence is a set of essential or necessary properties of human. Necessary

[96] Gizbert-Studnicki et al. (2016), p. 43.

[97] Gizbert-Studnicki et al. (2016), p. 43.

[98] Robertson and Atkins (2018).

[99] Fine (1994).

or essential features of human used to be regarded as a non-material aspect as soul or mind, free will and freedom or self-consciousness.[100] In contemporary philosophy, especially of an analytic orientation, the possession of mind is generally claimed to be a necessary or essential feature for human.

It is easy to form a falsifying test both for the modal and non-modal notion of human nature. Under the modal notion of nature, if a property is not possessed by every human being, it does not constitute human nature. Under the non-modal notion, if a property in a particular situation does not make a human to be human, it does not constitute human nature. For instance, it seems that under both notions of human nature, possessing intuitive (intuitive in the common sense meaning, I do not mean here any specific, epistemically significant intuitions) moral feelings will not constitute human nature as people with psychopathic personality do not have them. A person with a psychopathic personality is still a human, therefore, one can be a human being, despite not having intuitive moral feelings. Consequently, having them is neither necessary nor essential. As a result, having intuitive moral feelings does not constitute human nature understood as a set of necessary or essential properties. Plato's claim that human is a featherless biped animal cannot be regarded as describing the non-modal human nature. Even though there is no man possessing feathers, we can imagine an individual possessing all human capabilities yet having feathers instead of skin or hair. Such an individual would rather generally be labelled as a human. Thus, the lack of feathers is not essential for human—this is not the property of not having feathers that makes human to be human.

It may be discussable whether necessity or essentiality of a feature is *a priori* or *a posteriori* truth,[101] that is whether we should examine real-world instantiations (*a posteriori*) or rather some general conception of an entity (*a priori*). Andrei Marmor provides a very illustrative example:

> When we say that linguistic competence is an essential feature of humans, we are not committed to the idea that a person with serious brain damage that causes her to lose the ability to use language renders that person non-human. Essential conditions are not necessary features.[102]

Marmor, following Fine's analysis of essence, notices that if we argue that a property is essential for human, we do not state that it is also necessary. Someone may not have linguistic competence, but she is still a human.[103] Thus, the modal notion of human is not proper. Moreover, Marmor seems to notice that even if someone ceases to have linguistic competence, which seems to be an essential property, she does not cease to be human. It means that we rather operate, at least in case of linguistic competence as human nature, on the *a priori* level. Under the general conception of human, the loss of linguistic competence does not lead to the claim that someone ceases to be human. Perhaps, the roots of disagreement between proponents of the

[100] Stevenson and Haberman (1998, p. 96; p. 182); Searle (1984).

[101] Gizbert-Studnicki (2017).

[102] Marmor (2013), p. 223.

[103] Fine (1994).

analytic and the substantial (ontological) notion of "person", are based on the distinction between *a priori/a posteriori* analysis of essential properties. The debate on the concept of person seems to be close to the debate on "human nature" since the concept of person refers to properties that makes human a person. For instance, under the analytic notion of person, someone who loses essential properties, like higher cognitive functions, ceases to be a person.[104] It is an *a posteriori* analysis of real-world instantiations of the concept of human, i.e. actual humans. In turn, the proponents of the substantial notion of person believe that such a loss does not undermine one's being a person, for the reason that they assume a general, *a priori*, conception of person that is independent of the actual world scenarios. It is beyond the scope of this work to examine the debate on the concept of (human) person as I do not intent to analyse this concept but choose to examine the concept of human nature in order to seek in it the foundations for human dignity.

The notion of human nature as a set of necessary/essential properties of every human is sometimes applied in the philosophy of human rights. Jörn Reinhardt notices:

> Modern natural right theories still rest on the knowledge of human nature, and the term nature refers to what is not a mere product of practical reasoning, but its condition. Yet this condition is now interpreted in a different way. "Nature" does not refer to the perfect form of human life, but the imperfect matter that has to be dealt with in imposing the form upon the world (cf. also Korsgaard 1996, pp. 3–5). The human condition, natural impulses, and the natural dynamic of the human species are understood as the relevant factors in the process of realizing the form. The notion of human nature is not only detached from the metaphysical presuppositions, but also from the social and institutional embedding. Human nature refers to the "state of nature" as a state of life anteceding civil society, or, more or less, independent of social relations and political institutions.[105]

Reinhardt, using Aristotelian language, states that the content of the concept of "human nature" is constituted by the matter and not by the form (especially form as an aim—*telos*). In other words, for contemporary philosophers, the concept of human nature refers to some basic properties of every human and neither to properties acknowledged on the basis of a metaphysical inquiry, nor to ideal properties denoting some desired normative state of affairs of every human. Reinhardt calls the human nature understood as a set of basic properties the "first nature" due to its being developed by biological and evolutionary factors. In contrast, the "second nature" is researched by philosophical anthropology,[106] which also takes advantage of the concept of human nature as the set of necessary/essential properties, but in that case these properties are the product of socialisation processes. It is likely that these "second nature" properties are somehow dependent on the biological and evolutionary factors.[107] Reinhardt's account emphasises that the philosophers of

---

[104]The concept of person seems to be also broader than the concept of human as the concept of person can be conceived in the way that it includes non-human persons, as animals, AI, etc.

[105]Reinhardt (2014), p. 141.

[106]Reinhardt (2014), p. 143.

[107]For instance, they supervene on them, cf. Załuski (2009a, b).

human rights tend to understand human nature under the first of the described broad categories of meanings of "human nature"—as the set of necessary or essential properties—rather than under the second (nature as an ideal pattern), or the third one (nature are statistically dominant tendencies).

Notwithstanding the above discussion, I will not take advantage of the meaning of "human nature" as necessary or essential features. Under this notion, the determination of the content of human nature requires rather a purely philosophical, "armchair", method of inquiry. My aim is to conceive human nature in terms of empirical sciences. Although the distinction between necessary and essential features and *a priori* and *a posteriori* method of analysis can be somehow utilised in the debate on the foundations of human rights, the first understanding of human nature is far from fitting properly the scientific method of research. Sciences, especially those empirical sciences that research animal (including human) world, discover rather general tendencies than exact properties lacking any exceptions.

It should be noticed that the notion of human nature as a set of necessary/essential properties is descriptive in its character. Therefore, there arises a very serious problem: how we can justify human rights or human dignity, which are normative facts, by reference to human nature, understood as a set of necessary/essential properties, which is a descriptive fact? If one would like to use these concepts in reasoning and form an argument where the premise would be "Y is a set of necessary/essential properties that constitute human nature" and the conclusion would be "every human has human dignity/human rights", such an argument would fall into Hume's Guillotine. Descriptive sentences that include the concept of human nature could not logically entail normative sentences including concepts like "human rights" or "human dignity". The similar problem may arise in a more metaphysical sort of explanation. If one would like to explain human rights or human dignity by claiming that they are ontologically dependent on human nature (e.g. they are reduced to human nature), the problem occurs: how a normative fact can be dependent on a descriptive fact in such a way that the latter explains the former? I will come back later to this issue.

Moreover, the philosophical method of inquiry always raises many questions and tends to be inconclusive. There is no well-founded methodology with the criteria of falsification, especially in metaphysics. Each philosophical school has its own method and its means of justification (either internal and external). As for internal and external justification we can refer here to the distinction in legal theory between internal and external justification in the context of the justification of judicial or legal decision making.[108] Internal justification involves the proper logical form of argumentation—the inference from premises to a conclusion must be logically valid. In turn, external justification involves providing justification for the premises used in reasoning. I think this distinction can be easily extended to a wider scope than solely judicial or legal decisions and it can guide us in looking at what kind of thought should be used in the inquiry on the foundations of human rights. When we

---

[108] Wróblewski (1971) and MacCormick (1977).

deal with so important issue as the foundations of human rights, we should have very strong bases for our claims. Even the best understanding of human nature according to internal methods of one philosophical school can be totally opposed by others on the basis of disagreement concerning philosophical assumptions that are obvious or well-argued for some, but improper or highly controversial for others. In turn, the scientific method is well founded and has clear methodology and criteria of falsification.[109] It is also universal among every culture, whereas there is no universally accepted philosophical school. This is especially important as the justification of human rights should be universally accepted all over the world if we want to deeply ground the acceptance for human rights culture on grounds that are common for every culture. Historically, human rights are a Western idea and we should be cautious in using only Western terms and methods in the justification of human rights if we are to maintain the universally acceptable character of human rights. Therefore, I think that on the level of external justification there are good reasons to adopt the discoveries of natural sciences in the inquiry on the foundations of human rights.

3.3.2 Human Nature as an Ideal or Pattern

The second notion of nature refers to an ideal or pattern that every X can or should strive for.[110] This notion is by far normative in its characteristic. It is based on the view that what an object truly is, is what it should be. Only by knowing an ideal pattern we can truly identify an object. Under this account, human nature is constituted by an ideal of human. It seems that every notion defining human from a normative perspective is based on this account of human nature. Many religious notions of human nature are based on this account—firstly, a notion of an ideal human is established, and then, a duty to strive to reach this ideal. For instance, for Christian theology, there is a perfect ideal of human that existed before the original sin due to human's creation as an image of God. Human nature was created as entirely good and after the original sin, with the assistance of God's grace every human should strive to reach this true human nature, untouched by evil.

Human nature as an ideal or pattern is present also in teleological conceptions, which claim that there is a certain aim of human and its existence, which is morally good. Then, means to achieve this aim are indicated. Aristotelian *eudaimonia* is a good example of such an aim. The satisfaction of the criteria embedded in the concept of "good life", often used in the contemporary ways of justification of human rights developed by liberal political philosophy can also be classified as

[109] By the scientific method I mean the method that is based on observation and experiments that can be repeated, uses both inductive and deductive reasoning, tests hypotheses and finally produces theories, cf. Andersen and Hepburn (2020).

[110] Gizbert-Studnicki et al. (2016), p. 43.

such an aim.[111] For Aristotle virtues constitute the means that enable achieving this aim of a good life. For contemporary liberal political philosophers these means are constituted by e.g. capabilities[112] or normative agency.[113] *Prima facie*, human rights seem to be relatively easily justified by reference to human nature understood as the characteristics of an ideal human being. One needs to simply claim that in order to protect the possibility of reaching *eudaimonia* or the possibility of building one's conception of a good life, it is necessary to protect an individual. The function of human rights is to protect such possibilities. Human rights become justified as the means to achieve an ultimate goal.

However, with respect to the justifications of human rights presented by the contemporary liberal political philosophy, the inference from a set of claims about a concept of good life to claims ascertaining the possession of human rights is not straightforward. The object referred to by a concept of "good life" can be seen as a particular example of an idealised human nature. It is a normative concept requiring evaluation concerning one's plans, values and life. But often, it is a kind of goal that does not have to be already realised. If it were realised, good life would be a fact and means to realise this goal (human rights) would not be needed. However, in the Griffin's and Nussbaum's theories the protection of human rights is ascribed rather not to good life itself but to means that enable achieving it—normative agency for Griffin and capabilities for Nussbaum. And both normative agency and capabilities are already possessed by every human. Therefore, the problem mentioned in the previous paragraph is not present in Griffin's and Nussbaum's accounts of the foundations of human rights. They ascribe the necessity of protection by human rights to respective normative agency and capabilities, which are possessed by every human. A good life is a further step to which normative agency and capabilities lead. Nussbaum explicitly refers to the issue of human nature:

> The Capabilities approach is not a theory of what human nature is, and it does not read off from innate human nature. Instead, it asks, among the many things that human beings might develop the capacity to do, which ones are the really valuable ones, which are the ones that a minimally just society will endeavor to nurture and support?[114]

This citation clearly indicates Nussbaum's reluctance to regard some unchangeable properties of human as foundations of human rights. She would definitely oppose someone who would attempt to ground human rights in human nature understood as a set of necessary or essential features. Instead, Nussbaum prefers to regard some capabilities that we can develop as the justification for human rights. Yet, these capabilities are not the ultimate goal—they enable building one's conception of a good life. However, Harun Tepe argues that Nussbaum provides a concept of "human being", which she regards as a set of capabilities and opportunities worthy

---

[111] Nussbaum (2000, 2006, 2011) and Griffin (2008).

[112] Nussbaum (2000, 2006, 2011).

[113] Griffin (2008).

[114] Nussbaum (2011), p. 28.

of being developed.[115] This concept of human being seems to be close to the concept of human nature. Thus, it may be claimed that Nussbaum provides some hidden assumptions concerning the content of human nature, even though she believes that human rights are not justified by reference to some innate human nature.

The second notion of human nature as an ideal or pattern stands in sharp opposition to the first notion of human nature. Pursuant to the first notion, every human possesses the necessary/essential properties. Pursuant to the second one, human nature is an ideal pattern of the characteristic of human beings; a particular human beings can move very far from them. For instance, the claim that everyone can and should be subordinated to reason and live a perfectly moral life assumes that *de facto* not all people behave like this. If they behave according to this ideal, the obligation to strive to reach this ideal would be rather pointless. Of course, norms are basically created to guide human conduct and are useful if they are complied with. On their basis we are supposed to assess one's behaviour. If it is so, then what is the point of introducing (moral) norms to guide the behaviour of ideal human beings who always (or at least typically) behave morally. What is then a point of having human rights? What they are going to protect us from if no other person will behave immorally towards us?[116] Thus, from the ethical point of view, the understanding of human nature as an ideal may be very promising, however, paradoxically, from the point of view of the foundations of human rights, it is highly implausible. The core idea of human rights, expressed also directly in many international law documents, is that human rights are held by every human and are innate. If every human is a holder of such rights, they are to be held also by those who are far from the ideal of a perfect human. In fact, human rights are held even by those who do not aspire to achieve this ideal. Human rights protect every human, irrespective of her merits. Therefore, it is highly problematic to regard the foundations of human rights in human nature conceived as an ideal characterisation of human beings.

Methodologically, the justification of human rights (or human dignity) via human nature regarded as an ideal or pattern of human involves the least number of problems. The concept of human nature conceived in such a way is a normative concept. It can provide the proper justification for human rights, as the concept of human rights is normative as well. The reasoning from sentences describing human nature as an ideal to sentences describing the possession of human rights would be logically correct and would not fall under Hume's Guillotine. If one would like to propose a more metaphysical sort of explanation, human rights as normative entities can be ontologically dependent (irrespective of the exact type of metaphysical relation) on human nature, which is a normative entity. Nonetheless, although it is generally methodologically proper to justify a normative concept or entity by reference to some other normative concept or entity, one should bear in mind the

[115] Tepe (2014).

[116] As Raz argues (1999), pp. 157–162, even in such a situation we would need law for coordination of e.g. which part of the road we should drive a car. Notice, however, that human rights are not meant to play such a role.

particular problem mentioned a few paragraphs above. Human rights are innate and universal and their justification must be developed in such a way that it includes everyone as human rights holders. Including those who have not realised an ideal of human, that is those who do not satisfy the characteristics of an ideal human nature.

Moreover, looking from the metaphysical perspective, human nature understood as an ideal or pattern is a normative fact. But we have a strong intuition that normative facts do not constitute the basic furniture of the universe and that they are not metaphysically primitive. This intuition is the reason for the inquiry on the structure of reality by contemporary analytic metaphysics, which will be presented in the next part of this work. The basic furniture of the universe is rather constituted by some natural facts. In turn, I believe that normative facts tend to be dependent on natural facts. For instance, the fact that X is wrong, which is a normative fact, holds due to the fact that X causes pain, or due to the fact that X was performed solely with an intention of causing harm.[117] The fact that X causes pain and the fact that X was performed solely with an intention of causing harm are descriptive facts. Therefore, if one would like to use the concept of human nature as an ideal or a pattern in the justification of human rights, a question could be asked: but what makes such a human nature? Or in other words: why does such a human nature hold? There are two ways to answer such a question. The first is to refer to some self-evident normative concepts. I believe that Griffin's account of human rights pursues this path.[118] The worth of normative agency is rather self-evident and it does not require any further justification in terms of other, more basic concepts, reaching beyond the analysis of the properties of normative agency. One who understands what normative agency is, must accept its worth as the basis for building ethics upon it. Methodologically, such an approach is quite promising—it escapes an infinite regress in one's theory.

The second option to solve the problem of why a putative normative entity holds is to provide descriptive facts as its explanation. Following this route one must be aware of the of "is"-"ought" problem. Nonetheless, for those who do not prefer to base one's theory on self-evident normative truths, giving descriptive facts as explanation is another solution. We should not forget that alleged self-evident normative truths may not be so self-evident for everyone—in case of human rights, the acceptance for normative agency enabling choosing one's conception of a good life, including many moral choices, may not be so commonly accepted among cultures other than the Western culture. If someone from an Eastern culture does not accept the value of normative agency, the whole point of Griffin's argumentation in favour of human rights collapses.

---

[117]The exact nature of the relation of dependence can be questioned: one can claim that it is not a logical entailment due to Hume's Guillotine or that we cannot define normative truths by descriptive facts due to Moore's naturalistic fallacy. However, some general dependence is quite clear to hold between normative facts and descriptive facts.

[118]Griffin (2008).

Therefore, although I see many methodological advantages of using a normative concept or a normative entity as a foundation in an ethical theory, including a theory of human rights, my aim is to follow the argumentative path where normative facts are dependent on, and explained by, descriptive facts.

3.3.3 *Human Nature as a Statistically Dominant Tendency*

The third understanding of nature claims that the nature of X is a statistically dominant tendency (or tendencies) characterising all X-es as species, although not always characterising every individual X.[119] This notion of nature is descriptive in its character. It differs from the first notion of nature as it does not require that every member of a defined category must possess a given tendency. Therefore, finding a member of a category X that does not possess a tendency that most X-es generally possess does not falsify the statement that a given tendency constitutes the nature of X.

Under this notion of nature, the concept of human nature refers to a statistically dominant tendency (or tendencies) concerning human. But what exactly is "a dominant tendency concerning human"? It is best understood as a dominant tendency in human thinking or human behaviour, since thinking and behaviour are areas where human tendencies are most apparent. A tendency must be somewhere realised, as for human it is realised in thinking or behaviour. The notion of human nature as a dominant tendency (or a set of dominant tendencies) is applied in empirical sciences dealing with human beings. These empirical sciences provide naturalistic and psychological conceptions of human claiming that humans can be determined by external, environmental factors[120] or that human nature is a conglomerate of types of behaviour acquired evolutionary.[121] Such views do not deny that a concrete individual human can break out from behavioural or evolutionary schemes—a behaviour contrary to a dominant one is possible in some particular scenarios. Therefore, only the demonstration that a putative tendency is not a dominant tendency will falsify the thesis that it constitutes human nature.

3.3.3.1 Human Nature According to Evolutionary Psychology

One of the most developed empirical sciences that is dedicated to researches concerning human is evolutionary psychology. Evolutionary psychology is a rather new science, quickly developing since 1990s, that intends to find what humans are from the evolutionary perspective, i.e. by looking how we developed in the process

---

[119] Gizbert-Studnicki et al. (2016), p. 43.

[120] Stevenson and Haberman (1998), p. 195.

[121] Stevenson and Haberman (1998), p. 210.

of evolution to be what we are now. Evolutionary psychology needs to be distinguished from biological anthropology. Whereas the latter deals with anatomic changes, the first deals with mental changes and with explaining why and how our behaviour and ways of thinking developed in time. Evolutionary psychology rejects the so-called Standard Social Science Model the dominant view in social science since 50s and 60s, which regards the human mental sphere as *tabula rasa*, open for development in any direction via the contact with the environment.[122] For the Standard Social Science Model, the way we think and perceive other people and the world, as well as the way we behave are purely contingent outcomes of the society we live in. Thus, there is nothing universal in human nature. Behaviourism is one of the main instantiations of the Standard Social Science Model. In contrast, evolutionary psychology claims that there exist some basic aspects of our mental sphere and our behaviour we all universally share. Yet, it is not a deterministic theory, like the nineteenth and early twentieth century social Darwinism. Evolutionary psychology recognises the fundamental and universal level of our being. Nonetheless, our behaviour is not limited by any deterministic "natural laws". Evolutionary psychology takes advantage of the concept of nature as a set of dominant tendencies. Therefore, even if a particular human does not behave in accordance with a given dominant tendency, this does not undermine that this tendency constitutes human nature.

As for the method, evolutionism is the basic assumption of evolutionary psychology. Human beings, as they are today, have developed in the course of evolution not only in physical but also in mental aspects. Physical changes are easier to be proved as we can simply find the bones of our ancestors in the ground and track changes. Yet, the way our ancestors thought, and to a large extent the way they behaved, cannot be simply dug from the earth. The method of evolutionary psychology involves therefore (1) the comparative analysis with other primates;[123] (2) the examination of the brain size of skulls that are found, especially the size of the prefrontal cortex, which is the crucial part of the brain that corresponds to higher cognitive functions and the scope of mental and social capabilities; (3) the construction of evolutionary models consistent with the found data.[124] The method of evolutionary psychology is empirical as it starts from observations and experiments and then builds models and tests hypotheses that can be corroborated or falsified by the results of further observations and experiments. I would like to present two evolutionary psychology theories—Michael Tomasello's and Wojciech Załuski's and make use of their discoveries in my further philosophical research on the foundations of human rights.[125] I choose Tomasello's and Załuski's theories since they provide comprehensive accounts of human nature, and are based on scientific data and empirical way of thinking.

[122]Tooby and Cosmides (1992) and Załuski (2009a, b).

[123]Tomasello (2009).

[124]Dunbar (2014).

[125]Tomasello (2009) and Załuski (2009a, b).

Tomasello, one of the contemporary leading primatologists, implicitly employs the notion of human nature as a dominant tendency as he claims that human nature is constituted by a tendency to cooperate.[126] By cooperation he means:

(1) Altruism: one individual sacrificing in some way for another; and
(2) Collaboration: multiple individuals working together for mutual benefit.[127]

He reaches this conclusion on the basis of multiple experiments comparing natural, innate behaviour of human and our closest relative—chimpanzee. In order to exclude patterns of behaviour learnt by us in the process of socialisation Tomasello's experiments involve young human infants. To mention a few most prominent examples of his experiments: human infants, if they assume a piece of information is needed by an adult, they pass this piece of information by pointing as early as from twelve months of age. This occurs even before linguistic capacities are developed. In turn, chimpanzees and other apes do not inform others by pointing at all.[128] Apes help by pointing to an adult the place where a tool, which opens a box, is located only when the box contains food for the ape, while human infants point the tool even if an infant is not going to get anything from the box.[129] In a situation when a reward can be achieved either by one person or by two, young children tend to choose an option where both the chooser and the colleague obtain a reward, whereas chimpanzees never choose this option.[130] Great apes do not engage in joint attention, a crucial feature for collaboration, whereas young children do.[131]

In more details, here are the outcomes and the criteria of experiments that justify the claim about the existence of the innate tendency to cooperate. The study on 12- and 18- months infants measured the helping level of infants in two experiments.[132] The first one measured help level when an object was not intentionally dropped by an adult. The object had no stimulus features for children and it was additionally measured whether an infant would demand the object for itself.[133] In turn, the second experiment included the scenario where an adult needed the object that had been dropped. In the first experiment, 88% of 12-month-olds and 93% of 18-month-olds pointed at least once,[134] while the number was 88% in the second one.[135] Worth noting, only 14% of infants performed actions coded as wanting the object for

[126]Tomasello (2009).

[127]Tomasello (2009), p. XVII.

[128]Tomasello (2009), pp. 14–15; Liszkowski et al. (2006), pp. 173–187; Liszkowski et al. (2008), pp. 732–739.

[129]Tomasello (2009), p. 16; Bullinger et al. (2011).

[130]Tomasello (2009), p. 23; Hare et al. (2006), pp. 1013–2021.

[131]Tomasello (2009), pp. 71–72; Tomasello and Carpenter (2005).

[132]Liszkowski et al. (2006).

[133]Liszkowski et al. (2006), p. 175.

[134]Liszkowski et al. (2006), p. 175.

[135]Liszkowski et al. (2006), p. 183.

themselves.[136] As we see, the level of help is very high and is not triggered by actions done by the adult (like asking where the object is). Researchers interpret it as showing evidence for the claim on the existence of the natural, altruistic, tendency to help that is not learnt in social environment or triggered by adults' authoritative actions.[137] These claims were collaborated by another study.[138] There, the study on 12 months old human infants was conducted in order to measure the helping level to point an object that falls down to an adult (1) if the adult seems not to know where the object fell (experimental condition) and (2) if the adult is still looking at the object (control condition).[139] In the experimental condition 70% of the infants pointed, while this number is 27% on the control condition. Moreover, 70% of the pointing in the experimental condition was done by a clear finger gesture and 80% of them occurs in the very first phase of the experiment.[140] These studies are very interesting as they measure the help level before children linguistic capacities are developed. Thus, they give experimental grounds that it is not language that enables collaboration and cooperation. Rather, as Tomasello argues, language itself is enabled by, or based on, some more natural propensity, which is the tendency to cooperate.[141]

Let me know compare it with a comparative study on chimpanzees and human infant that measured the level of cooperation in pointing a tool that an adult needed in two scenarios: (1) when one that points, either chimpanzee or human infant, is going to receive a reward if the tool is pointed (help "for-me" scenario), or (2) is not going to receive a reward (help "for-You" scenario).[142] Two modes of experiments were introduced in the chimpanzees' experiment: when the tool was going to be used by the pointing chimpanzee, or by the asking adult. In the mode of experiment when it was a chimpanzee that later used the tool the chimpanzees level of pointing was 57% in the first scenario (help "for me") and 29% in the second one (help "for-You".[143] In the mode where the tool was later used by the adult, the levels were 72% in the first scenario (help "for me") and 14% in the second scenario (help "for-You") (2011, p. 62).[144] In turn, where young children are tested, there is no difference in scenarios: in both of them children pointed on the level of 89%, moreover, the help level of 86% was established in two first phases of experiments where the looking

[136] Liszkowski et al. (2006), p. 182.

[137] Liszkowski et al. (2006) and Tomasello (2009).

[138] Liszkowski et al. (2008).

[139] Liszkowski et al. (2008).

[140] Liszkowski et al. (2008), p. 738.

[141] Tomasello (2009).

[142] Bullinger et al. (2011).

[143] Bullinger et al. (2011), p. 61.

[144] Bullinger et al. (2011), p. 62.

adult only expressed surprise and was looking for the tool without directly asking the child where the tool is.[145]

As we see, the children's level of helping does not differ on the basis of any factor—adult directly asking for the object, children receiving reward, etc. In turn, chimpanzees rather help when they will receive a reward from their helping (however even here the numbers are not significant), but clearly do not help if they do not benefit from their help. Consequently, the claim can be established: humans have an innate tendency to cooperate (innate as it comes before linguistic and later social factors can shape behaviour), while our closest biological relatives do not have such a tendency. These and other experiments have provided empirical background for the Tomasello's thesis that the human nature is constituted by the tendency to cooperate. It is the *differentia specifica* distinguishing us from our closest evolutionary relatives—big apes, chimpanzees in particular. I believe that this account of human nature implicitly takes advantage of "nature" understood as the dominant tendency. The tendency to cooperate is the dominant tendency in our behaviour, although sometimes it is not followed. For instance, some children chose an option where only the chooser obtained the reward in the third of the above-mentioned experiments. We know from experience that sometimes we do not help others and reject to work together, even though it would be for a mutual benefit. Still, these are exceptions on a practical level of instantiations of our natural tendencies. Contemporary evolutionary psychology does not propose a deterministic view on human behaviour—we are able to behave in real live not in accordance with our natural tendencies. In fact, as Tomasello argues, humans not cooperating is rather a product of socialisation—children learn that in some situations it is better not to help, e.g. when an individual may help someone who does not help others, or tends to exploit help given to.[146] Nonetheless, our "default software" is to cooperate with others.[147]

Such an approach to human nature has one major methodological advantage—it is developed by the scientific method, which can provide results with a high degree of certainty on the basis of experiments. Moreover, there are widely accepted

[145]Bullinger et al. (2011), p. 66. Tomasello's researches provide of course much more statistical data flowing from his experiments. The most important is the p value, or probability value, which is a number describing how likely it is that data would have occurred by random chance. A *p*-value less than 0.05 (typically $\leq$0.05) is statistically significant. It indicates strong evidence that there is less than a 5% probability that the results are random, and the so-called null hypothesis can be rejected. There are other statistical values as well like t and F, but p value is the most important—it means that statistical tests indicated that the effect is statistically significant. It is satisfied in Tomasello's experiments.

[146]Tomasello (2009), pp. 29–30, 82–84.

[147]Tomasello's researches are profound and have not been falsified. To by best knowledge, there is no evidence against his claims. Of course, evolutionary psychology hosts various debates, both empirical and theoretical or methodological (e.g. Pinker vs Tomasello debate on the status on linguistic competences) but claims drawn by Tomasello from his experiments are rather uncontroversial.

methods of falsification in empirical sciences.[148] That is a substantial advantage over purely philosophical inquiry where conclusions are dependent on philosophical views and the disagreement over the possible way of falsification is likely to occur.

Another thinker within evolutionary psychology is Wojciech Załuski.[149] He develops his account of human nature from evolutionary perspective by analysing experimental data and building a general model with strong employment of evolutionary game theory.[150] He argues that from the evolutionary perspective the question on human nature is constituted by two questions: (1) what is the dominant moral motive of human behaviour? and (2) what is the dominant human mode of acting? The form of those questions is, just as in Tomasello's theory, implied by the notion of nature as the dominant tendency.

As for the dominant moral motive, he distinguishes four possible answers: genuine morality, narrow altruism, egoism and malice (immorality). They are all defined by the occurrence of three forms of altruism that can be empirically measured: kin altruism, reciprocal altruism and pure altruism.[151] Kin altruism means that "an agent sustains high costs for the good of a relative without expecting the return of these costs in the future"; reciprocal altruism means that "an agent sustains high costs for the good of an unrelated person expecting the return of these costs in the future", while pure altruism means that "an agent sustains high costs for the good of an unrelated person without expecting the return of these costs in the future".[152] Załuski defines egoism as engaging in reciprocal exchanges with the goal of promoting one's interests and malice as acting against another's interests even when one's interests can be violated.[153] Załuski distinguishes four possible views on human nature as the dominant moral motive of human behaviour is concerned:

- Extremely optimistic: human beings are genuinely moral – they tend to manifest in many circumstances kin altruism, reciprocal altruism and pure altruism.
- Moderately optimistic: human beings are narrowly altruistic – they tend to manifest in many circumstances kin altruism and reciprocal altruism.
- Moderately pessimistic: human beings are egoistic – their dominant moral motive is egoism.
- Extremely pessimistic: human beings are malicious (immoral) – their dominant moral motive is malice.[154]

For him, the question of the dominant moral motive of human behaviour under evolutionary psychology can be answered by demonstrating which of these views is correct. On the basis of wide empirical evidence and evolutionary game theory,

---

[148] Andersen and Hepburn (2020).

[149] Załuski (2009a, b).

[150] I will cite the English language work as it is easier accessible for a non-Polish speaker than the Polish one.

[151] Załuski (2009a), p. 4.

[152] Załuski (2009a), pp. 3–4.

[153] Załuski (2009a), p. 5.

[154] Załuski (2009a), p. 6.

Załuski argues that the human dominant moral motive is narrow altruism. It is narrow since we tend to behave altruistically towards our relatives and people we assume will reciprocate our help. Consequently, it means that human nature, as for the part of the dominant moral motive, is moderately optimistic.

As for the dominant mode of acting, there are two possible answers: perfect prudence and imperfect prudence. Human dominant mode of acting is imperfect prudence—understood as the game theory rationality—one is rational in the basic sense if and only if she maximizes her utility function; one is fully rational over time if she does not discount her utility hyperbolically.[155] As for prudence over time, simply, one is rational if she does not prefer a lesser good in the nearer future over a greater good in the more remote future. Humans are not fully rational—we tend to prefer achieving a smaller amount of goods now over a bigger some time later, provided that a closer good is not substantially smaller than a future one, or if a future good is highly remote in time. Therefore, the dominant mode of human action is imperfect prudence—we often tend to behave not fully rationally in terms of game theory.

These two dominant tendencies together form human nature. The narrow altruism is the dominant moral motive of human behaviour and the imperfect prudence is the dominant mode of human action.

Załuski, unlike Tomasello who does not draw moral conclusions from his research, explicitly provides conclusions about the moral considerations about human nature. He argues that it is moderately optimistic.[156] He proposes an interesting framework for drawing moral conclusions from discovered natural facts about human nature. He combines the possible answers on the dominant moral motive and the dominant mode of acting. Jointly, there are eight combinations that lead to the following moral facts concerning human nature:

- Extremely optimistic (1): human beings are genuinely moral and perfectly prudent.
- Extremely optimistic (2): human beings are genuinely moral and imperfectly prudent.
- Moderately optimistic (1): human beings are narrowly altruistic and perfectly prudent.
- Moderately optimistic (2): human beings are narrowly altruistic and imperfectly prudent.
- Moderately pessimistic (1): human beings are egoistic and imperfectly prudent.
- Moderately pessimistic (2): human beings are egoistic and perfectly prudent.
- Extremely pessimistic (1): human beings are malicious (immoral) and imperfectly prudent.
- Extremely pessimistic (2): human beings are malicious (immoral) and perfectly prudent.[157]

Notice how the moral view on human nature changes on the basis of different possible forms of basic tendencies in human behaviour. For Załuski, the ultimate proper answer is the second version of the extremely optimistic notion of human nature. Human nature might be claimed to be extremely optimistic if the dominant moral motive of our behaviour were the genuine morality and the dominant mode of

155 Załuski (2009a), pp. 40–41.

156 Załuski (2009a), p. 50.

157 Załuski (2009a), p. 14.

our behaviour were the perfect prudence. However, they are not. Human nature might be claimed to be pessimistic if we tended to behave egoistically or maliciously, and not prudently (irrationally), nonetheless it is false as well.[158] Załuski argues that the evolutionary approach to human nature falsifies some philosophical theories on human nature that were developed without the use of scientific method over time. He believes that the pessimistic view on human nature that can be found in A. Schopenhauer's or S. Freud's works is wrong: we are not innately evil. In turn, the ultra-optimistic notion of human nature, defended by J. J. Rousseau is wrong as well.[159] Of course, evolutionary psychology is aware of the problem of evil in human behaviour (I address this issue in Sect. 7.3, where I discuss the origins of human evil behaviour from evolutionary perspective). In that part, I will analyse whether the fact of human evil behaviour can undermine the claim of evolutionary psychology that human nature is (moderately) optimistic.

I think that certain moral conclusions can be drawn from the Tomasello's account of human nature in a similar way. His account of human nature is optimistic as well. In a different wording and by slightly different methods he builds the very similar notion of human nature as Załuski. Tomasello argues that human nature is constituted by the tendency to cooperate, whereas Załuski rather claims that the tendency to cooperate is built upon narrow altruism and imperfect prudence.[160] In fact, these two accounts propose an almost identical notion of human nature in evolutionary perspective. Human nature described by evolutionary psychology can be recognised as optimistic since the tendency to cooperate or narrow altruism and imperfect prudence are good. Tomasello's tendency to cooperate consists of altruism and collaboration. It is simply good to have a basic tendency to cooperate with others, to have a basic tendency towards altruism and towards collaboration. In my view, both components are simply good. The same goes for Załuski's narrow altruism and imperfect prudence. I believe that these tendencies are innately and inherently good. They are good also from a more consequential perspective, for someone who is an adherent of consequentialism. These tendencies, constituting our nature, are why we grow, why we developed culture and are able to behave morally in the society. All positive things we have developed as a species are a product of our tendency to cooperate. Our culture and all its achievements could not exist without a cooperation of various individuals, which is enabled by the fact that we have an evolutionary tendency to cooperate.[161] It is not difficult to see our nature as optimistic. Surely, it is not perfect, if it were so, we perhaps would not need a theory of human rights.

[158] Załuski (2009a), p. 14.

[159] Załuski (2009a), pp. 60–66. As he believes that law emerges upon our natural tendencies, similarly he claims that it is possible to falsify some views on origins of law—both ultra-optimistic Hayekian view and pessimistic Hobbesian.

[160] Załuski (2009a), p. 85, p. 137.

[161] Of course I see evil that happened within human history and examples of the lack of cooperation, I address the problem of evil and evolutionary vision of human nature in Sect. 7.3. However, notice that as Załuski (2018) argues, evil in human behaviour is rather contrary to the basic evolutionary tendencies. What is more, Załuski (2009a) claims that no social order can in long term stand to the

I would like to notice that if we understand human nature as the tendency to cooperate or as a tendency to behave in a narrowly altruistic and in a narrowly prudent way, we can regard Nussbaum's capabilities as somehow dependent on and built upon human nature, which is our basic evolutionary furniture. Nussbaum's capabilities are real opportunities to choose and to act in order to achieve certain states of affairs. Capabilities must have some deeper fundament since by far they are not fundamental entities. Both Tomasello's collaboration as well as Załuski's narrow altruism and imperfect prudence are a plausible and well-fitting fundament for capabilities. Imperfect prudence means that we are able to behave rationally in the game-theory sense (although not fully rational), that is that we can plan our future actions and achieve some goals. Collaboration means we can work for mutual benefit. Narrow altruism means that in making decisions we focus not only on ourselves but also on other individuals, although mainly on our relatives and those that we believe will reciprocate our help. Altruistic behaviour is a very important component of our choices. The possibility of existence of capabilities is dependent on the existence of some more fundamental aspect of human being that enables their emergence. The tendencies constituting our nature can be regarded as this aspect. Let me recall Nussbaum's claim that the capabilities approach to human rights is not about what human nature is and what can be entailed by an innate human nature. According to her, human nature is rather about what capacities may be developed and how they are to be protected.[162] This claim is actually consistent with evolutionary claims about human nature, which is an innate human property/entity. Capabilities are real opportunities to choose and to achieve some things that must be protected by human rights. They do not constitute an innate human nature. But, they are dependent on human nature: in other words, the tendencies that form human nature enable humans to have capabilities. Nussbaum refers to capabilities as entities that directly justify or explain human rights, and she does not need to go one level below. However, this level below exists and it is the level of evolutionary human nature that underlies the existence of capabilities.

Let me emphasise that the evolutionary notion of human nature is a descriptive one, despite the fact that altruism is argued to be the part of the natural tendencies that create human nature. However, altruism is understood here in purely descriptive terms: it is a feature that an individual sustains high costs for the good of another person.[163] Evolutionary notion of human nature does not mean per se that altruism is morally good or that we should behave altruistically. It simply states our natural tendency that is defined in non-normative way. One may here wonder how I want to argue that such a descriptive human nature is the foundation of human dignity, which is normative. I will refer to this problem in Sect. 6.5.1.

contrary with our evolutionary tendencies and must finally collapse, totalitarian regimes are such examples.

[162] Nussbaum (2011), p. 28.

[163] Załuski (2009a), p. 4.

There is a very interesting connection between the discoveries of evolutionary psychology and the claim made in the art. 1 of UDHR that says: "All human beings are born free and equal in dignity and rights. They are endowed with reason and conscience and should act towards one another in a spirit of brotherhood".[164] Notice especially the second sentence that ascribes reason, conscience and acting in a spirit of brotherhood to every human. In some sense, it can be regarded as describing what might be called human nature. And the second sentence may be understood as being the reason for the first sentence—so having reason, conscience and the norm of acting in a spirit of brotherhood is the reason for having (human) dignity and (human) rights. Looking from the perspective of naturalisation, the evolutionary psychology claims on human nature provide justification for the second sentence of art. 1—acting in the spirit of brotherhood can be understood as collaboration and altruism (and the provision from art. 1 claiming that all human beings *should* act towards one another in a spirit of brotherhood can be regarded as the duty to follow a good natural tendency); conscience as a moral faculty can have basis in altruistic tendencies; reason as a rational thinking and ability to make choices is clearly visible in Załuski's analysis of prudence (although it is limited in some situations) and in collaboration as acting together to the common goal. In such a way, the claims on human nature found in art. 1 are very consistent with the notion of human nature developed by evolutionary psychology and this notion can serve as their justification. This is not to say that fully-fledged ethics can be derived from evolutionary tendencies—that would be an invalid derivation of "ought" from "is", what I want to say is that the traits from art. 1 mentioned are very consistent with what evolutionary psychology says about human nature. So, what was formed as a philosophical or common-sense claim has very plausible basis in the recent scientific discoveries.

A philosophical question ca be posed whether tendencies discovered by evolutionary psychology themselves form human nature or rather they are just the *differentia specifica* and some more general *genus proximus* should be added. The second notion would follow the classical definition based on *genus proximus* (most closest, general genre) and *differentia specifica* (the difference distinguishing from *genus proximus*), while the first notion would be rather in line with modern philosophy way of thinking starting from Descartes and Locke who regarded human (or rather precisely person as for Locke) as a being defined by its essential characteristics (mind/ability to doubt as for Descartes, mind/reason and self-reflection[165]) without referring to any wider genre. Consequently, following the classical notion human nature would is to be an animal, or more concretely, a primate (*genus proximus*) with tendency to cooperate (let me use here Tomasello's notion for brevity) (*differentia specifica*). In turn, under modern philosophy notion human nature is the tendency to cooperate.

[164] Universal Declaration of Human Rights (1948), art. 1.

[165] This is of course very brief reference of the very main ideas of these two philosophers. Their claims and methods are much more detailed.

This may seem a rather conceptual difference but such differences have impact on way of thinking and philosophical discrepancies between times and schools of thought. I don't want to refer here to such general philosophy problematics but let me note one area of difference that may be important for the question of human rights. This is having body. Following classical way of thinking, human must have body as human is a connection of mind/soul and body. Consequently, with only mind/soul and without body one is not a (full) human. It can be seen in the *genus proximus* part where being a primate/an animal (so necessarily a being with body) is stated. Such a view have consequences in a clear claims on bodily areas of human rights like for instance the right to (bodily) security—if body forms a part of human nature, and we want to make claims on human rights starting from it, bodily aspects of human will be included in claims about human rights. However, conversely, a being with human mind/soul but without body is not so clearly to be claimed to be a holder of human rights. This may seem a purely conceptual discussion one some may connect it with scholastic debates on angels (not-bodily beings) and human souls without body (like those after death and before resurrection) but assume transhumanistic development of science and new technologies that will lead to a possibility of extracting one's mind from body to another place (like machine, cloud or computer)—will such a human mind have human rights? Following classical notion this question is not obviously answered, or at least some theoretical adjustments should be made, like stating that body is a part of contingent social and environmental facts. Meanwhile, by following the modern philosophy notion the problem seems to disappear—human nature is the tendency to cooperate and having body doesn't play a significant role. As such, body is a contingent feature and its having or not having is not crucial for human nature, so as a result, also for the link between human nature and human rights (however, as we will see in later parts of the book I don't make a simple claim that what is in human nature should be protected by human rights). Therefore, as for the transhumanism issue of a human mind extracted from one's body, the notion of human nature as the tendency to cooperate would be much easier to base non-bodily aspects of human rights upon it.

I don't want to deeply go into the discussion on classical versus modern notion of human nature, rather I wanted to notice this area and its possible consequences for the philosophy of human rights. As we can see, the evolutionary notion of human nature is agnostic as for this discussion—it can understood in both ways so I will keep this point open in later parts of the book.

To sum up, Tomasello's thesis is that the tendency to cooperate constitutes human nature. Załuski's thesis is that the dominant moral motive of human behaviour is narrow altruism and the dominant human mode of action is imperfect prudence. These are the tendencies of our behaviour that form human nature. Tomasello's and Załuski's positions, despite slightly different terms, lead to highly similar claims about evolutionary discovered human nature. In fact, Załuski himself proposes that narrow altruism and imperfect prudence are the basis for the tendency to cooperate.[166] Tomasello's and Załuski's theses are formulated within the common methodological approach of evolutionary psychology and substantially connected. There are of course some differences as for the exact method. While Załuski based his conclusions on game theory and experiments conducted by other scientists, Tomasello conducted experiments himself. Yet, the common framework of evolutionary psychology is shared and the conclusions drawn by two thinkers are highly coherent. Therefore, later in the work, by evolutionary understood human nature, I will mean both Tomasello's and Załuski's discoveries simultaneously.

3.3.4 Conclusions

Every version of the naturalistic (orthodox, substantial) approach in the philosophy of human rights must adopt some views concerning who a human is. The often discussed views concerning who a human is refer to the content of human nature. However, these views on the content of human nature are rarely formulated explicitly. Even if they are, they are not based on a more general theory about human but rather on some intuitive assumptions concerning human beings, or on obsolete, armchair inquiry that has nothing to do with the modern discoveries of empirical sciences. Yet, following the project of (methodological) naturalisation I believe it is the most plausible to base the conception of human rights not on *assumptions* concerning human nature but on *facts* concerning human nature. I think that this criterion is best fulfilled by the conception of human nature developed from the evolutionary perspective. The scientific approach to human nature in the philosophy of human rights has been underlined by Chris Brown:

> For some thinkers a scientific account of what human nature actually is (if such could be provided) would provide us with an account of how we should live our lives – would be, in effect, a theory of the good life upon which the idea of human rights could be directly based. Others argue that there is no link at all between a scientific account of human nature and a moral account of how we should live. A third position is that there is no direct, but a strong indirect, connection between human nature, the good, and human rights; our rational capacities (themselves part of our nature) allow us to determine how to live our lives but our nature is the starting point for this process.[167]

Brown distinguishes three types of relation between the scientifically understood concept of human nature and the moral conception of a good life, which includes or entails a conception of human rights. The first position is that there is a direct link from human nature to human rights. It seems that the first position can be extended not only on scientific notions of human nature but on every notion of human nature, especially philosophical ones. Such a position might be ascribed to those who attempt to justify human rights by reference to some necessary or essential features

[166] Załuski (2009a), p. 85, p. 137.

[167] Brown (2013), p. 25.

of human, like e.g. possessing soul, being rational or possessing consciousness. From the analytical point of view, such a position would have to face the "is"-"-ought" problem. The same goes for purely scientific notions of human nature: how can a sentence describing certain scientific, empirical facts about human nature entail a sentence ascertaining normative human rights? The second position is the negation of the first one: there is no such a direct link. The second position distinguished by Brown, which is that there is no link between human nature and human rights, can be ascribed to Nussbaum's approach. She believes that human nature has nothing to do with her justification of human rights.[168]

The third position lies in between the first one and the second one: there is no direct relation between human nature and human rights, however, scientifically understood human nature can provide us with many useful facts about the basic functioning of human. Taking those facts into consideration in a theory of human rights enables to build a conception of human rights in accordance with empirical facts about how humans really are. Yet, the employment of the scientific facts does not limit a theory of human rights only to those issues that can be directly entailed by human nature. The third position can be ascribed to those who attempt to regard the relation between human nature and human rights not as a logical entailment, but as a weaker relation, e.g. a sort of a rational justification.[169]

To sum up, I have presented three most general conceptions of the concept of human nature: (1) human nature as a set of necessary/essential features of human, (2) human nature as an ideal or pattern of human and (3) human nature as a dominant tendency (or tendencies) characterising all humans as species, although not always characterising every individual human. The first and the third notion are descriptive, while the second is normative in its character. All of them are applied in the philosophy of human rights, although often implicitly, as every theory of human rights must assume some facts about human (and this is "human nature").

In my view, the third notion of human nature, which most adequately suits to the scientific accounts of human nature, is best employed in the inquiry of the foundations of human rights. The scientific accounts of human nature are based on empirical facts and developed on the basis of the scientific method, which is more reliable than the purely philosophical method due to its empirical basis and determined means of falsification. Among the scientific accounts of human nature the most promising are proposed by the adherents of evolutionary psychology. The aim of evolutionary psychology is to demonstrate the basic tendencies of human by scientific method under the broad evolutionary theory, which claims that everything

[168] Nussbaum (2011), p. 28.

[169] Herbert's Hart conception of the minimal content of natural law is an instantiation of the third view. Hart claims that there are certain characteristics that every legal system must possess in order to be effective. These characteristics comprise human vulnerability, approximate equality, limited altruism, limited resources, and limited understanding and strength of human's will (1994, pp. 192–197). They must be taken into consideration while determining the content of legal norms, however, they do not constitute any reasons for legal norms (Hart 1994, p. 192). Similarly, as for human rights, one should take into consideration facts about human nature.

we possess, including mental aspects, is a product of evolution. The evolutionary conception of human nature is important for the philosophy of human rights also for the reason that human rights are rights that *humans* and only humans possess. It must be something in humans that causes that only they possess human rights.[170] If human rights hold in virtue of being human, whereas "being human" refers to human nature, it is human nature that is the difference making only humans have human rights. The evolutionary notion of human nature explicitly provides the theory of only human nature. Tomasello's notion of human nature is a proper example—he explicitly seeks the tendencies that distinguish humans from their closest biological relatives, which are chimpanzees. Evolutionary understood human nature is a natural, scientific, fact.

References

Alston P (1984) Conjuring up new human rights: a proposal for quality control. Am J Int Law 78: 607–621

Andersen H, Hepburn B (2020) Scientific method. The Stanford Encyclopedia of Philosophy (Winter 2020 Edition). https://plato.stanford.edu/archives/win2020/entries/scientific-method/

Brown C (2013) Human rights and human nature. In: Holder C, Reidy D (eds) Human rights. The hard questions. CUP, Cambridge, pp 23–38

Bullinger AF, Zimmermann F, Kaminski J, Tomasello M (2011) Different social motives in the gestural communication of chimpanzees and human children. Dev Sci 14:58–68

Complak K (2014) Komentarz do art. 30. In: Bartoszewicz M, Haczkowska M, Ławniczak A, Complak K, Balicki R, Masternak-Kubiak M (eds) Konstytucja Rzeczypospolitej Polskiej. Komentarz. Lexis Nexis, Warszawa

Cranston M (1973) What are human rights? Taplinger Publishing Company, New York

Cruft R, Liao SM, Renzo M (2015) Philosophical foundations of human rights: an overview. In: Cruft R, Liao SM, Renzo M (eds) Philosophical foundations of human rights. OUP, Oxford, pp 1–44

Donnelly J (2003) Universal human rights in theory and practice. Cornell University Press, Ithaca

Dunbar R (2014) Human evolution. Pelican Books, London

Fine K (1994) Essence and modality. Philos Perspect 8:1–16

Gizbert-Studnicki T, Dyrda A, Grabowski A (2016) Metodologiczne Dychotomie: krytyka pozytywistycznych teorii prawa. Wolters Kluwer, Warszawa

Griffin J (2008) On human rights. Oxford University Press, Oxford

Griffin J (2011) Human rights: questions of aim and approach. In: Ernst G, Heilinger JC (eds) The philosophy of human rights: contemporary controversies. De Gruyter, Berlin, pp 3–16

Hage J (2016) Facts, values and norms. In: Taekema S, van Klink V, de Been W (eds) Facts and norms in law. Edward Elgar, Cheltenham, pp 23–49

Hare B, Call J, Tomasello M (2006) What's in it for Me? Self-Regard Precludes Altruism and Spite in Chimpanzees. Proc Royal Soc London Series B Biol Sci 273:1013–1021

Hart HLA (1994) The concept of law. Oxford University Press, Oxford

[170] I do not claim that other species do not possess rights, probably (at least some) animals possess animal rights. Yet, the foundations of animal rights must be different from the foundations of human rights, which is quite trivial, although there are no reasons not to regard both human and animal rights via a coherent philosophical framework.

Hill T (2013) In defence of human dignity: comments on Kant and Rosen. In: McCrdudden C (ed) Understanding human dignity. OUP, Oxford, pp 312–326

Hohfeld W (1913) Fundamental legal conceptions as applied in judicial reasoning. Yale Law J 26: 710–770

Kant I (1785) The groundwork of the metaphysics of morals. Yale University Press

Korsgaard C (1996) The sources of normativity. Cambridge University Press, Cambridge

Lee P, George LP (2008) The nature and basis of human dignity. Ratio Juris 21:173–193

Liao SM (2015) Human rights as fundamental conditions for a goof life. In: Cruft R, Liao SM, Renzo M (eds) Philosophical foundations of human rights. OUP, Oxford, pp 79–100

Liszkowski U, Carpenter M, Striano T, Tomasello M (2006) 12- and 18-month-olds point to provide information for others. J Cogn Dev 7:173–187

Liszkowski U, Carpenter M, Tomasello M (2008) Twelve-month-olds communicate helpfully and appropriately for knowledgeable and ignorant partners. Cognition 108:732–739

MacCormick N (1977) Legal reasoning and legal theory. OUP, Oxford

Macklin R (2003) Dignity is a useless concept: it means no more than respect for persons or their autonomy. Br Med J 327:1419–1420

Marmor A (2013) Farewell to conceptual analysis (in Jurisprudence). In: Waluchow W, Sciaraffa S (eds) Philosophical foundations of the nature of law. Oxford University Press, pp 209–229

Mazurkiewicz S (2018) Czy natura człowieka może być podstawą praw człowieka – ujęcie analityczne. Avant IX:129–144

McCrudden C (2008) Human dignity and judicial interpretation of human rights. Eur J Int Law 19: 655–724

McNeill W (1998) History and the scientific world-view history and theory. Stud Philos Hist 38:1–13

Miller D (2007) National responsibility and global justice. OUP, Oxford

Miller D (2012) Grounding human rights. Crit Rev Int Soc Polit Philos 15:407–427

Mulligan K, Correia F (2017) Facts. The Stanford Encyclopedia of Philosophy (Winter 2017 Edition). https://plato.stanford.edu/archives/win2017/entries/facts/

Mulligan K, Simons P, Smith B (1984) Truthmakers. Philos Phenomenol Res 44:287–321

Nickel J (2019) Human Rights. The Stanford Encyclopedia of Philosophy (Summer 2019 Edition). https://plato.stanford.edu/archives/sum2019/entries/rights-human/

Nussbaum M (2000) Women and human development: the capabilities approach. Cambridge University Press, Cambridge

Nussbaum M (2006) Frontiers of justice: disability, nationality, species membership. The Belknap Press Harvard University Press, Cambridge

Nussbaum M (2011) Creating capabilities, the human development approach. The Belknap Press of Harvard University Press, Cambridge/London

Orend B (2002) Human rights: concept and content. Broadview Press

Pendelton MD (1999) A new human right – the right to globalisation. Fordham Int Law Rev 22: 2052–2095

Piechowiak M (1999) Filozofia Praw Człowieka. Prawa Człowieka w świetle ich Międzynarodowej Ochrony. Towarzystwo Naukowe KUL, Lublin

Piechowiak M (2011) Klasyczna Koncepcja Osoby jako Podstawa Pojmowania Praw Człowieka. Wokół św. Tomasza i Immanuela Kanta propozycji ugruntowania godności człowieka In: Dardziński P, Longchamps de Bérier F, Szczucki K Prawo Naturalne – Natura Prawa. C.H. Beck, Warszawa, pp 3–20

Piechowiak M (2019) Plato's conception of justice and the question of human dignity. Peter Lang, Berlin

Pinker S (2008) The stupidity of dignity: conservative bioethics' latest most dangerous ploy The New Republic, 28th May 2008

Rachel J (1986) The elements of moral philosophy. McGraw Hill, New York

Raz J (1999) Practical reasons and norms. OUP, Oxford

Raz J (2010) Human rights without foundations. In: Besson S Tasioulas J (eds) The philosophy of international law. OUP, pp 321–338

Reinhardt J (2014) Human rights, human nature, and the feasibility issue. In: Albers M, Hoffmann T, Reinhardt J (eds) Human rights and human nature. Springer, Dordrecht, pp 137–160

Renzo M (2015) Human needs, human rights. In: Cruft R, Liao SM, Renzo M (eds) Philosophical foundations of human rights. OUP, Oxford, pp 570–587

Robertson T, Atkins P (2018) Essential vs. Accidental Properties. The Stanford Encyclopedia of Philosophy (Spring 2018 Edition). https://plato.stanford.edu/archives/spr2018/entries/essential-accidental/

Rosen G (2017) What is a moral law? In: Schaffer-Landau R (ed) Oxford studies in metaethics, vol 12. OUP, Oxford, pp 135–159

Rosen M (2012) Dignity: its history and meaning. Harvard University Press, Boston

Rosen M (2013) Dignity: the case against. In: McCrdudden C (ed) Understanding human dignity. OUP, Oxford, pp143–154

Searle J (1984) Minds, brains and science. Harvard University Press, Cambridge

Shue H (1996) Basic rights: subsistence, affluence and U.S. Foreign Policy. Princeton University Press, Princeton

Stevenson L, Haberman D (1998) Ten theories of human nature. OUP, Oxford

Tasioulas J (2011) On the nature of human rights. In: Ernst G, Heilinger JC (eds) The philosophy of human rights: contemporary controversies. De Gruyter, Berlin, pp 17–59

Tasioulas J (2013) Human dignity and the foundations of human rights. In: McCrdudden C (ed) Understanding human dignity. OUP, Oxford, pp 291–312

Tasioulas J (2015) On the foundations of human rights. In: Cruft R, Liao SM, Renzo M (eds) Philosophical foundations of human rights. OUP, Oxford, pp 45–70

Tepe H (2014) Rethinking human nature as a basis for human rights. In: Albers M, Hoffmann T, Reinhardt J (eds) Human rights and human nature. Springer, Dordrecht, pp 57–78

Tomasello M (2009) Why we cooperate? A Boston Review Book, Cambridge, London

Tomasello M, Carpenter M (2005) The emergence of social cognition in three young chimpanzees. Monogr Soc Res Child Dev 70:1–132

Tooby J, Cosmides L (1992) The psychological foundations of culture. In: Batkow J, Cosmides L, Toob J (eds) The adapted mind: evolutionary psychology and the generation of culture. OUP, Oxford, pp 19–136

Waldron J (2012) Dignity, rank and rights. OUP, Oxford

Waldron J (2015) Is dignity foundation of human rights? In: Cruft R, Liao SM, Renzo M (eds) Philosophical foundations of human rights. OUP, Oxford, pp 117–137

Wellman C (1999) The proliferation of rights: moral progress or empty Rhetorics? Westview Press, Boulder

Wellman C (2010) The moral dimensions of human rights. OUP, Oxford

Wolterstorff N (2008) Justice: rights and wrongs. Princeton University Press, Princeton

Wróblewski J (1970) Natura a reguły postępowania. Etyka 6:51–78

Wróblewski J (1971) Legal decision and its Justification. Logique et Analyse 45:409–419

Załuski W (2009a) Evolutionary theory and legal philosophy. Edward Elgar, Cheltenham

Załuski W (2009b) Ewolucyjna Filozofia Prawa. Wolters Kluwer, Warszawa

Załuski W (2011) Pojęcie Osoby w świetle Osiągnięć Nauk Biologicznych. In: Brożek B, Mączka J, Grygiel W, Hohol M (eds) Oblicza Racjonalności. Copernicus Centre Press, Kraków, pp 83–98

Załuski W (2018) Law and evil. The evolutionary perspective. Edward Elgar, Cheltenham

Chapter 4
Contemporary Analytic Metaphysics

I base my inquiry of the foundations of human rights on two frameworks of the contemporary analytic metaphysics, which can be clearly presented.[1] These are: the project of naturalisation (or simply naturalisation) and relational metaphysics (the latter could be called "theory of grounding" bearing in mind that it is not limited only to the inquiry on the relation of metaphysical grounding). As for the latter, I understand relational metaphysics as the inquiry on how different entities exist dependently on other entities. Metaphysics has been often understood as investigation on what exists, which focuses on debating particular entities, like the issue of identity. In turn, in the recent three decades, there has been a movement within analytic metaphysics that emphasises the debate on the structure of the universe and various relations between different entities, rather than on the question of identity of particular entities. It is sometimes referred to as "meta-metaphysics", although I decide not to use this highly technical and perhaps unclear term.[2] The term "theory of grounding" could also be here used but with putting strong emphasis that I do not limit it only to the relation of metaphysical grounding.[3] In order to avoid potential confusion, I prefer to use the term "relational metaphysics" for the debate on how and why various entities depend on one another. I am aware of the fact that metaphysics in general, including analytic metaphysics, covers more questions than just this one but I find this the best terminology to be used.

Let me first briefly present the project of naturalisation. It is sometimes understood as an epistemological inquiry, rather than a metaphysical one. As we will see, the ontological version of naturalisation is by far a metaphysical issue as it provides

[1] Contemporary analytic metaphysics discusses metaphysical problems by employing analytic tools. I do not want to elaborate on the issue of analytic metaphysics in general, there is also no generally accepted metaphysical theory.

[2] Notice also that the meta-metaphysics is most often seen as the inquiry on the foundational issues for whole metaphysics (Manley et al. 2009).

[3] Also, broadly conceived "theory of grounding" understood as the inquiry on relations between various entities does not have to presuppose the relation of metaphysical grounding.

S. Mazurkiewicz, *Grounding Human Rights in Human Nature*, Law and Philosophy Library 141, https://doi.org/10.1007/978-3-031-30734-8_4

claims about what and why exists. In turn, there can are concerns about the methodological naturalisation, which will be addressed below.

4.1 Naturalisation

Human nature, as understood in evolutionary psychology, will be employed in this work as the basis for the justification of human rights. Within analytic philosophy, there is a conception concerned with utilising natural facts in philosophical inquiry. This conception is philosophical naturalism or, in another wording, naturalisation. The notion dates back to late 1960s[4] although, of course, naturalistic positions in philosophy are as old as philosophy itself. The term "naturalism" has many connotations and means different things in different philosophical areas. However, two forms of naturalism are well defined.

The first one is ontological naturalism.[5] Brian Leiter and Matthew Etchemendy define it by the claim that "there exist only *natural* or *physical* things".[6] In other words, there are no supranatural entities in the world. Everything that exists is a physical, natural entity. Natural entities are entities that can be discovered and described by empirical sciences. Natural facts are constituents of natural entities. For example, pursuant to ontological naturalism, mind in fact *is* a neuro-physical state of the brain. In turn, naturalism concerning moral domain—moral naturalism—is characterised by the claim that "moral facts are natural facts", or on the semantic level by the thesis that "our moral claims are *synonymous* with certain (highly complex) claims in the natural sciences".[7] It is widely accepted that natural facts have an impact on moral facts, e.g. an act that causes someone's pain (natural fact) makes this act wrong (moral fact).[8] But many claim that we cannot fully define moral facts in terms of natural facts and, thus, they are not identical.[9] Such a position is an anti-naturalistic view.

Consequently, moral naturalism in the context of human rights and human dignity would boil down to the claim that human rights are actually identical to certain natural facts. The view that human rights and human dignity are not identical, but only somehow dependent on, or constituted by, natural facts is a non-naturalistic position.

The second form of naturalism is methodological naturalism.[10] It refers to the method of philosophical inquiry. Methodological naturalisation means that in

[4]Quine (1969).

[5]Leiter and Etchemendy (2017) and Papineau (2020).

[6]Leiter and Etchemendy (2017).

[7]Lutz and Lenman (2018).

[8]McPherson (2019).

[9]Moore (1903).

[10]Leiter and Etchemendy (2017), Nolan (2017) and Papineau (2020).

philosophical investigations we should start from scientific knowledge and develop one's philosophical theory on its basis and in accordance with it.[11] For instance, if one investigates the issue of determinism, she should start her inquiry from physics, probably quantum physics if she researches determinism in general, or from neuroscience if she researches the particular issue of determinism in human behaviour. Methodological naturalism does not claim that everything is a natural fact, however, it claims that natural facts can falsify philosophical claims and every philosophical investigation should begin from the claims about the relevant natural facts. For example, one's claim that mind has no connection to the neuro-physical state of brain would be false as it is in contradiction to the claims about natural facts provided by scientific knowledge. Methodological naturalism is thus a normative principle about the method of philosophical inquiry.

There are a few arguments in favour of methodological naturalisation. First, it is the scientific method that gives the proper knowledge of the world. From the beginning of the scientific revolution the scientific method has provided scientific explanation of many facts that used to be previously considered on a purely philosophical basis. The same is likely to happen as for the issues we debate nowadays by purely philosophical methods. Second, the scientific method is well-established and provides clear ways of corroboration and falsification. Therefore, we should think of entities we discuss in philosophy as either identical to natural entities, or constituted by them. We should develop our knowledge about entities discussed in philosophy with the strongest possible reference to the known relevant natural facts. As for the moral domain, one can be an ontological non-naturalist and a methodological naturalist. This happens if one claims that the scientific knowledge provides the relevant data for determining the content of moral facts and builds one's theory in accordance with these natural facts, however without claiming that moral facts are actually identical to natural facts. One can have concerns that methodological naturalisation is still a part of metaphysical inquiry since it deals with the issue of how we should discover the reality, which belongs to epistemology. Surely, methodological naturalism provides directives on how to conduct philosophical research. But its consequences are of a metaphysical character, at least in some parts. If a given philosophical question can be methodologically naturalised, it means that natural facts researched by natural sciences are relevant for this philosophical topic. For instance, if the question about mind is answered by making use of neuro-physical studies, mind of course does not necessarily become a purely neuro-physical natural fact, yet, in some sense, it is dependent on the neuro-physical natural facts. And that is a metaphysical claim since it is about the way of existence. Therefore, I believe that methodological naturalism is in its further consequences relevant for metaphysical questions.

It seems that naturalism is one of the main key concepts discussed in contemporary analytic philosophy and contemporary analytic metaphysics. Debates between

---

[11] Papineau (2020).

naturalists and non-naturalists are conducted not in general but rather on specific fields, like the philosophy of mind, philosophy of mathematics, or metaethics.

Naturalistic positions are also present in the philosophy of law, mainly in the general jurisprudence debate on the nature of law. Leiter argues that jurisprudence should be naturalised just as other philosophical domains.[12] He and Etchemendy believe that American Legal Realists and Scandinavian Legal Realists were the precursors of naturalisation in the philosophy of law.[13] Leon Petrażycki's claim that law is constituted by specific sorts of emotions defined by psychology of that time is a notable precursor of legal naturalism.[14] The rapid development of cognitive studies has provided new foundations for legal naturalism; e.g. Bartosz Brożek claims that law emerges upon social regularities and mental states.[15] According to the further parts of Załuski's evolutionary theory, which were not discussed here, that law is an emergent entity supervening on the tendency to cooperate is a naturalised theory of law *per se*.[16]

Nonetheless, naturalism has been almost entirely absent in the philosophy of human rights is. Leiter and Etchemendy claim: "The 'naturalistic turn' that has swept so many areas of philosophy over the past four decades has also had an impact in the in legal philosophy".[17] However, my observation is that it has had almost no impact in the philosophy of human rights. It surely had no impact on the major accounts in the philosophy of human rights, like Griffin's, Nussbaum's, the political approach, etc. The debate on the foundations of human rights is in no worse position to be naturalised than other philosophical debates. There is no direct reference to ontological moral naturalism, which in the philosophy of human rights constitute a hypothetical claim that human rights are identical to natural facts. This is quite understandable as human rights belong to the wider class of moral rights and the naturalistic position in metaethics raises serious difficulties. The main accounts of philosophy of human rights present implicitly non-naturalistic position. Yet, problems appearing on the transition from "is" sphere to "ought" sphere, like Hume's "is"-"ought" problem or Moore's naturalistic fallacy, arise only with respect to such relations that are proposed to connect a descriptive sentence or concept with a normative sentence or concept (as in case of logical entailment in the context of Hume's Guillotine) and inferences where certain descriptive and normative attributes are taken to be identical on the premise that certain classes of objects, possessing both of these attributes, are identical, as in case of Moore's naturalistic fallacy.[18] These mistakes can, however, be avoided by the careful scrutiny of relations holding between the discussed objects (relata). Philosophers of human

[12] Leiter (2007).

[13] Leiter and Etchemendy (2017).

[14] Petrażycki (1904).

[15] Brożek (2012).

[16] Załuski (2009a, b).

[17] Leiter and Etchemendy (2017).

[18] cf. White (1956), pp. 174–177.

rights seem to be unaware of the possibility of considering the character of putative relations more thoroughly, thus they fall prey to the above mentioned inferential, "is"-"ought" and identity problems.

However, the lack of reference to methodological naturalism is not so easily understandable. To my best knowledge, there is no major theory of human rights that would refer to natural facts, either under ontological, or methodological naturalism. The references to empirical science are present in few papers. Mikhail proposes to adopt the project of Universal Moral Grammar in arguing for the justification of human rights.[19] Universal Moral Grammar is related to the theory of Universal Grammar which claims that some basic linguistic structures are innate in humans.[20] Consequently, there are some basic common linguistic competences, especially structural, that are independent of experience and not learnt in the process of socialisation. The correctness of this theory is debated in linguistics, psychology and philosophy of mind. In turn, according to proponents of Universal Moral Grammar, we have basic, moral competences that are not being learnt in the processes of socialisation, but are innate.[21] Adherents of the Universal Moral Grammar believe that there are scientific arguments in its favour, especially delivered by cognitive sciences.[22] According to Mikhail human rights can be understood as an instantiation of the natural morality we all share.[23] There are some works that analyse how concepts referring to natural facts are used by philosophers of human rights, but such works are very rare.[24] Herbert Gintis arguing from the historical and evolutionary perspective, suggests that the development of human rights should be understood as a manifestation of valuing individuality that fights against hierarchy.[25] The mainstream of the philosophy of human rights is still attached to a solely conceptual, armchair mode of philosophising.

The absence of naturalised notions of human rights becomes even more striking when we recall that the prevailing approach in the philosophy of human rights is called the *naturalistic* approach. To recall, the naturalistic approach claims that human rights are possessed by every human simply in virtue of being human or in virtue of humanity.[26] This "being human" or "humanity" is understood differently by different philosophers: as human dignity and human interests,[27] normative agency[28] or capabilities,[29] but it generally denotes something humans inherently

---

[19] Mikhail (2012).

[20] Chomsky (1964, 1986).

[21] Mikhail (2007).

[22] Mikhail (2007, 2012).

[23] Mikhail (2012).

[24] Brown (2013).

[25] Gintis (2012).

[26] Griffin (2008), p. 2; Tasioulas (2011), p. 26.

[27] Tasioulas (2015).

[28] Griffin (2008).

[29] Nussbaum (2000, 2006, 2011).

possess or innately are. As we see, the putative foundations of human rights are understood by major philosophers of human rights with no reference to empirical sciences. The justification of human rights is developed by a purely armchair mode of thinking, as it has been presented in Chap. 2. In fact, it turns out that the naturalistic approach in the philosophy of human rights is not naturalised at all.

My aim is thus to naturalise the *naturalistic* approach. The concepts "being human" or "humanity" that, in the naturalistic approach, are claimed to be the grounds of the (concept of) human rights can be understood by reference to the discoveries of empirical sciences. In other words, these concepts can be naturalised. Consequently, the naturalistic approach will be naturalised. The concepts "being human" or "humanity" can be labelled "human nature". I believe this is an uncontroversial turn since "being human" or "humanity" refer to the same reality as the concept of "human nature". Then, following naturalism, I will understand human nature as it is conceived in evolutionary psychology. As a result, the philosophy of human rights will become naturalised—the foundations of human rights will be conceived by the reference to natural facts.

4.2 Moral Naturalism and Autonomy of Ethics

The issue of moral naturalism requires a deeper elaboration. Moral naturalism, which is the ontological naturalism position in the moral domain, claims that moral facts are identical to natural facts. In simple words, moral facts are natural facts. According to moral naturalism, we have two different semantics for discussing the reality—one for the moral domain, the second for the natural domain. Our moral language enables fast communication by introducing words like "good", "right", "wrong", etc. In the ordinary language usage terms like "good" and "unpleasant" are rather not equivalent. Of course, language has many contexts and the synonymy of the natural languages terms is discussable.

However, following moral naturalism, it turns out after a deeper examination that the terms like "good", "right", "wrong", etc. most often either denote solely natural facts, or if such a denotation cannot be proven, they have no precise meaning other than an emotive sense (i.e. they represent only emotions). For instance, the claim that X is wrong is often equivalent to the claim that X causes pain once a thorough analysis is done. Perhaps, in this aspect we could interchangeably use sentences: "It is wrong" and "it causes pain", even though in many situations natural language descriptions are much more sophisticated and complicated. Yet, it turns out that moral claims are often synonymous with descriptive claims.[30] Consequently, moral claims do not have any special and independent meaning in relation to natural facts. According to the proponents of moral naturalism, it entails that moral facts are actually identical to natural facts.

[30]Lutz and Lenman (2018).

The question whether moral naturalism is sound is of great significance to the philosophy of human rights. Human rights obviously belong to the moral domain, they can be classified as moral facts as it was presented in Sect. 3.1. If moral naturalism is true, it is so for every normative fact, including human rights. Therefore, if moral naturalism is true, human rights are identical to certain natural facts. In order to justify or explain them, we would only need to find and describe these natural facts. No reference to human dignity, human autonomy or any other non-natural entity would be needed. It would not mean that we should abandon the language of human rights—it is useful in our communication, as moral language in general is useful. Yet, in fact, human rights would be just some natural facts. I will analyse whether human rights are identical with some natural facts in Sect. 4.4, here I would like to focus on moral naturalism in general. If moral naturalism is true for every moral fact, it is so for human rights. I will present this issue on the basis of the discussion on the autonomy of ethics.

The debate on the autonomy of ethics aims to illuminate the issue of moral naturalism.[31] It is a conception that takes together all problems concerning the natural and the moral domains and discusses the status of ethics in relation to the natural world. Charles Pidgen proposes the following structure of the autonomy of ethics.[32] First, there is logical autonomy, noticed by Hume and known as Hume's Guillotine or "is"-"ought" gap. It claims that moral conclusions cannot be logically derived from non-moral premises. In order to form logically proper reasoning, wherein the conclusion has a moral character, at least one of the premises must have moral character as well. This is rather universally accepted. Second, there is semantic autonomy: moral properties cannot be defined in natural terms. It was demonstrated by G. E. Moore and its violation is known as the naturalistic fallacy.[33] White distinguishes two forms of Moore's argumentation about committing a naturalistic fallacy. According to the first one, the naturalistic fallacy is committed when goodness is deemed to be confused with another, natural concept. Moore's argument is that if one claims that X (e.g. pleasure) is good, we can still wonder why is that and ask "Is it true that X is good?" And this question is meaningful. It would be meaningless if it were equivalent to asking "Is it true that good is good?"[34] However, we intuitively feel there is a difference and the first question is valid. Since it is meaningful, goodness and any natural property and different concepts. According to the second form distinguished by White, the naturalistic fallacy in about "passing from the statement that the class of good things is identical with the class of things conductive to pleasure to the statement that the attributive of being good is identical with the attribute of being conductive to pleasure".[35] According to White, this form of fallacy has nothing to do solely with moral investigation, it is a

[31] Pidgen (1989) and Makowski (2014).

[32] Pidgen (1989).

[33] Moore (1903).

[34] Moore (1903) § 13.

[35] White (1956), p. 174.

case of much wider mistake of inferring from the fact that two classes are identical (i.e. they denote the same objects) the conclusion that the attributes are identical. White gives a few examples: the class of creatures having a kidney is identical with the class of creatures having a heart, but it does not entail that having a kidney is identical with having a heart; the class of featherless biped animals is identical with the class of man, but it does not mean that being a featherless biped animal is identical with being a man.[36] Looking from the perspective of the debate on the autonomy of ethics, Moore's arguments are considered to prove that semantic autonomy holds, i.e. moral properties cannot be defined in terms of natural properties. However, the crucial issue is whether there exists also ontological autonomy: moral judgments, to be true, must correspond to a realm of *sui generis* non-natural properties.[37] In other words, the truth of a moral claim does not depend on the natural world. Consequently, moral facts are ontologically different than natural facts. The key issue is that logical autonomy and semantic autonomy does not necessarily entail ontological autonomy. Moore would rather claim that his conceptual inquiry gives conclusions not only on semantic, but also on ontological level. However, the contemporary debate distinguishes semantic autonomy and ontological autonomy and tends to regard that Moore's analysis does not directly gives basis for a claim on ontological autonomy.[38] And in order to decide whether moral naturalism is true, we need to justify whether ontological autonomy holds.[39] We cannot derive "ought" from "is" and we cannot define "ought" in terms of "is". Yet, it does not directly leads to any position defending ontological autonomy. One of the following positions is still possible: that "ought" actually cannot be reduced to "is" (ontological autonomy holds), or that "ought" actually can be reduced to "is" (ontological autonomy does not hold).

The main argument against the claim that logical autonomy and semantic autonomy entail ontological autonomy is that the argumentation in favour of ontological autonomy is based on a certain kind of implausible conceptual analysis. However, we rather discover the nature of the universe not on the basis of philosophical inquiry of concepts, but on the basis of empirical study. For instance, we know that water actually is H2O not on due to the conceptual analysis of the concept of water, but due to the development of chemistry.[40] By examination of the concept of water we could never discover what water actually consists of.[41]

[36] White (1956), p. 174.

[37] Piotr Makowski (2014) also distinguishes epistemic autonomy: ethical method is different from natural method, consequently, we cannot know moral facts on the basis of natural facts.

[38] cf. Pidgen (1989) and Makowski (2014).

[39] cf. Maguire (2015).

[40] Lutz and Lenman (2018) and Papineau (2020).

[41] Of course, I am aware of the difference between the chemical composition of water and the meaning or function of water. One does not have to know the chemical composition of water in order to know the function of water and the concept of water. I assume here that sense sets reference. I am aware that this is, as well as the relation between conceptual analysis and scientific method and

Advocates of naturalism claim that the same may happen with moral facts and natural facts. The development of science may enable us to discover what actually moral concepts mean, irrespective of our conceptual analysis of moral terms.

Nonetheless, the problem is that such a development of science has not yet occurred. And we do not know if we have to simply wait for such a development, or due to a specific nature of ethics, science will never be able to a provide full picture of rightness and wrongness. In my view, the status of current scientific knowledge provides rather a sceptical argument against moral naturalism.

There is another, much stronger argument, against naturalism. Assume that we know that X causes pain. The fact that X causes pain is a natural fact. X is wrong, which is a moral fact. So, a moral fact actually appears to be fully described by natural language—that it causes pain—and therefore moral fact is a natural fact. But how do we know that X is wrong? One can answer: "because pain is wrong". But how do we know that pain is wrong? Some may claim that it is self-evident. It seems right, but reference to self-evidence is far from the way of thinking we would like to employ in a naturalistic view, for there is no reference to solely natural, scientifically known facts. It turns out that X is wrong because (1) it causes pain, which is a natural fact, but also (2) because pain is wrong, which we consider as self-evident, non-natural fact. It is not the case that natural facts alone constitute the moral fact that X is wrong, and consequently naturalism fails.

Another solution might be to attempt to naturalistically explain that pain is wrong. A possible analysis might be that pain has such and such negative consequences on the functioning of a being. These consequences lead to such and such state of an organism that for instance is improper from the biological perspective for the functioning of an organism. Here, the answer is developed on a purely scientific level. We can even claim that such a state of an organism may lead to death or may diminish evolutionary powers. Such a deeper examination may lead us to the thesis that an improper biological state of the organism or its death, or a limitation of its evolutionary powers are wrong. But still, the question arises: why are these states of affairs actually wrong? On what basis is the death of an organism wrong? Biology or an evolutionary theory has no capability to determine the results of an action outside the theory—the death of an organism can ultimately lead to the extinction of a whole species, but then most probably certain new species will fit into this ecological gap. The claim that such a state of affairs is wrong is rather made from the perspective external to a given empirical science.

However, let us assume someone finds a well-argued definition of wrongness on the basis of an empirical science. Therefore, the fact that X is wrong would be the natural fact that it causes pain. But then, another key question emerges: why should we avoid causing X? What is the ground of the normative power of a natural fact? The answer may be: you should not do the wrong. Yet, the problem comes back: how do we know that we should not do wrong. In other words: what is the nature of

its discoveries, are debated issues in philosophy, however, I do not aim to enter this discussion in this work.

the claim that you should do what is good and avoid what is wrong? If the answer is that it is simply self-evident or intuitive, it is actually the proof for non-naturalism: the basis of moral claims is partly constituted by non-natural aspects.[42] If the answer refers to some natural facts, we come back to problems mentioned few sentences above and fall into regress ad infinitum. This line of argumentation is similar to Moore's argument for naturalistic fallacy but I believe that taking into consideration the current state of scientific knowledge it can be placed not only on the definitional, semantic level but on the ontological level, which is the most important from the metaphysical point of view.

Therefore, as for now, there are strong arguments against moral naturalism and I find the non-naturalistic position more convincing. The aim of this work is not to debate various metaethical positions. I am of course aware of other stances, like noncognitivism, or the error theory and moral scepticism (mentioned in the footnote). Solving metaethical problems is left outside the scope of this work. My aim was to present the outline of the discussion between moral naturalism and non-naturalism in light of the debate of the autonomy of ethics and explain why I choose to follow non-naturalism.

Human rights belong to the normative sphere and they are moral facts. Consequently, if non-naturalism is plausible in general, so it is in the particular issue of human rights. Therefore, due to the general implausibility of naturalism in the moral domain, it is implausible to suggest that human rights are identical with natural facts. Nonetheless, in my view, the issue of naturalism, especially in the moral domain, is still open for debate. The development of empirical sciences may provide new insights into this issue. However, as for now, I believe that moral non-naturalism is more plausible.

Notwithstanding, the implausibility of naturalism in the philosophy of human rights as a consequence of the rejection of the general moral naturalism refers only to ontological naturalism. The above-mentioned arguments do not undermine the methodological version of naturalism. Methodological moral naturalism boils down to the thesis that we should start the philosophical inquiry of the moral domain from the relevant state of scientific knowledge and develop theories in accordance with it, although without claiming that moral facts are identical with relevant natural facts. Consequently, the rejection of (reductive) ontological moral naturalism as for human rights does not undermine methodological naturalism in the philosophy of human rights.

I will follow this path which begins with the acceptance of methodological naturalism in the philosophy of human rights. However, before that, there is one topic left within the contemporary analytic metaphysics that requires careful presentation. This is the very idea of relational metaphysics, which deals with the issue of

[42] Of course, there are other views on the nature of moral claims. Proponents of error theory believe that all moral claims are indeed truth apt, yet all moral claims are false. Adherents of scepticism argue against the possibility of moral knowledge. It can happen that the development of science will question the existence of any morality. I am aware of such metaethical position, but they are outside the scope of this work.

why and how some entities are dependent on other in their existence. In other words, why and how metaphysical dependence relations hold and, especially, what is the nature of these relations.

4.3 Relational Metaphysics (Theory of Grounding)

For many years analytic metaphysics has been focused on the issues of identity of facts. Considerations from the previous sections are a good example—they aim to answer the question: what are moral facts? This question is answered by determining whether they are identical with natural facts. But in the last two or three decades another general issue has emerged in analytic metaphysics: how different facts are dependent on one another? For Quine the task of metaphysics was to say what exists;[43] this task was related to the observation that our talk commits us ontologically to the existence of various types of objects. Quine also thought that the terms like "being" and "existence" have only one meaning and there is only one way of existence (ontological univocalism). For Jonathan Schaffer, a strong proponent of the new insight into metaphysics, the task of metaphysics is to say what grounds what.[44] In other words: which facts (entities) depend in their existence on which other facts (entities).[45] This kind of metaphysical inquiry I call "relational metaphysics" or "theory of grounding", bearing in mind that it is not limited only to the research about the relation of metaphysical grounding.[46] This second approach does not preclude (but also is not committed to) the view that various types of entities, belonging to different domains (e.g. descriptive, normative) may exist in different ways.

For instance, if we hold the moral non-naturalism position and reject the claim that moral facts are identical to natural facts, still, there remains a strong possibility that natural facts have some impact on moral facts, even though the mode of existence of moral facts may be very different from the one we attach to natural facts. There is a particle of truth in the claim that the existence of the fact that X causes pain influences the existence of the moral fact that Y is wrong, although we cannot say that the moral fact that Y is wrong *is simply identical* or *reduced to* the

---

[43] Quine (1953).

[44] Schaffer (2009) and Wallner (2016).

[45] Analytic metaphysics makes use of "facts", which I mentioned earlier. I put the term "entities" in the brackets to indicate what is meant to someone not accustomed to this usage. In fragments devoted to analytic metaphysics I will make use of the term "facts".

[46] In literature, this kind of inquiry does not possesses its own name as is simply called metaphysics. However, I prefer to use more narrow term to emphasise that I am interested in a particular, narrow and well defined part of a very broad metaphysical inquiry. In turn, "theory of grounding" is rather associated solely with the relation of metaphysical grounding whereas in this work I test also other relations in order to assess what is the relation between human rights, human dignity and human nature.

fact that X causes pain. This general impact that facts from different levels or different domains have on some other facts is called ontological dependence.[47] There are important examples of putative ontological dependencies in other domains than moral as well. Mental facts seem to be ontologically dependent on neurophysical facts: my feeling of happiness is dependent on such and such neurophysical state of my brain. The facts about a set ontologically depend on the facts about its members;[48] in other words: the facts about the whole depend on the facts about it parts.[49] Legal facts seem to ontologically depend on social facts: the content of law is such and such due to facts about what we collectively think and how we collectively behave.[50] For example, the fact that a statute is a binding law holds due to the fact that a certain number of people simultaneously raised their hands and another person signed a piece of paper, as well due to the fact that other people apply rules contained by this piece of paper and society generally accepts them.

We have similar intuitions about holding of facts we discuss in the philosophy of human rights: human rights depend on human dignity and human dignity depends on some more basic facts about human that can be called human nature. Let me recall here two slightly different formulations of the general thesis of the naturalistic approach to human rights: "human rights are moral rights possessed by all humans simply in virtue of their humanity"[51] or "human rights are rights we have simply in virtue of being human".[52] It is claimed that human rights are rights humans have due to some more basic fact like being human or humanity. At the beginning of Chap. 2, I named this central claim of philosophy of human rights "foundational claim". This claim has been so far analysed only from the ethical point of view. It can be, however, analysed also from the metaphysical point of view. Bear in mind that the discourse on human rights, found both in international and domestic law and in philosophical works on human rights, presupposes that human right and human dignity are not merely ideas or concepts found in legal text, but they exist independently of one's mind and of legal text. This is why it is justified to analyse dependency in ontological terms. Therefore, from the metaphysical point of view, foundational claim of the philosophy of human rights represents an idea that human rights are ontologically dependent in their existence on being human or humanity, which in my view should be labelled "human nature".

The foundational claim is visible also in international human rights law documents and many domestic constitutions. I have cited some of them at the beginning

[47] I speak here about facts from different level/different domains to underlie that there are domains, in which facts have impact on facts from the very same domain, and this impact is of a different kind than ontological dependence. For instance, as for natural fact, they can stand in relation of causality with other natural facts. In turn, semantic facts can stand in inferential relations with other semantic facts.

[48] Correia and Schnieder (2012), p. 1.

[49] Correia and Schnieder (2012), p. 1.

[50] cf. Gizbert-Studnicki (2015, 2016, 2021).

[51] Tasioulas (2011), p. 27.

[52] Griffin (2008), p. 2.

of Chap. 2, International Covenant on Civil and Political Rights claims in its Preamble that human rights *derive* from human dignity. In what sense do they derive? The Polish Constitution says that human dignity is a source of human rights. But what does it actually mean?

Of course, legal documents are not metaphysical treaties and such formulations do not constitute conclusive metaphysical arguments. Yet, they provide profound insight into the thoughts of international and domestic legislators concerning how they regard the foundations of human rights. Moreover, those formulations about human rights, which are supposed to be derived from human dignity (International Covenant on Civil and Political Rights) or from human dignity perceived as a source of human rights (Polish Constitution), are embedded in legal text. At least for this reason I believe it must be taken seriously in legal philosophy. As stressed earlier, legal documents are also a good departure point to reconstruct truisms about human rights. Although it may happen that after a deeper philosophical examination human dignity has a different meaning than we used to believe, or that it can be reduced to another entity that actually constitutes the foundations of human rights, I believe that at least the first steps in the philosophy of human rights should refer to human dignity as referred to in legal documents.

Among philosophers of human rights, Waldron provides a list of potential meanings of a claim that a concept α is the foundation of a concept β:

(i) as a matter of history and genealogy, β was generated out of α;
(ii) α is the source of β, in the way that the application of one legal proposition may be the source of the validity of another;
(iii) β can be derived logically from α, either deductively or with the help of empirical premises; or
(iv) α throws some indispensable light on β or helps in the interpretation of β.[53]

First, notice that Waldron explicitly regards the issue of foundations only in terms of how a concept is a foundation of another concept. He remains on a solely semantic level, without touching the metaphysical level. In my view, what we aim in the philosophy of human rights is to justify or explain human rights themselves and not just the concept of human rights. Nonetheless, irrespective of this main objection, each of these proposals raises serious drawbacks. The first one refers to the history of an idea. It may be useful to know the historical development of some concept, still, it does not necessitates that this concept actually can be justified in terms of its historical background. For instance, human rights can be regarded as having historical roots in natural law, yet contemporary philosophy of human rights does not follow this path due to various significant philosophical problems that theories of natural law involve. The second meaning operates on a solely legal level, which is of course not an ultimate level of explanation or justification. There is something beneath the legal level. The third one is logical entailment. The problem here is that the relata of logical entailment are not concepts, like Waldron proposes, but propositions. Gewirth tried to make use of this relation but he failed (as demonstrated

[53] Waldron (2015), p. 135.

in Sect. 2.1).[54] These failures were recognised by other philosophers of human rights, and now it seems to be widely accepted that one cannot justify human rights by reference to the relation of logical entailment.[55] The last notion requires interpretation. It is claimed that an understanding of one concept can provide a necessary insight into the understanding of another concept. If it were not considered on a solely semantic level, it could be useful (e.g. by means of a certain type of conceptual analysis). Yet, in my view the ultimate question of the philosophy of human rights is of metaphysical character. Metaphysical relations that I intend to test as relations between human rights and their foundations are quite close to this fourth notion, with a reservation that they hold between metaphysical entities—facts, and not between concepts (or their meanings). Looking from the perspective of relational metaphysics on the issue of foundations of human rights, the foundational claim should be understood as the claim that there is an ontological dependence between human rights and their foundation.

Two different levels of ontological dependence should be distinguished in the discussed context. The first one holds between human rights and human dignity. It means that human rights depend on human dignity in their existence, which is presented in legal documents on human rights. It is also widely claimed by philosophers of human rights.[56]

The second ontological dependence is between human dignity and human nature. Human dignity as an inherent worth of every human being must be possessed due to some aspect of being human. I name this aspect "human nature". Consequently, there is an ontological dependence between human dignity and human nature. This ontological dependence is also clearly seen by following the naturalisation of the question of the foundations of human rights—human dignity is a moral entity (a moral fact) and its more fundamental, natural grounds should be identified. Pursuant to ontological naturalisation, it would mean that human dignity actually is human nature. Pursuant to methodological naturalism, it would mean that there are some scientific, natural facts relevant for the existence of human dignity and the research on foundations of human dignity should be started from them.

These two ontological dependencies can be understood as transitive and lead to formulating a three-partial ontological dependence—between human rights, human dignity and human nature.

Therefore, we can understand and analyse the foundational claim of philosophy of human rights in terms of the contemporary analytic metaphysics conception of ontological dependence. However, ontological dependence is a general term. What does it precisely mean that human rights ontologically depend on human dignity, which in turn ontologically depend on human nature? What is a specific relation that holds between human rights, human dignity and human nature? Thus, I propose to

---

[54] Gewirth (1981, 1982).

[55] Raz (2010).

[56] Piechowiak (1999, 2019), Griffin (2008) and Tasioulas (2011, 2013, 2015).

test three specific, precisely defined relations. I will examine whether these relations can properly express and explain those ontological dependencies.[57]

These relations are reduction, supervenience, and metaphysical grounding.[58] The debates concerning these relations constitute a large part of contemporary analytic metaphysics, which I would like to adopt in my study of the foundations of human rights. The study of these relations is the key part of what I call "relational metaphysics".

4.4 Reduction Account: Ontological Naturalism

Reduction is the strongest relation possible relations of ontological dependence. Marmor distinguishes two types of reduction: semantic and metaphysical.[59] Semantic reduction occurs when an entire vocabulary of a discourse or a theory can be fully expressed in terms of another vocabulary, which is more basic. Metaphysical reduction occurs when a phenomenon is fully constituted by and fully reducible to some another, more fundamental phenomenon.[60] These phenomena can be simply called facts (recall the technical usage of the term fact discussed in Sect. 3.1.1). In short, reduction means that a reduced fact is not at any point "over and above" the fact that it is reduced to. In other words, a reduced fact simply *is* a fact that it is reduced to.[61] Under the idea of semantic reduction, whole theories are reduced to more basic or broader ones. For instance, Newtonian mechanics is reducible to quantum mechanics. It has been yet impossible to reduce chemistry to physics[62] or biology to chemistry.[63] At best, scientists believe that the increase of scientific knowledge will enable these and related reductions. On the other hand, under the

[57] A French speaker can also see my paper (Mazurkiewicz 2020).

[58] One can wonder why I do not test also emergence. However, in my view, emergence has nothing to do with explanation or justification. Emergence means that some properties or entities are emergent upon some others, which means that some novel, irreducible properties or entities arise (O'Connor and Wong 2005). Yet, emergence means that the way in which these new properties or entities emerge is impossible to be tracked. Before the discovery of DNA, British emergentists believed that life emerges upon physical and chemical structure (O'Connor and Wong 2005). Claiming that X emerges upon Y means that the grounds of the existence of X cannot be explained. Emergence alone does not explain anything. This is why in the contemporary philosophy while talking about emergence, the relation of supervenience is often adopted (Załuski 2009a, b; Brożek 2012), to precisely formulate the relation between an emergent entity and an entity upon it emerges. Supervenience will be analysed in this work.

[59] Marmor (2011), p. 216.

[60] Marmor (2011), p. 216.

[61] Reduction and identity are related and similar concepts. I do not want to discuss how they are related, let me just notice that a dominant view seems to be that reduction is a means that enables to justify the claim that two facts are identical (van Riel and van Gulick 2019).

[62] cf. Hettemma (2012).

[63] Brigandt and Love (2017).

idea of metaphysical reduction particular phenomena are being reduced. So, under metaphysical reduction we might hypothetically reduce mental facts to neurophysical facts, moral facts to natural facts, or legal facts to social facts. The proper reduction must be able to deduce or explain all properties of a reduced theory or fact from the theory or fact that they are reduced to.[64] This is the reason why we cannot yet reduce chemistry to physics: we are not able to deduce chemical laws from physical laws. Moreover, the proper reduction must not leave any property of a reduced fact not included in a fact to which it is reduced to. For instance, Marmor claims that legal facts can be reduced to social facts.[65] But legal facts have a property of being normative. Social facts are however descriptive facts (they are facts about what people think and how people behave). If one aims to reduce normative legal facts to descriptive social facts, that reduction is improper—there is a missing property of being normative in social facts, which legal facts are going to be reduced to.[66] The necessity of being able to deduce/explain every property of a reduced fact on the basis of the fact which it is reduced to, is the necessary condition of the proper reduction, yet not sufficient. It may happen that every aspect of an entity X can be explained by reference to another entity Y, yet the entity X is irreducible to Y—it means that X is something over and above Y.

Since my aim is to explore the relation of ontological dependence between human rights, human dignity and human nature, the proper version of reduction would be the metaphysical one. Semantic reduction might be provided on the level of a whole theory of human rights if someone would like to reduce it to some more basic theory, like a particular moral theory or a particular social theory. This lies however outside the scope of this work.[67]

Thus, under the hypothetical reductionist account of ontological dependence between human rights, human dignity and human nature, human rights would be reduced to human dignity and human dignity would be reduced to human nature.

Let me firstly examine whether human dignity can be reduced to human nature. Human dignity is a normative, moral entity (moral fact). Human nature on the other hand is a descriptive fact. If no moral entity or fact can be reduced to descriptive entity or fact as it was presented above, the same goes for human dignity and human nature. Such a potential reduction would mean that human dignity actually *is* human nature. In order to properly reduce human dignity to human nature, the normative

[64] Brigandt and Love (2017).

[65] Marmor (2011, 2013).

[66] Gizbert-Studnicki (2015), p. 27; Gizbert-Studnicki (2016), pp. 128–129; Gizbert-Studnicki (2021), p. 431. Sometimes, two forms of normativity are distinguished in this context—weak and strong (Finlay 2010). Weak normativity involves only being related to a norm, while strong involves providing reasons for action. One can also claim that legal facts are not normative in the strong sense, but only in the weak sense. Then, reduction to social facts would be much more plausible. However, I believe that legal facts are normative in the strong sense.

[67] Perhaps, some of those who research foundations of human rights by claiming that human rights hold due to some interest are close to semantic reduction of theory of human rights to interest theory of rights.

component of human dignity—the inherent worth of every human being—must be some part of human nature, descriptively conceived as in evolutionary psychology. But how can the inherent worth of every human being actually be some purely descriptive part of human nature? This reductive impossibility means that human dignity is in fact a different entity than human nature.

However, these problems concerning differences between normative and descriptive entities are absent as for as the relation between human dignity and human rights is concerned. Both human rights and human dignity are normative, moral entities (moral facts). One moral fact can be potentially reduced to another moral fact. Still, the requirement of being able to reduce every component of a reduced fact to some part of a fact that it is reduced to must be preserved.[68] In the case of human dignity and human rights, every component of human rights must be reduced to some part of human dignity. However, even though both human rights and human dignity belong to the normative sphere, there is a significant difference between them. Human dignity is an inherent worth of every human being, which is quite abstract. In turn, human rights, both universal and particular, are norms that directly say what should be done. This is obvious for particular human rights, however the same goes for universal human rights—even though they are less concrete than particular human rights, they entitle to something. Human dignity, although it must be realised practically, does not directly entitle to anything on its own. The right to autonomy, the right to liberty and the right to security are not simply inherent values (worth) of every human being. They follow from human dignity but they are not the same as human dignity.

Even if we add to the description of human dignity the point that it prohibits solely instrumental treatment of a human being, still it is quite vague and very often human dignity alone cannot determine the scope of the desired state of affairs.[69] On the other hand, human rights determine such a state. And this is an issue that differentiates human rights from human dignity. It results in the fact that the reduction of human rights to human dignity is impossible—the scope and content of various concrete human rights cannot be explained solely in terms of human dignity. Looking from a different perspective, particular human rights cannot be deduced solely from human dignity. Consequently, human rights, both universal and particular, are irreducible to human dignity.

Consider also an argument from human rights law. International and domestic human rights law are not restrained in establishing legal protections of human dignity. Such documents provide us with a catalogue of human rights that are derived from human dignity and are not identical to (or reduced to) human dignity. If drafters of legal documents thought that it was sufficient to introduce only the *legal* protection of human dignity in order to protect human beings from violations of basic rights, they would simply draft legal acts without a detailed catalogue of

[68] I use a rather non-philosophical but colloquial term "component" to grasp all possible issues like features, properties, relations, etc.

[69] cf. Piechowiak (1999), p. 283, p. 291, pp. 300–301.

human rights. It would be only sufficient to state that human dignity is protected. Yet, there are detailed catalogues of human rights. And a legal document on human rights with just a preamble and one article saying that human dignity is protected, we would rather find perplexing or weird.

Human dignity cannot be reduced to human nature and human rights cannot be reduced to human dignity. Both human dignity and human rights are something "over and above" human nature and human dignity (respectively).

The reduction relation where an entity is reduced to a natural fact is the metaphysical representation of ontological naturalism. Under ontological naturalism, a debated entity actually *is* a natural fact. Unfeasibility of reducing human dignity (philosophical entity) to human nature (natural fact) means that ontological naturalisation of the question of the foundations of human rights is impossible. This means that the generally analysed implausibility of moral naturalism is confirmed concerning particular moral entities—human rights and human dignity. If human dignity is irreducible to human nature, even if human rights were reduced to human dignity, still human rights cannot be reduced to natural fact—human nature.[70]

For this reason, only methodological naturalism may be recognised as a plausible position. Further parts of this work will be devoted to answering whether methodological naturalisation of foundations of human rights is feasible. Methodological naturalism does not operate by means of reduction relation—if it had operated this way it would have simply become a version of ontological naturalism. Methodological naturalism is compatible with two other non-reductionist relations of analytic metaphysics: supervenience and metaphysical grounding. Let me now analyse the plausibility of employing the relation of supervenience to describe the interconnections between entities in question.

References

Brigandt I, Love A (2017) Reductionism in biology. The Stanford Encyclopedia of Philosophy (Spring 2017 Edition). https://plato.stanford.edu/archives/spr2017/entries/reduction-biology/

Brown C (2013) Human rights and human nature. In: Holder C, Reidy D (eds) Human rights. The hard questions. CUP, Cambridge, pp 23–38

Brożek B (2012) Normatywność Prawa. Warszawa, Wolters Kluwer

Chomsky N (1964) Current issues in linguistic theory. Mouton, The Hague

Chomsky N (1986) Knowledge of language: its nature, origin, and use. C.T: Praeger, Westport

[70] Due to the short and conclusive argument against reduction account, which is complementary to the refutation of ontological naturalism as for human rights, I have decided to formulate it within one section after sections on analytic metaphysics and moral naturalism. The analysis of the feasibility of employing relations of supervenience and metaphysical grounding will be much longer and put in separate chapters.

Correia F, Schnieder B (2012) Grounding: an opinionated introduction. In: Correia F, Schnieder B (eds) Metaphysical grounding: understanding the structure of reality. Cambridge University Press, Cambridge, pp 1–36

Finlay S (2010) Recent work on normativity. Analysis 70:331–346

Gewirth A (1981) The basis and content of human rights. Nomos 23:119–147

Gewirth A (1982) Human rights: essays on justification and application. University of Chicago Press, Chicago

Gintis H (2012) Human rights: an evolutionary and behavioral perspective. In: Goodman R, Jinks D, Woods AK (eds) Understanding social action, promoting human rights. Oxford University Press, Oxford, pp 135–159

Gizbert-Studnicki T (2015) Metafizyka Pozytywizmu Prawniczego. Principia 61:19–40

Gizbert-Studnicki T (2016) The social sources thesis, metaphysics and metaphilosophy. In: Banaś P, Dyrda A, Gizbert Studnicki T (eds) Metaphilosophy of law. Hart Publishing, Oxford, pp 121–146

Gizbert-Studnicki T (2021) Social facts and legal facts: Perils of Hume's Guillotine. In: Spaak T, Mindus P (eds) The Cambridge companion to legal positivism. Cambridge University Press, Cambridge, pp 419–442

Gizbert-Studnicki T, Dyrda A, Grabowski A (2016) Metodologiczne Dychotomie: krytyka pozytywistycznych teorii prawa. Wolters Kluwer, Warszawa

Griffin J (2008) On human rights. Oxford University Press, Oxford

Hettemma H (2012) Reducing chemistry do physics: limits, models and consequences. Rijksuniversiteit Groningen, Groningen

Leiter B (2007) Naturalizing jurisprudence: Essays on American legal realism and naturalism in legal philosophy. OUP, Oxford

Leiter B, Etchemendy M (2017) Naturalism in legal philosophy. In: The Stanford Encyclopedia of Philosophy (Summer 2017 Edition). https://plato.stanford.edu/archives/sum2017/entries/lawphil-naturalism/

Lutz M, Lenman J (2018) Moral naturalism. In: The Stanford Encyclopedia of Philosophy (Fall 2018 Edition). https://plato.stanford.edu/archives/fall2018/entries/naturalism-moral/

Maguire B (2015) Grounding the autonomy of ethics. In: Shafer-Landau R (ed) Oxford studies in metaethics, Vol 10. OUP, Oxford, pp 188–215

Makowski P (2014) Moore i Semantyczna Autonomia Etyki. Principia 59:67–81

Manley D, Chalmers D, Wasserman R (2009) (eds) Metametaphysics: new essays on the foundations of ontology. OUP, Oxford

Marmor A (2011) Philosophy of law. Princeton University Press, Princeton

Marmor A (2013) Farewell to conceptual analysis (in Jurisprudence). In: Waluchow W, Sciaraffa S (eds) Philosophical foundations of the nature of law. Oxford University Press, pp 209–229

Mazurkiewicz S (2020) Que signifie que les droits de l'homme découlent de la dignité humaine? Utilisation des relations de la métaphysique analytique contemporaine Direito. Estado e Sociedade 56:270–291

McPherson T (2019) Supervenience in Ethics. The Stanford Encyclopedia of Philosophy (Winter 2019 Edition). https://plato.stanford.edu/archives/win2019/entries/supervenience-ethics/

Mikhail J (2007) Universal moral grammar: theory, evidence, and the future trends in cognitive. Sciences 11:143–152

Mikhail J (2012) Moral grammar and human rights: some reflections on cognitive science and enlightenment rationalism. In: Goodman R, Jinks D, Woods AK (eds) Understanding social action, promoting human rights. OUP, Oxford, pp 160–202

Moore GE (1903) Principia Ethica. Cambridge University Press, New York

Nolan D (2017) Methodological naturalism in metaethics. In: McPherson T, Plunkett D (eds) The Routledge handbook of metaethics. Talyor and Francis, New York, pp 659–673

Nussbaum M (2000) Women and human development: the capabilities approach. Cambridge University Press, Cambridge

Nussbaum M (2006) Frontiers of justice: disability, nationality, species membership. The Belknap Press Harvard University Press, Cambridge
Nussbaum M (2011) Creating capabilities, the human development approach. The Belknap Press of Harvard University Press, Cambridge/London
O'Connor T, Wong H (2005) The metaphysical emergence. Nous 39:658–678
Papineau D (2020) Naturalism. The Stanford Encyclopedia of Philosophy (Summer 2020 Edition). https://plato.stanford.edu/archives/sum2020/entries/naturalism/
Petrażycki L (1904) O Pobudkach Postępowania i o Istocie Prawa i Moralności
Pidgen C (1989) Logic and the autonomy of ethics. Aust J Philos 67:127–151
Piechowiak M (1999) Filozofia Praw Człowieka. Prawa Człowieka w świetle ich Międzynarodowej Ochrony. Towarzystwo Naukowe KUL, Lublin
Piechowiak M (2019) Plato's conception of justice and the question of human dignity. Peter Lang, Berlin
Quine WVO (1953) From a logical point of view. Harvard University Press, Cambridge
Quine WVO (1969) Epistemology naturalized. In: Ontological relativity and other essays. Columbia University Press, New York
Raz J (2010) Human rights without foundations. In: Besson S Tasioulas J (eds) The philosophy of international law. OUP, pp 321–338
Schaffer J (2009) On what grounds what. In: Manley D, Chalmers D, Wassrerman R (eds) Metametaphysics: new essays on the foundations of ontology. OUP, Oxford, pp 347–383
Tasioulas J (2011) On the nature of human rights. In: Ernst G, Heilinger JC (eds) The philosophy of human rights: contemporary controversies. De Gruyter, Berlin, pp 17–59
Tasioulas J (2013) Human dignity and the foundations of human rights. In: McCrdudden C (ed) Understanding human dignity. OUP, Oxford, pp 291–312
Tasioulas J (2015) On the foundations of human rights. In: Cruft R, Liao SM, Renzo M (eds) Philosophical foundations of human rights. OUP, Oxford, pp 45–70
Van Riel R, Van Gulick R (2019) Scientific reduction. The Stanford Encyclopedia of Philosophy (Spring 2019 Edition). https://plato.stanford.edu/archives/spr2019/entries/scientific-reduction/
Waldron J (2015) Is dignity foundation of human rights? In: Cruft R, Liao SM, Renzo M (eds) Philosophical foundations of human rights. OUP, Oxford, pp 117–137
Wallner M (2016) Metaphysical Grounding: On How to Explain Explanation. https://www.academia.edu/30475938/Metaphysical_Grounding._On_How_To_Explain_Explanation
White M (1956) Towards Reunion in philosophy. Harvard University Press, Harvard
Załuski W (2009a) Evolutionary theory and legal philosophy. Edward Elgar, Cheltenham
Załuski W (2009b) Ewolucyjna Filozofia Prawa. Wolters Kluwer, Warszawa

Chapter 5
Supervenience Account

5.1 Supervenience

The conceptualisation of the relation of supervenience dates back to R. M. Hare[1]; however, it spread into many fields of analytic inquiry after J. Kim's paper (1984).[2] Supervenience is a relationship between two objects or sets of objects—A and B, called resp. supervenient and subvenient objects.[3] In discussing supervenience, the usage of properties as the relata of these relations prevails, rather than entities or facts, however, there is no difficulty in regarding entities or facts as relata of supervenience relations. In a short, slogan way, supervenience is defined by the claim that there cannot be a difference in A without a difference in B (McLaughlin and Bennett 2018). In other words, there cannot be a difference in a supervenient object (A), without a difference in a subvenient object (B).[4] For instance, mental

[1]Hare (1952).

[2]Kim (1984).

[3]Several philosophers of law made use of supervenience in their researches on the foundations of law. Załuski (2009a, b) claims that law is an emergent entity that supervenes on the human natural tendency to cooperate. Bartosz Brożek also makes of supervenience (2012, 2017) and claims that law supervenes on social regularities and mental states (2012). Gizbert-Studnicki (2015, 2016) excludes supervenience as the proper relation between legal facts and social fact due to its lack of explanatory force.

[4]There is a more formal definition of supervenience provided in logical terms, however, I do not believe that introducing it would be necessary for this work. I think that the shortened natural language notion of supervenience as "no difference in A, without difference in B" is fully sufficient. This logical notion of supervenience has the following form in two slightly different versions connected to the notions of weak and strong supervenience:

> *A weakly supervenes$_m$* on *B* if and only if necessarily, if anything *x* has some property *F* in *A*, then there is at least one property *G* in *B* such that *x* has *G*, and everything that has *G* has *F*, i.e., iff

S. Mazurkiewicz, *Grounding Human Rights in Human Nature*, Law and Philosophy Library 141, https://doi.org/10.1007/978-3-031-30734-8_5

facts are highly likely to supervene on neuro-physical facts: there cannot be a difference in one's mental state without a difference in one's neuro-physical state of his brain.

Supervenience can be therefore regarded as a kind of a necessary covariance.[5] From logical point of view, supervenience is reflexive (for any entity A, there cannot be a difference in A without a difference in A), non-symmetric (A can supervene on B, and simultaneously, B can, but does not have to, supervene on A) and transitive (if A supervenes on B, and B supervenes on C, then A supervenes on C).[6] Non-symmetricality means that supervenience for some given entities when A supervenes on B can be symmetrical (B supervenes on A), while for some other entities it can be asymmetrical (B* does not supervene on A*),[7] of course A and A* as well as B and B* are not the same entities—for the same entities A and B supervenience can only be either symmetrical or asymmetrical.

Being non-symmetric makes supervenience a weak relation—we cannot generally decide which object is prior in an ontological sense. Also, the statement that A supervenes on B does not mean that it is because of B that A is A.[8] Supervenience does not involve ontological dependence; it is actually only a necessary covariance. That makes supervenience a weak relation in terms of the analysis and explanation of the structure of reality. Supervenience does not entail that a further explanatory claim holds—even though A supervenes on B, it does not mean that it is because of B that A exists. In other terms: it does not mean that B explains the existence of A. Coming back to the example of mental facts supervening on neuro-physical facts, it means that we can neither claim that mental facts hold *due to* neuro-physical facts, nor that the neuro-physical facts explain the existence of mental facts.[9] Although this example may look like a sort of a causal relation, supervenience has nothing to do with causality. It is so not only because of the fact that causality provides explanation, but due to the fact that supervenience is a metaphysical relation, while causality is a relation holding between natural facts. If mental facts were natural facts just like neuro-physical facts, a causal relation between them could be properly established.

$$\Box \forall x \forall F \in A[Fx \rightarrow \exists G \in B(Gx \& \forall y(Gy \rightarrow Fy))]$$

A strongly supervenes$_m$ on *B* if and only if necessarily, if anything *x* has some property *F* in *A*, then there is at least one property *G* in *B* such *x* has *G*, and necessarily everything that has *G* has *F*, i.e., iff

$\Box \forall x \forall F \in A[Fx \rightarrow \exists G \in B(Gx \& \Box \forall y(Gy \rightarrow Fy))]$ (McLaughlin and Bennett 2018; cf. Kim 1993, pp. 58, 65).

[5]Kim (2003), p. 564.

[6]McLaughlin and Bennett (2018).

[7]McLaughlin and Bennett (2018).

[8]McLaughlin and Bennett (2018); Berker (2018).

[9]This issue is connected with the so-called explanatory gap in the philosophy of mind.

However, they are not,[10] and consequently, the relation between them and natural facts is of a different kind. This is a metaphysical relation. Historically, the application of supervenience in the philosophy of mind seems to have foundations in the failure of the reductive project of the relation between mental and natural spheres. After discovering that the relation between those facts cannot have a form of reduction, supervenience has been introduced. It has one significant advantage over reduction—mental facts are different objects from neuro-physical facts. However, due to the lack of explanatory force of supervenience, this was only a partial development—still, no claim about *why* mental facts hold can be provided in terms of supervenience.

Later, supervenience has been implemented into moral philosophy for the purpose of expressing the relationship between moral facts and natural facts.[11] Similarly as in the philosophy of mind, supervenience became regarded as the proper relation between moral and natural facts by anti-naturalists who claimed that moral facts are different from natural facts.[12] Moreover, *prima facie*, supervenience seems to express a widely shared general intuition about the nature of moral sphere—that in some sense moral facts are such and such due to descriptive natural facts, e.g. an act is wrong due to its causing pain. It can be easily formulated by the use of supervenience—there cannot be a difference in moral facts with no difference in natural facts. Consider an act causing pain; if it is done with intention of causing pain (difference in natural fact), its moral wrongness increases (difference in moral fact). Looking from a different perspective: two acts having the same natural description (natural facts) have the same moral assessment (moral facts)—the principle of impartiality is actually based on the supervenience account in ethics. However, the statement that a moral fact A supervenes on a natural fact B means only that A cannot change without a change in B.[13] This statement does not, however, claim that A holds because of B, or that B explains the existence of A. Moreover, logical properties of supervenience lead to certain undesired consequences. First, due to being non-symmetric, it turns out that although moral facts supervene on natural facts, the reverse claim cannot be excluded on the basis of supervenience alone: it cannot be logically excluded that natural facts can supervene as well on moral facts. Yet, the change of natural facts on the basis of moral facts seems to be false. Second, moral facts supervene on themselves, which logically is correct, but metaphysically is quite a weird claim. Third, we also cannot claim in terms of supervenience that natural facts are ontologically prior to moral facts.

---

[10] Nagel (1974); Jackson (1982).

[11] McPherson (2019).

[12] Cf. McPherson (2019). There are many other fields where some relations have a form of supervenience. For instance, the surface areas of perfect spheres supervene with on their volumes (and *vice versa*) (Lombard 1986). It is highly likely that aesthetics facts of e.g. a sculpture supervene on physical facts (but not *vice versa*) (cf. Gizbert-Studnicki 2015).

[13] I will use interchangeably terms "difference" and "change" since although the first one is used in the philosophical debate on supervenience, the second one—"change"—reflects the same issue and I find it better representing the ideas concerning the philosophy of human rights.

For those reasons, the lack of explanatory force being the most important, supervenience is not a proper relation in the exploration of the foundations of moral facts. After all, what is the core of this inquiry is answering the question of what makes moral facts to be moral facts. An answer that there is a necessary covariance relation is true but is too weak to answer the core of the question.

Therefore, the above general analysis on the inadequateness of adopting supervenienceas relation between moral facts and their foundations consequently holds on the level of particular moral facts—human rights and human dignity—and particular natural facts that constitute their foundations—human nature. If something is true generally, it is so as for particular instances of these general truths. Therefore, I believe that making use of supervenience in expressing and explaining the foundational claim (ontological dependencies between human rights, human dignity and human nature) is implausible. Yet, perhaps some interesting claims can be developed and some truth about foundations of human rights can be revealed. Let me therefore analyse this issue in detail.

5.2 Supervenience Between Human Rights, Human Dignity and Human Nature

Can therefore the ontological dependence between human nature, human dignity and human rights be properly expressed and explained in terms of supervenience? This question can be split into two more detailed questions: do human rights supervene on human dignity and does human dignity supervenes on human nature? Two conditions must be met in order to prove these claims. The first one is to satisfy the general account of supervenience, according to which there cannot be a difference in a supervenient fact without a difference in a subvenient fact. The second one is to satisfy the logical properties of supervenience.[14] By the lack of difference or lack of change for every entity debated below I mean change in scope, content, holders, etc. To maintain the readability of the next sections, I will refer to all such situations by "change in X", where X is a given debated entity: particular human rights, universal human rights, human dignity and human nature.

In turn, in order to determine that supervenience properly expresses ontological dependencies between human rights, human dignity and human nature, there must be demonstrated that supervenience fully expresses and explains these ontological dependencies.

[14] I will analyse whether logical properties of supervenience are met for debated entities. It can seem to someone overly technical, however I believe it is required to prove the claim that certain entity supervenes on some other entity and to avoid a possible objection that some claim is not justified. Similarly, I will do it for the logical properties of metaphysical grounding in Chap. 6.

5.3 Supervenience of (Universal) Human Rights

A question arises: is there a supervenience relation between human rights and human dignity? Human rights are of course considered as the supervenient facts while human dignity is the subvenient fact. As for the first condition, the question is whether it is true that there cannot be a difference in human rights without a difference in human dignity. As mentioned above, by change or difference in human rights I mean change of scope, content, holders, etc. Following the first condition of supervenience, for human rights to change, there must be some change in human dignity. *Prima facie*, the claim that human dignity must change to trigger a change in human rights seems to be false—we witness historical changes in human rights, as e.g. extending the scope of human rights holders to slaves, women, children etc. that begun in the late eighteenth century and had its peak in the late nineteenth and early twentieth century, or the development of new human rights (like the third generation of human rights conceptualised in the late twentieth century). Yet, human dignity is universal, innate and inherent—it is the same for every human being irrespective of time and space. Human dignity does not depend on any historical or social issues. If every human being possesses human dignity equally, the first members of the homo sapiens species had the same human dignity as we have today. But they did not have same the human rights as we have, like for instance the right to elementary free of charge education. So, there is a difference in human rights whereas there is no difference in human dignity. Does this difference make the claim that human rights supervene on human dignity false? The difference in human rights while there is no difference in human dignity certainly does so, but only with respect to particular human rights like the right to vote, the right to healthcare, the right to due process etc. These human rights in fact change while human dignity remains unchanged.

This short analysis demonstrates why distinguishing universal human rights and particular, human rights that are their instantiations in practical environmental and social conditions is useful.[15] Shortly reminding it (more detailed analysis is presented in Sect. 3.1), I regard three general human rights—the right to autonomy, the right to liberty and the right to security—as fully universal in terms of time and space that together with some contingent social or natural facts instantiate particular human rights. For instance, the human right to elementary free education holds due to the universal, general right to liberty and the fact that with the progress in human knowledge and complexity of our societies, education becomes necessary to live a decent life. In order to be able to make choices in one's life and prosper, the amount of necessary knowledge became so big that it requires formal teaching provided by qualified persons. In the Bronze age, those facts did not occur, therefore there was no human right to free elementary education, although the human right to liberty already existed.

[15] Cf. Griffin (2008), Tasioulas (2011).

If we differentiate between universal human rights and particular human rights, the application of supervenience can be maintained with respect to universal human rights—there can be no difference in them without a difference in human dignity. To shortly remind, universal human rights are the most abstract and general human rights that are possessed regardless of particular time and place. In turn, particular human rights are instantiations of universal human rights in concrete circumstances. Particular human rights can differ across different times and places, however for the same time and place, e.g. Europe in 1550 or South East Asia in 2021 they are the same for every human being. Universal human rights are, as the name suggests, universal, so no change is possible as for them. Human dignity is universal too, thus, it cannot change as well. Therefore, it is true that there can be no difference in universal human rights without a difference in human dignity, since neither universal human rights can change, nor human dignity.[16] As a result, the first condition of determining whether universal human rights supervene on human dignity is met. Looking on the foundations of human rights by supervenience presents clearly the problem of universality of human rights and how the distinction of universal moral rights and particular human rights solves this dilemma. Supervenience enables to express this problem briefly, as well as clarify and explain it. As for the satisfaction of the logical properties, being reflexive is met—there cannot be a difference in universal human rights without a difference in human rights. This is quite trivial—if there occurs a change in universal human rights, there simply occurs a change in universal human rights. Since no change in universal human rights is possible, this property is satisfied. There cannot be change in universal human rights without change in universal human rights, since, in fact, there can be no change in universal human rights. It is a formal requirement that has nothing to do with any deeper metaphysics, however, it is met for human rights.

The second logical property of supervenience is being non-symmetric. Being non-symmetric means that in some supervenience relations, B supervenes on A (symmetrical relation), while in some cases B* does not supervene on A* (asymmetrical relation); A and A* as well as B and B* are different entities in these cases. For satisfying the logical property of being non-symmetric, one of these situations must be true for a particular supervenience relation. Consequently, in order to be satisfied that supervenience of universal human rights on human dignity is non-symmetric one of the following claims must be true: human dignity supervenes on universal human rights or human dignity does not supervene on universal human

[16] Someone might find this form of necessary covariance trivial; it may be trivial metaphysically or explanatorily but is still formally true. It is similar to the problem found in the general application of supervenience to discussions on foundations of moral facts—if moral realism is true, which is the claim that there exist at least some fully objective moral facts, those fully objective moral facts cannot change (like the fact that killing innocent people is always wrong). But mathematical facts, like the fact that $2 + 2 = 4$ cannot change as well. Consequently, moral facts supervene on mathematical facts, which seems to be quite a weird claim, yet formally correct. This is one of the reasons why supervenience ceased to be regarded as a useful relation to express ontological dependencies, at least in moral inquiry.

rights. Consequently, it must be true that either there cannot be a change in human dignity without a change in human rights, or that there can be a change in human dignity with no change in human rights. I believe that the first claim is correct. Since both human dignity and universal human rights have been determined as unchangeable, it is also true that there can be no change in human dignity without a change in human rights. Therefore, the logical property of being non-symmetric is satisfied—universal human rights supervene on human dignity and simultaneously human dignity supervenes on human rights. It means that as for the supervenience relation of universal human rights on human dignity, this supervenience relation is symmetrical—human dignity supervenes on universal human rights as well.

The third logical property is transitivity. However, in order to check whether this property is satisfied, there must be three entities to be analysed. For two, like universal human rights and human dignity, it is impossible to determine the meeting of this requirement. Nonetheless, I do not leave this issue unanswered; it will be further analysed after exploring supervenience of particular human rights and the supervenience relation between human dignity and human nature.

The conclusion to be drawn from the above analysis is that both the general supervenience claim—no difference in supervenient fact, without difference in subvenient fact—and the logical properties of supervenience are satisfied for universal human rights as the supervenient fact and human dignity as the subvenient fact. Thus, the claim that human rights supervene on human dignity is true. There can be no change in human rights without change in human dignity.

However, there is also another condition beyond those formal requirements—in order to answer the question on why universal human rights exist, making use of supervenience must be able to fully express and explain the foundational claim (ontological dependencies between human rights, human dignity and human nature). While presenting supervenience relation in general it was already stated that this is rather a weak relation of only a necessary covariance with no explanatory force. Not surprisingly, if supervenience generally cannot provide explanation of why some facts exist dependently on other facts, this lack of explanatory force is maintained on the level of particular facts, like human rights and human dignity. Notwithstanding, I will analyse this issue in detail after determining whether supervenience holds between other entities—particular human rights and their basis, as well as between human dignity and human nature.

5.4 Supervenience of Particular Human Rights

I concluded that universal human rights supervene on human dignity. Particular human rights are concrete instantiations of universal human rights dependent on environmental and social facts that differ in time and space. The foundations of particular human rights can be analysed in terms of supervenience as well. Particular human rights can be seen as supervenient fact, whereas both universal human rights and environmental and social facts can be regarded as subvenient facts.[17] Can therefore be no change in particular human rights without change in universal human rights and environmental and social facts? Universal human rights cannot change so they are irrelevant for the changes of particular human rights. In fact, if someone claimed that particular human rights depend solely on universal human rights and present it in terms of supervenience, such a claim would be false—universal human rights are unchangeable whereas particular human rights differ in time and place. Therefore, there can be a change in particular human rights (i.e. in their content, scope, holders, etc.) without a change in universal human rights, which means that particular human rights do not supervene on universal human rights.

However, I propose, similarly to many philosophers of human rights,[18] that there are also environmental and social facts that constitute foundations of particular human rights. As universal human rights are immutable (they cannot differ), the difference in particular human rights must be associated with a difference in environmental and social facts. But, is it true that always, when there is a change in particular human rights, some contingent environmental and social facts must change? I believe this question is to be answered in the affirmative. My notion of particular human rights is that they are instantiations of universal human rights that realise them in specific conditions dependent on environmental and social circumstances. If certain environmental and social circumstances (environmental and social facts) occur, respective particular human rights change (for instance they come to existence or change their content). It means that the change in environmental and social facts triggers the change in particular human rights. Nonetheless, this is too little to establish supervenience relation. Supervenience requires that the supervenient fact cannot change without a change in the subvenient fact and not that when the subvenient fact changes, the supervenient fact changes as well. In this context, the situation when particular human rights change when environmental and social facts change is insufficient for establishing the supervenience relation. It does not exclude a scenario when human rights change with no change in environmental and social facts.

Nonetheless, I claim that particular human rights arise *only* when certain environmental and social facts occur. Only when primitive hunter-gatherer societies started shifting into the settled form of life and the specialisation of labour with a possibility of being subjected to someone's rule occurred, the human right to not be held in slavery or servitude emerged as a practical instantiation of the universal human right to liberty. Only after the development of judicial institutions the human right to "a fair and public hearing within a reasonable time by an independent and impartial tribunal established by law"[19] arose. With no progress in medicine and the growth of wealth, especially public wealth, the human right to (public) healthcare

---

[17] More than one fact or entity can constitute subvenient level, e.g. Brożek (2012) claims that law supervenes on social regularities and mental states.

[18] Griffin (2008), p. 50; Tasioulas (2011), p. 33.

[19] European Convention of Human Rights (1950), art. 6.

would not exist. These examples can be multiplied. Therefore, it is true that there cannot be a change in particular human rights with no change in environmental and social facts. It means that the general form of a supervenience relation is satisfied. There cannot be a difference in the supervenient fact—particular human rights, without a difference in the subvenient facts, namely environmental and social facts and universal human rights (the latter actually can never differ).

As for the logical properties of supervenience, reflexivity is trivially satisfied. There cannot be a difference in particular human rights without a difference in particular human rights. The reflexivity of supervenience is a formal property with no further metaphysical consequences, similarly to the reflexivity of universal human rights.

With respect to non-symmetricality, I showed that particular human rights can supervene on universal human rights and environmental and social facts. Being non-symmetric means that in some supervenience relations, B supervenes on A (symmetrical relation), while in some relations B* does not supervene on A* (asymmetrical relation). In order to meet the logical property of being non-symmetric, one of these situations must occur for a particular supervenience relation. In the case of particular human rights and universal human rights with environmental and social facts, it holds that universal human rights and environmental and social facts do not supervene on particular human rights. There can be a change in environmental and social facts while no change in particular human rights occurs. This possibility of change means that the asymmetrical variant of non-symmetricality of supervenience is fulfilled. For instance, the shifts from monarchy into the republican form of government after World War I (change in social facts) occurred with no change in particular human rights. The Little Ice Age in the 17th–18th century (change in environmental facts) was not followed by any change in particular human rights.[20] Therefore, being non-symmetric is satisfied.

Transitivity of supervenience can be analysed because universal human rights supervene on human dignity and there are three entities to possibly form the transitive relation: human dignity, universal human rights and particular human rights. It might therefore appear that particular human rights supervene on human dignity since universal human rights supervene on human dignity and particular human right supervene on universal human rights. But particular human rights supervene also on environmental and social facts, which do not supervene on human dignity. As it was demonstrated, changes in environmental and social facts trigger changes in particular human rights. Particular human rights would supervene on human dignity if both universal human rights and environmental and social facts supervened on human dignity. However, with only one part of the subvenient level supervening on human dignity, transitivity cannot be maintained. This is the issue similar to the problem of the transitivity of causality: if A is caused by B and C, and

[20] This is similar to the supervenience of mental facts on neuro-physical facts—there cannot be a change in mental facts with no change in neuro-physical facts, however, neuro-physical facts can change with no change in mental facts.

C is caused by D, it is not true that A is caused by D.[21] Thus, particular human rights do not supervene on human dignity. This claim, developed on the basis of the analysis of transitivity, is consistent with the previously made claim that particular human rights do not supervene on human dignity, which has been developed on the basis of the analysis of the holding of the direct supervenience relation between particular human rights and human dignity (beginning of the Sect. 5.3).

Particular human rights supervene on environmental and social facts. For this reason, other unchangeable facts, like universal human rights, can be added on the subvenient level. If there can be no change in particular human rights without change in environmental and social facts, there also can be no change in particular human rights without change in environmental and social facts *and* universal human rights, since the latter can never change. From formal point of view, if A supervenes on B, there can be added C along with C, if C cannot differ. Thus, we can conclude that particular human rights supervene on environmental and social facts and on universal human rights. Supervenience allows such operations since it is only a relation of necessary covariance with no explanatory force itself.

To conclude, particular human rights supervene both on universal human rights as well as on environmental and social facts. Particular human rights do not supervene on human dignity, even though universal human rights supervene on human dignity.

5.5 Supervenience of Human Dignity

Now, I will analyse the relation of ontological dependence between human dignity and human nature in terms of supervenience. As it was demonstrated several pages above, human dignity cannot be reduced to human nature. It leaves the space for seeking another metaphysical relation that is able to express and explain the ontological dependence of human dignity on human nature. Supervenience is a possible relation to hold between human dignity and human nature. In order to demonstrate that it holds, the general condition of supervenience must be satisfied—"no difference in supervenient fact, without difference in subvenient fact" as well as the logical properties of supervenience.

I remind that I understand human dignity as an inherent worth of every human being. It is a moral fact. Looking from the perspective of both a common intuition and the naturalisation project, human dignity has roots in something positive about human. In a slightly more precise philosophical formulation: human dignity has origins in something positive in human nature. In turn, I conceive human nature as it is regarded by evolutionary psychology, which is the tendency to cooperate[22] or

[21] Cf. Schaffer (2012).

[22] Tomasello (2009).

narrow altruism and imperfect prudence, which are foundations for cooperative tendencies.[23]

Is it therefore true that there cannot be a difference in human dignity without a difference in human nature? In my view, following also the project of naturalisation, human dignity exists due to human nature. With no change in evolutionary understood human nature, there cannot be a change in human dignity. Since the time when evolution shaped the current state of our nature, we possess human dignity. If we had evolved differently as for our basic natural tendencies, human dignity would have differed. For instance, if we had evolved in a much more egoistic way, with no cooperative and altruistic tendencies, we would not have had human dignity at all. If we evolve in the future into such a non-cooperative and non-altruistic species (it is however highly unlikely), similarly, human dignity will cease to exist. On the other hand, if we had evolved into a purely altruistic and cooperative species, the positive moral component of human dignity would have been even higher. We could then talk about human dignity not as just "an inherent *worth* of every human being" but as "an inherent *perfection* of every human being". Interestingly, it might happen that in such a scenario, no one would conceptualise human rights as they would not be needed—we would behave perfectly morally and no one's rights would be violated. Human dignity in my approach is therefore not absolute—it has come to existence due to the current state of human nature. The current state of human nature is estimated to last from circa 0.2–1 million years ago.[24] Thus, the same goes for the existence of human dignity. My notion is therefore free of the objection of "metaphysical Platonism"—human dignity has foundations in natural, changing world. By metaphysical Platonism I mean an objection that is often ascribed to some kinds of metaphysical inquiry. Metaphysical Platonism occurs when there are proposed highly abstract entities that do not exist in time or space, consequently these entities are non-physical and non-mental.[25] This is of negative assessment from the point of view of epistemology and methodology.[26] It is not my claim that the objection of metaphysical Platonism is sound, what I want to point is that my proposal is immune to the objection of metaphysical Platonism, irrespective of philosophical soundness of this objection.

The supervenience relation is able to partly grasp this claim on the foundations of human dignity. There cannot be a change in human dignity without change in human

[23]Załuski (2009a, b).

[24]Dunbar (2014).To avoid confusion: the concept of human nature is the set of dominant tendencies in human behaviour. The actual content of human nature humans have is the tendency to cooperation and altruism. But, if evolution had occurred differently and shaped our tendencies in a different way, then of course, it would have been a different set of tendencies that would constitute human nature. A philosophical question out of the scope of this book is whether we would be able to call this, differently shaped species, humans, and consequently, whether it would still be *human* nature, or perhaps the nature of some other species.

[25]Balaguer (2016).

[26]Cf. Balaguer (2016).

nature, although it cannot grasp the fact that is *due to* the lack of changes in human nature that human dignity cannot change.

In fact, if there was another species with its natural tendencies constituting its nature, which could lead to the same positive vision as our nature, members of that species would also possess dignity. For instance, if aliens landed one day on Earth and we discovered that their natural tendencies can be found as optimistic or good, they would possess their dignity, which might be called "alien dignity". Imagine that aliens have exactly the same tendencies that constitute their nature, just as we have. Following the general and widely accepted by analytic moral philosophers claim of supervenience in the moral domain, which is that moral facts supervene on natural facts, aliens would possess exactly the same dignity as we possess. If two facts are the same as for their natural properties, moral facts that supervene on them are also the same. I believe that this makes my approach immune to the speciesism objection about human rights.[27] It makes my approach open for dignity of non-human creatures, and consequently rights, of animals, or aliens that we can meet one day. The metaphysical view on human rights and the application of supervenience as the relation between (human) dignity and (human) nature is able to express it. Since dignity supervenes on natural facts concerning one's nature, the existence of these natural facts in a form that gives the basis for a positive moral fact about one's nature leads to the existence of dignity. It holds no matter which species, human or not, possess these natural facts about its nature. Human dignity cannot change with no change in human nature, but similarly, if another species had a comparably positive nature, it would possess dignity as well. This work is not devoted to animal rights and I do not want to investigate which currently existing species have their evolutionary nature such that it warrants a positive view of their nature. It seems that those animals that possess higher mental capabilities (self-consciousness and consciousness of what others think about their thoughts) are most likely to have their nature assessed positively.

As we see, there are significant theoretical consequences of the application of the supervenience relation, which help to understand and explain better the foundations of human dignity and human rights. Nonetheless, the main conclusion is that the general form of supervenience—no difference in supervenient fact, without a difference in subvenient fact—is satisfied for human dignity as the supervenient fact and human nature as the subvenient fact. As for the logical properties, reflexivity is trivially satisfied—there cannot be a difference in human dignity without a difference in human dignity. Similarly to reflexivity for human rights, meeting this criterion is a formal, logical one with no metaphysical consequences. Being non-symmetric means that in some cases of supervenience relations, where A supervenes on B, B supervenes on A, while in some A supervenes on B. For satisfying the logical property of being non-symmetric, one of those situations must be true for a particular supervenience relation. In this context, it must be true that either human nature supervenes on human dignity (symmetrical relation), or that

[27] Singer (1975); Steinbock (1978).

human nature does not supervene on human dignity (asymmetrical relation). In other words, either human nature cannot change without a change in human dignity or human nature can change without a change in human dignity. I believe that the second claim is correct. Human nature can change without triggering any changes in human dignity. For instance, human nature may contain a tendency that is morally neutral—a tendency that does not change anything as for moral vision of human. Consequently, nothing changes with respect to the content of human dignity, however, there is a change in human nature. As a result, human nature does not supervene on human dignity. In this context, supervenience of human dignity on human nature is asymmetrical.

The last logical property is transitivity. For instance, if human nature supervenes on some other facts, e.g. genetic facts—facts about certain genes we all share—it would mean that human dignity supervenes on those genetic facts. This issue lies however outside the scope of this work. I will however later analyse the transitivity of supervenience of all entities that were analysed—particular human rights, social and environmental facts, universal human rights, human dignity and human nature.

To sum up, with respect to the issue of the logical properties of supervenience, all of them are satisfied. Therefore, altogether with satisfying the general requirement of sueprvenience—i.e. no change in supervenient fact without change in subvenient fact—it can be concluded that human dignity supervenes on human nature.

5.6 Consequences of the Supervenience Account

The foundational claim that there are ontological dependencies between human rights, human dignity and human nature, has been analysed in terms of supervenience. It was explored whether relations between human rights and human dignity, as well as between human dignity and human nature, have a form of supervenience. The answer is affirmative with some minor comments. Universal human rights supervene on human dignity, while particular human rights supervene on universal human rights and environmental and social facts. Human dignity supervenes on human nature. It means that there cannot be any change in universal human rights without a change in human dignity and that there cannot be any change in human dignity without a change in human nature. Moreover, particular human rights cannot change without a change in environmental and social facts (universal human rights on which they supervene too cannot change at all, so the change in particular human rights must be attributed to other facts on which they as well supervene). Nonetheless, the crucial issue is whether these necessary covariances are sufficient to express and explain the foundational claim. Is the supervenience relation able to express and explain the ontological dependencies between human rights and human dignity as well as between human dignity and human nature?

Let me analyse the transitivity between the supervenience relations of universal human rights-human dignity and human dignity-human nature. Particular human rights neither supervene on human dignity, nor on human nature, since they supervene not only on universal human rights but also on social and environmental facts. This is because of the same reasons while partial causality and partial metaphysical grounding are not transitive—if A supervenes on B and C, and B supervenes on D, it is not true that A supervenes on D.[28]

Since universal human rights supervene on human dignity and human dignity supervenes on human nature, due to transitivity, universal human rights supervene on human nature. It means that there cannot be any change in universal human rights without a change in human nature. It means that for the universal human rights to change, there must be a change in human nature. For instance, in order not to have universal human rights, our human nature must have been of a sort that no positive vision had ever been possible. If our human nature were constituted by a tendency to behave egoistically or even maliciously,[29] no positive moral vision of such a human nature would be possible. Consequently, human dignity would not hold and, as a result of transitivity of supervenience, universal human rights would not hold as well. But the ultimate basis for not possessing human rights (change in human rights: the lack of existence of human rights) would be the change in human nature. In turn, if we evolved differently and the differences in that state of human nature in comparison to human nature as it is in our world were significant from the moral point of view, the universal human rights might be different.[30] Notwithstanding, not every change in human nature would lead to a change in human dignity and consequently in universal human rights. Some changes in our basic natural tendencies would be irrelevant for the moral domain. This is consistent with the properties of supervenience—human rights cannot change without a change in characteristics of human nature, while human nature can change without a change in human rights. This is true as the supervenience relation of human dignity on human nature is asymmetrical—supervenience in "another direction" (human nature on human dignity) does not necessarily hold. Consequently, human nature may differ with no differences in universal human rights.

The conclusion that universal human rights ultimately supervene on human nature is a remarkable consequence of the metaphysical reading of the foundations of human rights and the application of the supervenience relation. Due to one of the logical properties of supervenience, it can be stated that there is a necessary covariance relationship between (universal) human rights and human nature. In some sense (its scope will be discussed soon), human nature itself can be regarded as a basis of human rights. In this way, the issue of foundations of human rights becomes methodologically naturalised—the natural facts that are the basis of human rights have been identified. Universal human rights supervene on human dignity and human dignity supervenes on human nature. Due to the logical property of

---

[28] Schaffer (2012).

[29] Cf. Załuski (2009a).

[30] Notice that this is consistent with the notion of universality of universal human rights. They are universal irrespective of time and place but this holds only in our world. In another possible world where e.g. human nature was of negative moral assessment, universal human rights would not exist.

transitivity, universal human rights supervene on human nature. There can be no change in universal human rights without a change in human dignity and that there can be no change in human dignity without a change in human nature. Consequently, there can be no change in universal human rights without a change in human nature. Particular human rights supervene on both universal human rights and on social and environmental facts but they do not supervene on human dignity. These theses are metaphysical claims: the relation of supervenience is a metaphysical relation that holds between metaphysical objects. The relata of these supervenience relations are metaphysical entities—human rights, human dignity—and natural entity—human nature. The meaning of supervenience is that for some entities to change there must be a change of some other. In the context of foundations of human rights, it means that for human dignity to exist, human nature must exist. For universal human rights to exist human dignity must exist. Consequently, for universal human rights to exist, human nature must exist. In other words, there is a necessary covariance between the existence of universal human rights, human dignity and human nature. The case of the analysed supervenience relations is an example of the view on the nature of morality claiming that moral facts ultimately supervene on natural facts.

However, are these supervenience theses, albeit true, sufficient to express and explain the foundational claim of the philosophy of human rights? Are these supervenience relations sufficient to express and explain the ontological dependence between human rights, human dignity and human nature? First, let me check whether supervenience is able to express the foundational claim. If we think that there is something beneath human rights that is their foundation, we assume that in some sense this foundation is prior to human rights., It is not priority in terms of time as it would be in causal relations. Rather, it is priority in terms of metaphysical fundamentality[31]—that the foundation of human rights is more fundamental, more metaphysically basic or primitive than human rights. For instance, probably all legal philosophers would agree that social facts are more fundamental in relation to legal facts. Social facts are more basic and while we can imagine societies without law (legal facts), if there exist certain legal facts (like the fact that there is a legal system in a given society), there must be some underlying social facts.[32] If human dignity is conceived as the foundation of human rights it must be metaphysically fundamental in relation to human rights. If an entity is a foundation of another entity, it must be more basic, more primitive in its existence than the entity that it founds.

Looking from a different point of view, I believe that human dignity is in fact more metaphysically basic than human rights. Human dignity is an inherent worth of every human being whereas human rights are much more determined in their normative dimension. Human rights, especially particular human rights, enable to formulate direct claims on what should be done. Such claims cannot be made solely on the basis of human dignity. Similarly, human nature is metaphysically

[31] Tahko (2018).

[32] I do not presuppose that only social facts determine legal facts so this description is I believe equally acceptable for non-positivists.

fundamental in relation to human dignity. Human nature belongs to the natural sphere. In turn, human dignity comes as something positive about human nature. It means that human nature is more primitive and more basic in its existence—it is constituted of descriptive, natural facts. Human dignity holds as an entity dependent on this natural facts, which means that these natural facts are metaphysically more fundamental.

Human dignity is thus metaphysically fundamental in relation to human rights and human nature is metaphysically fundamental towards human dignity. It means that human nature is more basic, more primitive in its existence than human dignity, which in turn is more basic, more primitive in its existence than human rights. Is supervenience able to express these issues? I believe that it is not. Notice that supervenience is non-symmetrical. It means that if A supervenes on B, in some cases B supervenes on A and in some cases B does not supervene on A. It depends on entities that constitute A and B in a particular supervenience relations. For instance, it was concluded that while universal human rights supervene on human dignity, human dignity supervenes on universal human rights as well. However, while human dignity supervenes on human nature, human nature does not supervene on human dignity. Each of these claims has been formulated on the basis of the analysis of the features of these entities and relations holding between them and not on the basis of the properties of supervenience itself. It means that supervenience alone does not entail whether in case of A supervening on B, B supervenes or does not supervene on A. The determination of this issue is crucial for the determination of metaphysical fundamentality. If A supervenes on B and B supervenes on A, we do not know which entity is fundamental. Therefore, supervenience cannot express metaphysical fundamentality between human rights, human dignity and human nature. For this reason, supervenience is not sufficient to express the aspect of fundamentality of the ontological dependencies holding between human rights, human dignity and human nature.

Moreover, there is another aspect of the foundational claim (ontological dependencies), which is of greater importance. Human rights hold *due to* their foundation, which I regard to be human dignity, and, consequently, human dignity holds *due to* its foundations, which I propose to be human nature. This is the core of what I call "foundational claim". The proper formulation of the foundational claim must be able to provide the explanation or justification of why human rights exist due to human dignity and why human dignity exists due to human nature. However, supervenience is only a relation of a necessary covariance stating that there can be no change in a supervenient entity without change in a subvenient entity. Supervenience does not cover the fact that this lack of change in the supervenient entity holds *due to* the lack of change in the subvenient entity. For this reason, supervenience is a weak metaphysical relation with no explanatory force. Most probably it is true that moral facts cannot change without a change in natural facts, however, it does not mean that moral facts cannot change *because of the fact that* natural facts do not change. This lack of change cannot be explained by reference to supervenience, but only by other means. The lack of explanatory force of supervenience explains why one should not be confused with some intuitively weird particular supervenience relations, as e.g. that moral facts under moral realism supervene on mathematical facts. Truly, if certain moral facts cannot change (like the fact that slavery is always wrong), they supervene on other facts that cannot change as well (like all mathematical facts). But there is nothing in this supervenience relation that those moral facts cannot change *due to* mathematical facts. In fact, under moral realism, human rights, at universal human rights, supervene on mathematical facts as well, but it does not mean that mathematical facts constitute foundations of human rights. Therefore, supervenience is not able to express the foundational claim of the philosophy of human rights. By reference to supervenience we are not able to express the claim that human rights hold due to human dignity and that human dignity holds due to human nature. The statement that universal human rights supervene on human dignity and human dignity supervenes on human nature does not mean that human dignity explains the existence of human rights or, respectively, that human nature explains that human dignity exists. Supervenience is a too weak relation for that purpose.[33]

5.7 Conclusions

Despite the lack of explanatory force, the reference to supervenience illuminates certain aspects of the question of the foundations of human rights. It is a conceptually clear relation, precise and well analysed by analytic philosophy. Supervenience holds in the following way: (1) particular human rights supervene on universal human rights and contingent environmental and social facts, (2) universal human rights supervene on human dignity and (3) human dignity supervenes on human nature. It means that between each of the above relata there is the necessary covariance what means that the supervenient entity cannot change without a change in the subvenient entity. I believe it is an important feature, which partly covers the basic views on the foundations of human rights. Making use of supervenience enables to express these views in a brief and clear way

Due to the fact that supervenience is transitive, it can be concluded that universal human rights supervene on human nature. I find it to be an interesting and important claim. It is established on the basis of the logical property of relation that is used. The reference to supervenience also shows that the reference to metaphysical relations increases our understanding of issues in the philosophy of human rights. Moreover, I believe that certain interesting claims can be formulated by making use of supervenience while interpreting the views of various philosophers of human rights. Under Nussbaum's capabilities approach human rights do not read off from innate,

[33] For analogous reasons, Gizbert-Studnicki (2015, 2016) rejects supervenience as the proper relations to express and explain the legal positivism claim that legal facts are determined only by social facts—even though legal facts supervene on social facts, which means that there can be no change in legal facts without change in social facts, supervenience cannot express and explain the core of this legal positivism claim, which is that legal facts hold due to social facts.

unchangeable, human nature.[34] Under the capabilities approach, human rights protect central capabilities and the list of capabilities (life, bodily healthy, bodily integrity etc.) indicates that they are universal due to being unrelated to any contingent circumstances.[35] The employment of the "supervenience interpretation" to Nussbaum's theory seems to suggest that human rights, which mirror the capabilities, do not supervene on human nature. But since she explicitly regards human nature as *innate*, thus unchangeable and universal, human rights technically supervene on it. If there can be no change in both human nature and human rights, universal human rights must supervene on human nature. It is a technical and perhaps trivial claim, yet it is true. Yet, Nussbaum most probably means a stronger relation than supervenience as *reading off* of human rights, not merely a necessary covariance.

The second position of philosophers of human rights that may be interpreted in terms of supervenience that I would like to discuss is Waldron's view on the relation between human rights and human dignity.[36] As it was said in Sect. 3.2.3, he analyses three notions about what kind of entity human dignity is in relation to being the foundation of human rights. The first is that human rights have foundations in human dignity understood as value, while the second and the third accounts regard human dignity as status with differences related to what this status means. Under the second one, human dignity is seen as status understood as a package containing rights. The third is that human dignity is status understood as an idea underlying human rights.[37] The third understanding of human dignity as status implies that a given status is actually undistinguishable from rights that it contains and abbreviates. As for human dignity and human rights, it means that human dignity is a package of human rights undistinguishable from human rights. Human dignity simply comprises these rights and abbreviates them into one concept. This notion can be analysed from philosophical, or more specifically, metaphysical point of view.

One idea is to claim that under this conception human dignity is reduced to human rights. Then, human dignity in fact not different from human rights. The term "human dignity" is easier to use in certain situations, but it refers only to human rights. Yet, if one would prefer to regard human dignity and human rights as separate entities, supervenience can be applied as well. As supervenience is non-symmetric, human rights can supervene on human dignity and simultaneously human dignity can supervene on human rights. This account also represents the idea that human dignity is a package of human rights containing and abbreviating them. If human dignity contains human rights (all human rights, including particular human rights, because Waldron does not differentiate between universal and particular human rights), it obviously cannot change without a change in (content, scope, holders of, etc.) human rights. In turn, since human rights are abbreviated by and contained in

[34] Nussbaum (2011), p. 28.

[35] Nussbaum (2011), pp. 33–34.

[36] Waldron (2015).

[37] Waldron (2015, pp. 134–135).

human dignity, they cannot change without a change in human dignity. As we see, supervenience holds in both directions, which is possible under its logical properties. Making use of supervenience enables to clearly represent this conception: human dignity as a package containing and abbreviating human rights supervenes on human rights. In turn, human rights simultaneously supervene on human dignity. In such a way, the relations between various entities debated in the philosophy of human rights can be philosophically precisely described. As it was analysed in the Sect. 3.2.3, Waldron rejects this notion of status, I also believe it is the improper conception of what human dignity is. Nonetheless, I wanted to present that making use of metaphysical relations, in this scenario supervenience, enables to clarify and clearly express difficult issues of philosophy of human rights.

Although it is true that (1) particular human rights supervene on universal human rights and environmental and social facts, (2) universal human rights supervene on human dignity and (3) human dignity supervenes on human nature, making use of supervenience is not sufficient to express and explain the foundational claim of philosophy of human rights. The ontological dependences between human rights, human dignity and human nature cannot be properly expressed and explained by supervenience. Therefore, another relation must be tested. This relation is metaphysical grounding.

References

Balaguer M (2016) Platonism in metaphysics. The Stanford Encyclopedia of Philosophy (Spring 2016 Edition). https://plato.stanford.edu/archives/spr2016/entries/platonism/

Berker S (2018) The unity of grounding. Mind 127:729–777

Brożek B (2012) Normatywność Prawa. Warszawa, Wolters Kluwer

Brożek B (2017) Law, normativity and supervenience. In: Brożek B, Rotolo A, Stelmach J (eds) Supervenience and normativity. Springer, Dordrecht, pp 123–138

Dunbar R (2014) Human evolution. Pelican Books, London

Gizbert-Studnicki T (2015) Metafizyka Pozytywizmu Prawniczego. Principia 61:19–40

Gizbert-Studnicki T (2016) The social sources thesis, metaphysics and metaphilosophy. In: Banaś P, Dyrda A, Gizbert Studnicki T (eds) Metaphilosophy of law. Hart Publishing, Oxford, pp 121–146

Griffin J (2008) On human rights. Oxford University Press, Oxford

Hare RM (1952) The language of morals. Oxford University Press, Oxford

Jackson F (1982) Epiphenomenal Qualia. Philos Q 32:127–136

Kim J (1984) Concepts of Supervenience reprinted. In: Kim J (1993) Supervenience and mind: selected philosophical essays. Cambridge University Press, Cambridge, pp 53–78

Kim J (1993) Supervenience and mind: selected philosophical essays. Cambridge University Press, Cambridge

Kim J (2003) Supervenience, emergence, realization, reduction. In: Loux M, Zimmerman D (eds) The Oxford handbook of metaphysics. OUP, Oxford, pp 556–584

Lombard L (1986) Events: a metaphysical study. Routledge, London

McLaughlin B, Bennett K (2018) Supervenience. The Stanford Encyclopedia of Philosophy (Winter 2018 Edition). https://plato.stanford.edu/archives/win2018/entries/supervenience/

McPherson T (2019) Supervenience in Ethics. The Stanford Encyclopedia of Philosophy (Winter 2019 Edition). https://plato.stanford.edu/archives/win2019/entries/supervenience-ethics/

Nagel T (1974) What is it like to be a bat? Philos Rev 83:435–450

Nussbaum M (2011) Creating capabilities, the human development approach. The Belknap Press of Harvard University Press, Cambridge/London

Schaffer J (2012) Grounding, transitivity, and contrastivity. In: Correia F, Schnieder B (eds) Metaphysical grounding: understanding the structure of reality. Cambridge University Press, Cambridge, pp 122–138

Singer P (1975) Animal liberation: a new ethics for our treatment of animals. Avon Books, New York

Steinbock B (1978) Speciesism and the idea of equality. Philosophie 53:247–256

Tahko T (2018) Fundamentality. The Stanford Encyclopedia of Philosophy (Fall 2018 Edition). https://plato.stanford.edu/archives/fall2018/entries/fundamentality/

Tasioulas J (2011) On the nature of human rights. In: Ernst G, Heilinger JC (eds) The philosophy of human rights: contemporary controversies. De Gruyter, Berlin, pp 17–59

Tomasello M (2009) Why we cooperate? A Boston Review Book, Cambridge, London

Waldron J (2015) Is dignity foundation of human rights? In: Cruft R, Liao SM, Renzo M (eds) Philosophical foundations of human rights. OUP, Oxford, pp 117–137

Załuski W (2009a) Evolutionary theory and legal philosophy. Edward Elgar, Cheltenham

Załuski W (2009b) Ewolucyjna Filozofia Prawa. Wolters Kluwer, Warszawa

Chapter 6
Metaphysical Grounding Account

6.1 Metaphysical Grounding

Metaphysical grounding (which I sometimes refer to simply as "grounding") is a vividly discussed relation of the XXI century analytic metaphysics.[1] It is a metaphysical relation holding between facts (or objects[2])—where a grounded fact holds due to a grounding fact. Fabrice Correia and Benjamin Schnieder (2012, p. 1) give the following list of claims developed in various areas of philosophy where the relation holding between relata can be at least *prima facie* considered as metaphysical grounding:

1. *Mental facts obtain because of neurophysiological facts.*
2. *Legal facts are grounded in non-legal, e.g. social, facts.*
3. *Normative facts are based on natural facts.*
4. *Meaning is due to non-semantic facts.*
5. *Dispositional properties are possessed in virtue of categorical properties.*

[1]Fine (2001, 2010, 2012a, b); Rosen (2010, 2015, 2017a); Schaffer (2009, 2010, 2012); Audi (2012a, b); Rodriguez-Pereyra (2015). My description of the metaphysical grounding relation, as well as by current status of its application into legal positivism is partly based on my description of this relation in my paper (Mazurkiewicz 2019a).

I am aware of the philosophical background standing behind this relation, especially in terms of certain ontological views. In my view, this background consists mainly of the view that relations between entities can be researched in comparison to the view that would suggest that we can research only ideas or concepts, especially those that we have in minds. I do not want to discuss the philosophical debate between idealism and realism, what I want to note is that as the debate on human rights presupposes or implies moral realism (of course it is not the same as realism in metaphysics) and taking into consideration the discussion on the contemporary analytic notion of "fact" mentioned in Sect 3.3.1, I do not see any opposition between philosophical background of the relation of metaphysical grounding and the question on the foundations of human rights.

[2]Schaffer (2010).

S. Mazurkiewicz, *Grounding Human Rights in Human Nature*, Law and Philosophy Library 141, https://doi.org/10.1007/978-3-031-30734-8_6

6. *What accounts for the existence of a whole is the existence and arrangement of its parts.*
7. *A set of things is less fundamental than its members.*
8. *What makes something beautiful are certain facts about the reception of its beholders.*
9. *A substance is prior to its tropes or modes.*
10. *That snow is white is true because snow is white.*[3]

Quite interestingly, the claim of the general philosophy of law is presented right at the second place. All these situations described by the above claims refer to the scenario when one fact is the basis for the existence of another fact. The relation of metaphysical grounding is able to explain why a grounded fact holds due to a grounding fact. Therefore, a proposition that "mental facts hold in virtue of neuro-physical facts" means that neuro-physical facts ground mental facts, and the former explains the obtaining of the latter. In a grounding relation, the facts that are among the grounds are called "grounding facts", whereas the facts that they ground are called "grounded facts".

Jonathan Schaffer describes grounding by revealing its similarity to causation. He writes that "Grounding is something like metaphysical causation. Just as causation links the world across time, grounding links the world across levels".[4] What causality is in the natural world, metaphysical grounding is meant to be in the metaphysical sphere. Such a characteristic assumes a multi-layer structure of the universe. There are many levels of reality, and facts on a higher level are grounded in facts existing on a lower one. For instance, if it is the case that mental facts are grounded in neuro-physical facts, the former exist on a higher level of reality than the latter and are irreducible to the latter. Grounding provides metaphysical explanation: if A holds in virtue of B, it means that B explains why A holds. If one wonders about the foundations of A, one can refer to the fact that B is grounded in A in order to explain the holding of A. I believe it is a proper argument in favour of the view that grounding provides explanation: ultimately, if one wonders why a certain fact holds (let's say A), the explanation of the existence of A is to be done by referring to an entity that makes that it holds (let's say B) along with justifying that A holds due to this fact B. The logical properties of grounding: irreflexitivity, asymmetricality, and transitivity—are shared by grounding with the relation of explanation: A can never explain itself; if A explains B, it means that B can never explain A; if A explains B and B explains C, it means that A explains C. It is claimed that natural language phrases like "because of" and especially "in virtue of" represent the holding of metaphysical grounding between objects denoted by concepts found in sentences with these phrases.[5] Obviously, there are many relations that share the logical properties of explanation. However, what is believed to be the key of the

[3]Correia and Schnieder (2012), p. 1.

[4]Schaffer (2012), p. 122.

[5]Audi (2012b); Bliss and Trogdon (2016).

metaphysical explanation consists of providing why something (e.g. a fact) exists. If A is grounded in B, which means that A exists because of B, it enables to formulate a claim that the reference to B explains the existence of A.

The relation of metaphysical grounding is irreflexive (A never grounds itself), asymmetric (if A grounds B, B never grounds A), and transitive (if A grounds B and B grounds C, it means that A grounds C).[6] These logical properties involve significant metaphysical consequences: in the grounding relation, the grounding fact is ontologically prior to the grounded fact. Moreover, if a fact is grounded in another fact, there is no grounding relation in the opposite direction and, consequently, explanation goes only in one way. Transitivity is able to provide a chain of grounding relations, and consequently explanations, referring to deeper levels of the universe. If it is the case that biological facts are grounded in chemical facts and chemical facts are grounded in physical facts, it entails that physical facts ground biological facts. Thus, biological facts hold in virtue of physical facts. As we see, grounding has different logical properties than supervenience—while supervenience is reflexive (A can supervene on A), grounding is irreflexive; while supervenience is non-symmetric (A can supervene on B and B also can, but does not have to, supervene on A), grounding is asymmetric. These logical properties result in the fact that metaphysical grounding is a much stronger metaphysical relation than supervenience.

Grounding may seem similar to logical entailment. There are however important differences between them. While the relata of grounding are facts, which are metaphysical or natural entities, the relata of logical entailment are propositions, which are semantic entities. Logical entailment has also different logical properties—A logically entails itself (reflexivity) and while A entails B, B can entail A (non-symmetric). Logical entailment is transitive just like grounding. Metaphysical grounding is much stronger than logical entailment—it provides explanation while logical entailment alone does not. As Alfred Tarski argued, logical entailment (which he called logical consequence) relies on logical form of sentences, has a modal component and is formal (the term *a priori* perhaps represent it better), which means that no empirical evidence is required to its holding.[7] Logical entailment is therefore a relation about an inner structure of some reasoning (while premises of a reasoning can be not justified), while grounding enables to provide not only explanation in terms of an inner structure of a reasoning but also in terms of an external, metaphysical holding of the discussed fact or entity.

Grounding involves a specific kind of necessity of the existence of the grounded fact. As Fabrice Correia puts it, "Necessarily, if the fact that A is grounded in some given facts, then it is impossible that the latter facts all exist but fail to ground the fact that A".[8] In other words, when a particular grounding relation holds and the grounding fact holds, it is necessary that the grounded fact holds as well. Grounding

---

[6] Bliss and Trogdon (2016).

[7] Tarski (1936); cf. McKeon (2021).

[8] Correia (2005), p. 61.

does not mean that it is necessary that the grounding fact obtain, nor that it is necessary that the grounded fact obtain independently of the grounding relation and the grounding fact. For instance, if it is true that mental facts are grounded in neuro-physical facts and neuro-physical facts obtain, it is necessary that mental facts obtain as well. To give another example: if it is true that (1) legal facts are grounded in social facts and (2) there obtain certain social facts that ground legal facts, it means that legal facts necessarily hold.

Another important property of grounding is its hyperintentionality. Let me explain it by saying first what intenstionality is according to analytic philosophy. A concept that is intensional does not draw a distinction between contents that are necessarily equivalent.[9] Consequently, necessarily equivalent properties are treated as identical, for example triangularity is identical to trilaterality. Relations based on modal notions, like supervenience, are intensional. To the contrary, grounding is not intensional—it is hyperintensional, which means that necessarily equivalent properties are not considered identical. Let me illustrate it with an example of two sentences:

(1) *You have 40% chances of succeeding.*
(2) *You have 60% chances of failing.*[10]

They are equivalent, moreover, they are necessarily equivalent due to mathematics. But our psychological attitudes differ, it was shown that we are more likely to believe in a positive outcome while being presented with such sentences, in spite of their logical equivalence.[11] It means that the concept of belief is hyperintensional. Grounding is considered hyperintensional as well—certain fact (A) may necessarily lead to another fact (B), but these two fact are not the same. A grounds B, while A is not identical to B.

Two distinctions made by Fine are important.[12] The first is the distinction between full and partial grounding. While A and B both fully ground C, A partly grounds C and B partly grounds C. Obviously, a grounded fact may have many grounding facts. Let's assume that legal non-positivism is correct, then, under the metaphysical reading, legal facts are grounded in both social and moral facts.[13] It means that social facts and moral facts fully ground legal facts whereas social facts alone and moral facts alone partly ground legal facts.

The second among Fine's distinctions is a distinction between mediate and immediate grounding. Immediate grounding is a grounding relation that is not mediated by any other grounding relation. Fine describes it as follows:

---

[9] Berto and Nolan (2021).

[10] Berto and Nolan (2021).

[11] Berto and Nolan (2021).

[12] Fine (2012a).

[13] As far as I know, none of the contemporary non-positivists claim that social fact are irrelevant for determining law.

> The statement that A ∧ (B ∧C) is mediately grounded in the statements that A, B, C, since the grounding must be seen to be mediated through B, C grounding (B ∧ C) and A, (B ∧ C) grounding A ∧ (B∧C). The statements B, C, by contrast, immediately ground B ∧C, since the grounding in this case is not mediated through other relationships of ground.[14]

It may happen that a grounded fact is grounded immediately in its grounding fact. On the other hand, it may happen that a grounded fact is grounded in a mediated way. This happens when the basis of a grounded fact is also grounded in some other facts: there is a mediate grounding relation necessary to the grounding of the first fact. The distinctions between partial and full grounding, as well as between mediate and immediate grounding will be useful in further research of the relations holding between human rights, human dignity and human nature.

6.1.1 Why Does the Grounding Hold?

There is a debate among contemporary analytic metaphysicians on why grounding holds as an explanatory relation. The first historically given answer was that grounding is primitive and thus cannot be further analysed.[15] Ricki Bliss and Kelly Trogdon claim that the primitive nature of grounding prevails among its proponents:

> The more or less received view among proponents of grounding, however, is that the concept isn't analysable – the concept of grounding is ultimately primitive in nature [...], it's important to keep in mind that this doesn't mean that talk of grounding is obscure, or that grounding claims are confused or unjustified. It seems that many notions central to philosophy are unitary and unanalyzable (consider synchronic identity, for example), yet this leads few to dismiss them as obscure, confused, or unjustified.[16]

If grounding is an ultimate form of metaphysical explanation, one should not be confused that it is impossible to provide any further, deeper insight into this relation. Gideon Rosen argues

> We do not know how to say in more basic terms «what it is» for one fact to obtain in virtue of another. But that is obviously no reason for regarding the idiom as unclear or unintelligible.[17]

He does not see any problem in the primitive, unanalysable character of metaphysical grounding. As he argues, there are other key metaphysical notions, as metaphysical necessity, that cannot be defined in more basic terms, yet this does not undermine philosophical inquiry.[18] An argument for this position can be formulated by reference to other areas of knowledge. Mathematics does not feel anxious with axioms and concepts undefined in more basic terms. Physics seems to discover the

[14] Fine (2012a), p. 50.

[15] Fine (2001); Schaffer (2009); cf. Rosen (2010).

[16] Bliss and Trogdon (2016).

[17] Rosen (2010), p. 113.

[18] Rosen (2010), p. 113.

most basic particles of the whole universe—if they are the most basic, they obviously cannot be defined in terms of more basic entities. Reference to these particles will constitute the ultimate physical explanation. Why cannot the same go for metaphysics? If grounding is analogous to causality, it's the ultimate form of metaphysical explanation and does not have to be analysed and defined in more basic terms.

Nonetheless, some philosophers try to connect grounding with other concepts, like essence or metaphysical laws. The view that grounding holds due to relations between essences of grounding and grounded facts is proposed by Fine in his later writings[19] as well as by Gideon Rosen and Shamik Dasgupta.[20] For Fine, as it was mentioned, the essence of an object or property is the proposition that define it.[21] He argues that the essence of an object is not identical with its necessary properties—a property may be necessary for an object, yet still it does not have to make this object into that which it actually is.[22] Under the essentialist view on grounding, grounding holds because of essences of grounding fact and grounded fact. For example, if an essence of a natural fact is that it causes pain, it grounds the moral fact that it is wrong since there is a relation between essences of those facts that leads to this grounding relation. The problem with connecting grounding with essences is that the concept of essence is unclear and for many facts it can be difficult to identify their essence. For instance, the claim that legal facts are grounded in social facts, which will be discussed in the next section, is quite uncontroversial, yet if we have to add there the relation between essences of legal and social facts, it becomes much more problematic. It is highly debated what is the essence of legal facts, this debate is mostly formulated as the debate on the nature of law.[23] Moreover, I do not see a point in necessarily connecting the grounding version of explanation with explanations based on essence. Perhaps, for some facts that ground one another, there are also relations between their essences. But I am not so sure whether this occurs for every fact. Lastly, if there is a proper and working grounding explanation that explains why a given fact holds, I do not think it is necessary to refer to another layer—the layer of essences—in this inquiry.

Another view is that grounding holds due to metaphysical laws that back this relation. It is proposed by Jonathan Schaffer, Stephanie Leary and in recent Rosen's works.[24] Schaffer claims: "Just like causal explanation requires laws of nature, so metaphysical explanation requires *laws of metaphysics*".[25] While grounding is in general a form of metaphysical explanation, it also requires metaphysical laws that underpin it. The problems here are similar as in the essentialist version. Metaphysical

[19] Fine (2012a).

[20] Fine (2012a); Rosen (2010); Dasgupta (2014).

[21] Fine (1994a, b).

[22] Fine (1994a).

[23] Gizbert-Studnicki et al. (2016).

[24] Schaffer (2017), Leary (2017), Rosen (2017b).

[25] Schaffer (2017), p. 315.

laws can be difficult to identify for many facts, while the grounding relation between them is quite uncontroversial. For instance, what is the metaphysical law backing the relation between moral facts and natural facts, or between mental facts and neuro-physical facts? Such metaphysical laws are highly difficult to be identified, while the very grounding claims about these facts are much less controversial. Next, why should we refer to yet another level of explanation in trying to explain why a given fact holds? Let me here also recall the issue of *ad hoc* explanations and *ad hoc* hypotheses, which are "explanations" that "explain" a given instantiation of a situation with no providing any bigger picture that covers all the category. Maybe for some grounding relations there are correlated metaphysical laws, but I have doubts whether these laws could cover every grounding relation. There may be also particular metaphysical laws (related only to certain types of entities), but in these cases, there is a grave danger of falling into metaphysical speculation. I believe that while doing metaphysics we should avoid entering into obscure speculations and proposing controversial claims while simpler and less controversial forms of claims can be given.

I do not want to undertake my analysis on such deep metaphysical levels as the level of essences or metaphysical laws. I am aware of the debate on why grounding holds, however, I will follow, in my observation, the vastly majoritarian position that grounding is primitive.[26] I do not form conclusive arguments against each of the two others proposals, rather I present a list of serious concerns. Let me also notice that if it is determined that grounding holds between some facts, this observation cannot serve as a counter-argument from neither essentialist positions, nor from metaphysical laws positions. These positions can rather provide a new, deeper level for the currently researched grounding relation. Thus, I will follow the notion of grounding as a primitive notion.[27]

6.1.2 *Metaphysical Grounding in the Positivist Theory of Law*

Metaphysical grounding has already drawn the attention of some philosophers of law as a candidate for the possible relation explaining the existence of legal facts. Legal facts are simply facts about law, so every legal norm can be transformed into a fact about this legal norm. Usage of the term "legal facts" does not presuppose that legal facts are of the same category of facts as e.g. natural facts. To my best knowledge, David Plunkett is the first legal philosopher to claim that this relation

---

[26] In my paper (Mazurkiewicz 2019b) I tried to employ metaphysical grounding based on metaphysical laws to the grounding reading of the legal positivist social source thesis.

[27] Perhaps, the essentialist version might be adopted in this research since I clearly defined entities (human rights, human dignity, human nature). For instance, evolutionary understood human nature can be regarded as the essence of human under Fine's notion of essence. Human dignity may be grounded in human nature due to the essence of human nature that connects it with the essence of human nature.

of determination is something like metaphysical grounding when he argues against Mark Greenberg's view that moral facts are necessary in understanding the practice of law and, in particular, the legal relevance of some social facts.[28] However, Plunkett does not engage in the discussion on the metaphysical grounding and its application in legal philosophy. Rather, he simply finds that what he and Greenberg are discussing in legal theory is very similar to the general analytic metaphysics debate on metaphysical grounding.

Gizbert-Studnicki also aims to analyse the social source thesis of legal positivism, which claims that "legal facts are ultimately determined by social facts alone",[29] in terms of the proper metaphysical relation that constitutes this vague "determination".[30] Gizbert-Studnicki rejects reduction as normative legal facts cannot be reduced to descriptive social facts; he also disregards supervenience due to its weak explanatory force. He argues that the relation that holds between social facts and legal facts is metaphysical grounding. Due to the explanatory force of grounding, this relation provides explanation of why legal facts hold. Samuele Chilovi and George Pavlakos also argue that the adequate explanation of legal facts by reference to social facts can and should be done in terms of metaphysical grounding.[31] Actually, the debate between positivists and non-positivists can be briefly reconsidered in terms of grounding as a debate whether only social facts or also moral facts ground legal facts.[32]

Despite the manifold references to grounding within the field of general jurisprudence, the philosophy of human rights has not yet witnessed any application of the widely discussed relation. I will test whether grounding can express and explain ontological dependencies between human rights, human dignity and human nature.

[28] Plunkett (2012); Greenberg (2014). The relation of metaphysical grounding can also look similar to what Kelsen calls imputation—a normative category analogical to causality that links a condition with a (legal) consequence. Being analogical to causality, it was considered by Kelsen as a promising foundation for legal science as a proper science. Grounding is in contemporary analytic metaphysics also considered analogical to causation, so these two can be compared. However, one should not forget about the philosophical background of respectively Kelsen's pure theory of law and contemporary analytic metaphysics. Kelsen's theory is based on neo-Kantian philosophy and imputation is rather a cognitive category that serves the purpose of a necessary presupposition that makes knowledge of legal facts possible. In turn, the relation of metaphysical grounding has its background in the realistic part of the contemporary analytic metaphysics and is the objective relation holding between two facts, irrespective of an epistemic subject. So, while imputation and grounding can seem to be similar, they are categories from two different philosophical schools and are rather difficult to compare. Nonetheless, views on relations connecting various entities/ideas are to be found in different schools of thought, which shows the need to find plausible explanation of the debated entities/ideas.

[29] Shapiro (2011), p. 269.

[30] Gizbert-Studnicki (2015, 2016, 2021).

[31] Chilovi and Pavlakos (2019).

[32] Cf. Rosen (2010), pp. 113–114.

6.2 Metaphysical Grounding Between Human Rights, Human Dignity and Human Nature

Metaphysical grounding is a universal explanatory relation, which is not limited to any sphere of the metaphysical realm. It may also hold between human rights and their foundations and serve as explanation of human rights. In his classical approach to human rights, Piechowiak often uses the Polish term "ugruntowanie", which in English means "grounding".[33] He uses this term in a metaphysical way referring to states of affairs that form the foundation of human rights and human dignity. Many other philosophers of human rights often use terms like "ground" and "grounding". For instance in Griffin's book phrase "ground" is used 189 times,[34] while Miller's paper has it right in its name—"Grounding human rights" with words "ground", "grounding", "grounds" and "grounded" used 46 times on 20 pages.[35] In a profound volume edited by Cruft, Liao and Renzo "ground" is used 661 times, a "grounding" 93 times and "grounded" 139 times.[36] In my view, such a frequent usage of these phrases reveals the common intuition of philosophers of human rights about the foundations of human rights, which is that human rights have some deeper foundations, which can be referred to by such metaphysically-coloured terms. Yet, to my best knowledge, there is no reference to the specific relation of metaphysical grounding in any work on the philosophy of human rights.

Let me recall the main claim of naturalistic (orthodox, substantive) approach to human rights: "Human rights are moral rights possessed by all human beings simply *in virtue of* their humanity"[37] or "simply *in virtue of* being human".[38] There is used the phrase "in virtue of", which was said to be a strong indicator of a relation of metaphysical grounding. Also, the language used in the discourse of human rights suggests the occurrence of metaphysical grounding between human rights and their foundations. Let me test whether grounding holds between entities (facts) distinguished earlier, namely: particular human rights, environmental and social facts, universal human rights, human dignity and human nature.

[33] Piechowiak (1999).

[34] Griffin (2008).

[35] Miller (2012).

[36] Cruft et al. (2015).

[37] Tasioulas (2011), p. 26.

[38] Griffin (2008), p. 2.

6.3 Grounding of Particular Human Rights

Particular human rights have roots in both universal human rights and environmental and social facts. Just to remind, the distinction between universal human rights and particular human rights is necessary in order to maintain the universal character of human rights. While universal human rights, which I propose following Griffin consist of the right to autonomy, the right to liberty and the right to security, are universal in the sense that they do not depend on time and place, the particular human rights (the right to elementary free education, the right to rest and leisure, etc.) are universal but in relation to specific time and space. Everyone at the same time and/or location have the same human rights. Such a claim is quite common in the philosophy of human rights.[39] Particular human rights are, therefore, instantiations of universal human rights in some specific circumstances, which I call environmental and social facts. These environmental and social facts are contingent, which means that they do not have to obtain and they vary from time to time and from place to place.

The way in which particular human rights exist seems to fit well at a first glance the way in which metaphysical grounding can explain the existence of various entities. Let me explore this issue in detail. Are particular human rights metaphysically grounded in universal human rights and in environmental and social facts? For it to be true, logical properties of grounding must be satisfied by the relation between the proposed relata, but most importantly, the grounded facts—particular human rights—must hold in virtue of the grounding facts—universal human rights and environmental and social facts.

The logical properties of grounding relation—irreflexivity, asymmetricaly and transitivity must be satisfied. It must be, therefore, true that particular human rights are not grounded in themselves (irreflexivity), which is quite trivially true. It must be also true that universal human rights and environmental and social facts are not grounded in particular human rights (asymmetricality). This is true as well—universal human rights and environmental and social facts do not depend in their existence on particular human rights. Of course, we do not have the universal human right to liberty in virtue of having the particular human rights to elementary, free of charge education, rather vice versa. Similarly, global warming (an environmental fact) does not hold due to the right to healthcare. I will research transitivity after exploring all the possible grounding relations.

The main question is, however, whether particular human rights hold due to (exist because of) universal human rights and environmental and social facts.[40] In other

[39] Griffin (2008); Tasioulas (2011).

[40] A careful reader may notice that grounding holds between facts and I make use of entities here, not facts about these entities. Yet, grounding is seen to hold between objects themselves (Schaffer 2010), so my usage of entities, which are very similar to what Shaffer refers to as objects, is proper following Schaffer's notion. Looking on grounding as holding only between facts, if I were to use phrases "facts about universal human rights", "facts about particular human rights", "facts about

words, whether the existence of particular human rights can be explained by reference to universal human rights and environmental and social facts. I believe that this question can be answered by determining whether the grounded facts, which here are particular human rights, can be "metaphysically entailed" by the grounding facts, which in this case are universal human rights and environmental and social facts. By "metaphysically entailing" I mean a situation wherein the existence of A, which grounds B, necessarily leads to the existence of B.[41] Notice that I do not mean here logical entailment, which is the relation between propositions or sentences, but a relation holding between facts—metaphysical entities. This is why I speak about metaphysical entailment. For instance, following the analytic metaphysics reading of legal positivism, certain social facts metaphysically entail legal facts—the occurring of certain social facts necessarily leads to the existence of legal facts.

I earlier argued that universal human rights along with environmental and social facts determined the existence of particular human rights. Some examples have already been given in previous sections. Take for instance the human right to property (a particular human right). When society transforms from hunter-gatherers, who do not have a division on personal and common property, into a more settled way of living with one's cattle, land etc., in order to live a free life, be able to decide about oneself (the universal human right to liberty or the universal human rights to autonomy in relation to one's moral beliefs), it is necessary to have a claim to the things that are owned by a person. Without it, one cannot live a decent life. It follows that a particular human right to property emerges. In such a way, the particular human rights are metaphysically entailed by universal human rights and some contingent social facts.

We can also tell the above story conversely, i.e. by following the path from the particular human right to property to universal human right to liberty and social facts. From this point of view, the existence of the particular human right to property is being explained by reference to its basis. The requirement of explanation/metaphysical entailment is satisfied. Therefore, the particular human right to property is metaphysically grounded in universal human right to liberty and in the above-mentioned social facts.

Let me analyse the grounds of another particular human right, the human right to clean water. Clean water is necessary to live on a decent level, actually even on a basic biological level. The existence of a right must presuppose that there exists a

human dignity" etc. the whole work would become unintelligible. Notice also that the way from facts to entities is very short (Sect. 3.1.1). For these reasons I decide to make use of the terms human rights, human dignity and human nature instead of *facts about* human rights, human dignity and human nature. So, technically, it is that e.g. the fact that every human possess human dignity grounds the fact that that every human possess universal human rights (it will be discussed later). I do not see any problems in writing it as "human dignity grounds universal human rights". It is a common way to maintain readability of the work used in the papers on metaphysical grounding, wherein "p" actually refers to "the fact that p". I do the same here.

[41] Instead of metaphysical entailment there could be used terms like "generate", "produce", "lead to" etc. but I find metaphysical entailment the most accurate and precise.

possibility of its violation. If no such possibility exists, there is no point in the recognition of a given right. We do not have a human right to oxygen right now even though it may happen that in the future there will be shortages of oxygen and the human right to oxygen will arise. To give an example of a related particular human right that is held in many regions: in case of shortages of clean air that can undermine one's decent level of life, the right to clean air emerges as a human right. Notice that the right to clean, healthy and sustainable environment (that includes the right to clean air) started to be recognised as a human right in the second half of the 20th century when people realised the scale of degradation of the natural environment and the need for its protection.[42] Without the Industrial Revolution and subsequent degradation of the natural environment, the right to clean air would be pointless. Similarly, the human right to clean water holds only on those areas where there are shortages of clean water. It means that its universality is place-dependent across one time. Environmental facts about water shortages along with the universal human right to safety metaphysically entail the particular human right to clean water. Looking from a converse perspective—this particular human rights hold in virtue of the environmental facts about the shortages of water and the universal human right to safety, which means that the human right to clean water is metaphysically grounded in them.

In a similar way, every other particular human right can be explained. Some of them have been already mentioned with their foundations. The human right to free elementary education is grounded in the level of knowledge, which from around two centuries started to be necessary to live a decent life (social and environmental facts) and the universal human right to liberty. The particular human right to a fair trial is grounded in facts about modern states and their coercive powers and the universal human right to liberty. The particular human right to freedom from slavery is grounded in social facts about the possibility of losing one's freedom that emerged along with the transition to a settled form of life from hunter-gatherer communities and both the universal right to security and to liberty. The particular human right to recognition everywhere as a person before the law[43] is grounded in facts about the existence of legal system and in the universal human right to liberty. When there was no legal system, there was no point in having a right to be recognised as a person before the law. The particular human rights such as that everyone has the right to freedom of movement and residence within the borders of each state as well as that everyone has the right to leave any country, including his own, and to return to his country (art. 13 UDHR), are grounded in social facts related to the existence of states, modern borders and citizenship, as well as in the universal human right to liberty. Without borders, these right makes no sense. The human right claiming that everyone has the right to own property alone as well as in association with others[44] is

[42] Declaration of the United Nations Conference on the Human Environment (1972), so called "Stockholm Declaration".

[43] Universal Declaration of Human Rights (1948), art. 6.

[44] Universal Declaration of Human Rights (1948), art. 17.

grounded in social facts about certain social order and in certain facts about the economic development of a given society and in the universal human right to liberty. In a hunter-gatherer society that does not have the concept of "personal property" and of "ownership" (rather only of "possession"), this right is pointless. Similarly, the second part of the formulation of this right, about ones being able to own property in association with others, starts to exist only when the economic development achieves such a high level that concepts of corporations, societies, associations or companies emerge (in the Western world it seems to have happened along with the development of the Roman Empire). However, recall for example (it is an example, I do not debate here historical facts) that the collapse of civilisation after the fall of Rome was so consequential that economics came back to a very primitive stage with no monetary exchange for goods. Then, although a Roman person had this right in 2nd century CE, a Germanic lord in modern day France in seventh century CE did not, as this right did not provide him any means to live a decent life. Then, after the economic recovery, probably around 12–13th century, at least in regions like Northern Italy, this particular human right came back to existence.

To give one more example related to the universal human rights to autonomy: the particular human rights to freedom of thought, conscience and religion is grounded in the universal human right to autonomy and in certain social facts about the existence of religion, social oppression, etc. If there were no religion, there would be no right to freedom of religion. Let me now cite the art. 19 of UDHR: "Everyone has the right to freedom of opinion and expression; this right includes freedom to hold opinions without interference and to seek, receive and impart information and ideas through any media and regardless of frontiers".[45] One may imagine a sketch of argument in favour of the view that the above provision covers also a particular human right to the Internet access. Thanks to its rapid development, the Internet becomes a primary source of information, knowledge and an enabler for building links with others. Someone who has no access to the Internet is impaired in relation to those people who have access. This impairment is of such a level that without the Internet, it becomes extremely difficult to live a decent life, especially in comparison to others within the same society who enjoy such access. Therefore, the particular human right to Internet access emerges. It is grounded in any of two universal human rights: to autonomy (Internet enables shaping one's beliefs), and to liberty (Internet enables making choices in life), along with a given social, or civilisational, conditions.

The discussion on the human right to the Internet is a good point to address the problem of duties related to human rights. For instance, one can wonder whether state is obliged to provide everyone with the Internet access. If so, how? By subsidising Internet connections and handing smartphones to everyone, or perhaps by running a stated-owned not-for profit Internet service providing company? The issue of duties corresponding to rights is complicated and discussed in ethics.[46] I do

[45] Universal Declaration of Human Rights (1948), art. 19.

[46] Raz (1987); Griffin (2008), ch. 5.

not want to enter this debate in greater detail. Let me however notice a few issues concerning human rights and their corresponding duties. If A has a human right to X, it is not the case that state must provide X. Corresponding duties can be of different kinds, mentioned in Sect. 3.1 Hofheldian-based analysis of human rights already proves so. State can have a duty to refrain from certain actions, e.g. from infringement of the freedom of religion. State can have duty to undertake certain steps, for instance, enact laws regulating traffic that protect the right to live. As we see, the right to live does not trigger the duty that one is not killed by a state official, yet also other duties. And sometimes state has a duty to strive to a certain goal with no duty to provide particular instantiations of this goal. Notice the wording of article 2(1) of the International Covenant on Economic, Social and Cultural rights:

> Each State Party to the present Covenant undertakes to take steps, individually and through international assistance and co-operation, especially economic and technical, to the maximum of its available resources, with a view to achieving progressively the full realization of the rights recognized in the present Covenant by all appropriate means, including particularly the adoption of legislative measures.[47]

It is explicitly said that the duty of states is to undertake steps to achieve the full realisation of rights that are listed in this treaty. Therefore, if there is stated that every human has a right to X, the duty of state is not to provide X to every human being. Rather, the duty of state is to make all possible steps that enable every human being to achieve X.[48] To give an example and simultaneously come back to the human right to the Internet access that served as a beginning of these considerations: the duty of state that corresponds to this right is to undertake all possible steps to achieve the widest access to the Internet to everyone. However, if someone does not have access to the Internet, she cannot claim, both in legal and in moral terms, that state should provide it, if only the state fulfilled its general duty of enabling the Internet access. If the state fails to do so, that would be a basis for formulating different claims against the state.

Let me here refer to the idea of generations of human rights. It was proposed by a Czech-French jurist Karel Vašák.[49] Vašák distinguishes three generations of human rights. The first generation contains political rights and Vašák associates this generation with the value of liberty. They were first discovered and implicitly formulated as human rights. The human rights that are included in the first generation are rights like the right to life, the right to a fair trial, freedom of religion, etc. The second generation of human rights contains economic, social and cultural rights. Vašák identifies them with the value of equality. The human rights included in this generation are human rights like the right to free of charge elementary education, the right to basic social security, the right to work under certain level of conditions, etc. As we see, these rights can demand high costs to achieve them and it is this generation of rights where the notion of duty as taking all possible steps arises. The

[47] International Covenant on Economic, Social and Cultural rights (1976), art. 2(1):

[48] cf. with constitutional norms of similar character; cf. Gizbert-Studnicki and Grabowski (1997).

[49] Vašák (1977).

third generation of human rights, which is associated by Vašák with the value of solidarity, is quite unclear. It covers rights that at the moment of Vašák's analysis was progressive and not enacted in legally binding documents yet proposed and included in declarations that can be categorised as "soft law",[50] as Stockholm Declaration[51] or Rio Declaration.[52] Human rights that belong to the third generation are rights as "the right to a healthy and ecologically balanced environment, the right to peace, the right to ownership of the common heritage of mankind".[53] Human rights scholars see other rights in this generation like the right to self-determination, the right to economic and social development, the right to natural resources.[54] What differentiated the third generation is that they are collective, which means that they focus on groups rather than on individuals, and that their promotion can only be achieved on supra- or cross-state level as even a particular country's effort is not sufficient in delivering healthy and ecologically balanced environment.[55] Currently, there is an emerging debate on the existence of a fourth generation of human rights is. These rights are supposed to protect human beings in the digital environment related in particular to highly developing new technologies, like massive surveillance, that pose new threats to human functioning.[56]

I wanted to present the idea of (three) generations of human rights to demonstrate that the philosophical distinction on abstract, universal and more concrete, particular human rights, which I follow in this work, corresponds with a more juristic notion of (three) generations of human rights. By making use of the relation of metaphysical grounding I argued that particular human rights are metaphysically grounded in universal human rights and environmental and social facts. The basis of the idea of (three) generations of human rights is that at different times different types of human rights were recognised that were to serve the needs of particular times. Without the destruction of the natural environment that was a consequence of rapid industrialisation there would be no idea of protecting the environment and natural resources. Similarly, without the rapid development of new technologies that transform the way we live and the way our functioning can be threatened, there would be no current debate on the fourth generation of human rights.

Assume the correctness of the postulates in favour of the fourth generation of human rights. Here, the views on the existence of human rights of the fourth generation can be formulated by making use of the language of facts and grounding: the foundations of the human rights of the fourth generation are universal human rights and certain social or environmental facts about the development and impact of new technologies. It is that certain social or environmental facts about the

[50] Domaradzki et al. (2019), p. 425.

[51] Declaration of the United Nations Conference on the Human Environment (1972).

[52] Rio Declaration on Environment and Development (1992).

[53] Vašák (1977), p. 29.

[54] Domaradzki et al. (2019), p. 425.

[55] Domaradzki et al. (2019), p. 426.

[56] Soh et al. (2018).

development and impact of new technologies and universal human rights ground human rights of the fourth generation. One of the proposed rights of this generation is the right to maintain one's unique genetic code.[57] It is grounded in the fact that our genetic code can be changed and manipulated without our consent and that can have consequences for our functioning. It is grounded as well in the universal human right to liberty as one cannot have her genetic code modified without one's consent. I think that the human right to autonomy cannot here serve as the foundation among the universal human rights as it involves the protection of the lack of domination, including in the moral domain, of others. As such, the modification of genetic code can have an impact on one's autonomy, but does not have in every case—there can be many examples of the modifications of genetic code that have no impact on one's autonomy. I can propose a sketch of the framework of the argumentation in favour of some particular human right of the fourth generation: in order to propose a particular human rights of the fourth generation one should (1) demonstrate the traceability of such right from at least one universal human rights and (2) demonstrate concrete social or environmental facts that constitute the basis of the need of such a right.[58]

Summing up this whole section, I conclude that particular human rights are metaphysically grounded in universal human rights and environmental and social facts. It follows that universal human rights and environmental and social facts bring particular human rights into existence.

We can see that there are two entities among the facts that ground particular human rights. It means that, under Fine's distinction on full and partial grounding, universal human rights and environmental and social facts both fully ground particular human rights, while each of them partly grounds particular human rights.

---

[57] Stępniak (2019), p. 113.

[58] I am aware of the fact that I leave some problems related to human rights not answered, especially problems related to particular human rights that are most close to legal thinking about human rights as these are particular human rights that are enacted by legal documents. One of such problems is the problem of conflicts between human rights, which is a situation when two or more particular human rights cannot be simultaneously satisfied. Legal theory has developed frameworks to deal with similar problems, like balancing approach, balancing legal principles or legal values. However, even if from a strictly legal point of view human rights could be balanced against one another, this raises serious concerns from philosophical point of view on human rights. If human right are considered to always win against other rights or interests, what happens when it is another human right that is in a conflict? If human rights are inalienable and universal, how can they be balanced against one another? This becomes especially important when more and more moral rights are proposed to be human rights, which leads to a worry of many philosophers of human rights that there is an inflation of human rights (Cruft et al. 2015; Tasioulas 2015; Buchanan 2015, p. 245; Luban 2015, p. 264). There are certain solutions proposed, but mostly on the legal level (Smet, 2017), while the problem of conflicts between human rights on moral level (i.e. conflicts between human rights *per se*, rather than conflicts between legal norms enacting human rights) remains very problematic for the philosophy of human rights. Of course, my work cannot present in detail every problem of the philosophy of human rights. My work aims to present how human rights can be explained from the perspective of contemporary analytic metaphysics and as such, I focus on a more fundamental issue of the foundations of human rights in general and have to leave some points related to specific issues, like particular human rights.

Recall also the way in which metaphysical grounding is necessary—if grounding facts obtain and the grounding relation between them and grounded facts holds, grounded facts necessarily obtain. In the case of grounding of particular human rights it means that since particular human rights are metaphysically grounded in universal human rights and environmental and social facts, if some environmental and social facts start to obtain, some particular human rights corresponding to them necessarily start to obtain as well. The starting of obtaining of universal human rights can be skipped since they are universal in almost absolute sense (I will explore it later) and do not change as contingent environmental and social facts do. Therefore, humans have particular human rights just when the emergence of certain environmental and social facts reveals the need for protection a decent level of life in some specific area. In other words, if certain environmental and social facts emerge, necessarily some particular human right starts to exist.

One can wonder why just one of the grounding facts—either the set of universal human rights or of environmental and social facts is not sufficient to metaphysically entail particular human rights. In other words, the question is whether particular human rights are grounded only in one of those entities. In my view, only both ground particular human rights. Universal human rights are too abstract to ground the existence of various specific particular human rights. The right to free of charge elementary education cannot be metaphysically entailed solely by the universal human right to liberty without reference to any concrete conditions. If it were possible to metaphysically entail particular human rights out of universal human rights, we would know now all human rights that will be held in the future. But we do not know what, for instance, the rapid development of new technologies or climate changes will bring to human lives in 100 or 200 years. How can we know what particular human rights will we have then?

Nonetheless, environmental and social facts alone cannot metaphysically entail particular human rights as well. We do not have a right related to every circumstance described as social and environmental facts. Something more must be added as the fundament of human rights than just solely descriptive and contingent conditions of life. This is why universal human rights are necessary as the partial foundation of particular human rights. Tasioulas's notion of the foundations of human rights is of a similar character—he argues that we have human rights thanks to both having human dignity and the existence of human interests.[59] None of these fundaments could serve as the foundation of human rights on its own—there is no route from solely interests to rights, whereas human dignity is too abstract and vague to determine specific rights alone.

[59] Tasioulas (2011, 2013, 2015).

6.4 Grounding of Universal Human Rights

It was necessary to distinguish particular human rights and universal human rights to avoid problems with the universality of human rights. Yet, human rights in general are claimed to have their foundations in human dignity according to numerous international human rights documents[60] and many domestic constitutions.[61] The same is claimed by various philosophers of human rights.[62] I argued above that particular human rights are metaphysically grounded in universal human rights and in social and environmental facts. Nonetheless, if it turned out that universal human rights were grounded in human dignity, due to the transitivity of grounding (accepting Schaffer's contrastive treatment), particular human rights would be grounded in human dignity as well. Let me now discuss whether universal human rights are metaphysically grounded in human dignity.

As far as logical properties are concerned, universal human rights of course do not ground themselves (irreflexivity)—universal human rights do not hold on the basis of themselves but on the basis of a different, more fundamental entity. As for being asymmetric, if universal human rights are grounded in human dignity, human dignity is not simultaneously grounded in universal human rights. Human dignity does not hold due to universal human rights. The logical properties (irreflexivity and asymmetricality, I will discuss transitivity later) are thus satisfied.

More importantly, I believe that human dignity can metaphysically entail universal human rights and human dignity makes that universal human rights exist. Human dignity is the inherent worth of every human being. As a value associated with every human being, human dignity demands more practical realisation, just as I claimed in Sect. 3.2.3. This more practical realisation consists of human rights. Immediately, this more practical realisation consists of universal human rights. But since universal human rights partly ground particular human rights, this more practical realisation of human dignity consists mediately of particular human rights. In such a way human dignity metaphysically entails universal human rights—human dignity necessarily leads to (metaphysically entails) the existence of universal human rights. In other words, human dignity explains the existence of universal human rights. Human dignity has its normative, more concrete, consequences, which consists of universal human rights. If we have dignity, then liberty and security are necessary to live, at least, a decent life. Without security one's life is threatened, without liberty one cannot make choices and decide about one's life. By far, this is what is meant by practical realisation of human dignity. Looking from "another direction", universal human rights hold due to human dignity. The best way to understand this statement is that the relation holding between human dignity and universal human rights is metaphysical grounding. Universal human rights are metaphysically grounded in

---

[60] Universal Declaration of Human Rights (1948); Covenant on Civil and Political Rights (1966).

[61] (Basic Law for the Federal Republic of Germany (1949); Constitution of the Republic of Poland (1997).

[62] Piechowiak (1999); Tasioulas (2011, 2013, 2015).

human dignity. Human dignity and universal human rights are different entities and a reduction of universal human rights to human dignity has been proven as impossible. Even if universal human rights are quite abstract, they are still much more practical than a highly abstract idea of human dignity, for instance as reference points for legislators and acting agents. One should also not forget that the distinction of universal and particular human rights is necessary to maintain the universal character of human rights.

Some may wonder whether human dignity is sufficient as the foundation of universal human rights, especially whether other values shouldn't form the basis of human rights along with human dignity. Such values can be solidarity, reason, freedom, autonomy or liberty. Of course that depends on theoretical framework, but under the notion that I follow human dignity is the principal value and other values like especially autonomy and liberty have foundations in human dignity. It is clearly seen as these two values are mentioned in two of three universal human rights: the right to autonomy and the right to liberty. Notice however, that under other readings, like Kantian-analytic account, the relation would converse – autonomy and liberty would be the basis for dignity.

As for freedom, I think it's (best regarded as) a necessary condition of point of having human rights, rather than value as a foundation of human rights. Only a being that is free, so can act freely, can have some rights—the right to liberty or freedom of religion wouldn't make any sense if we were not able to choose among different things or think about our religious beliefs. Consider animals—it may be argued under the debate on animals rights that they have certain rights similar to human rights, like the right to life or the right not to be treated cruelly. But it's clear that they don't have the right to freedom of religion or the right to free choice of employment—they are not able to freely and rationally choose among such matters so such rights make no sense. As we see, freedom is a necessary pre-requisite of having (certain) rights, not a value being the foundation of these rights.

Concerning reason, as the ability to think in abstract and rational way, in one sense it's the analogical to freedom—it's a necessary condition of certain types of rights. Without being able to think rationally, some aspects of freedom of thought make no sense. But let me focus on a different aspect. Consider a being fully rational and fully free (to make sure it can also act, not only think). Will such being have human rights due to these values? The answer is not obvious, which on its own shows that the matter is not self-evident. And it's not only conceptual matter—consider Artificial Intelligence (AI) in strong sense, so a being that would be rational and would be able to choose different things (i.e. would be free). Will such an AI have (AI) rights solely on the basis of rationality and freedom? Those familiar with religious ideas or medieval philosophy can think about devil—under these areas of thought rational (much more than human) and free being. But devil is not discussed to be the holder of (devil) rights despite reason and freedom. This is in my view for the simple reason—it is (human) inherent worth that is the foundation of (human) rights, which we now is human dignity, not other values. Let me recall Załuski's framework for stating the moral view on human nature on the basis of possible types of natural tendencies. Perfect prudence (which is rationality) and egoism leads to moderately pessimistic notion of human nature while perfect prudence and malice (immorality) leads to extremely pessimistic notion.[63] As we can see, rationality on its own is not able to give even moderately optimistic notion of human nature, which would be able to make a claim about an inherent worth (dignity). This is why the question on AI's rights is not obvious—imagine fully rational, free but malicious, or even egoistic AI. Would we be eager to state that this AI has AI rights analogical to human rights? I don't think so. And the key reason for that is that to state one's inherent worth that can be the basis of rights we need to point to something morally good. Reason and freedom on their own are not enough, which is why I discuss human dignity and not other values as the foundation of human rights.

To conclude this part: universal human rights are metaphysically grounded in human dignity; human dignity is what grants the existence of universal human rights.

6.5 Grounding of Human Dignity

Human dignity is the inherent worth of every human being. It is a value and the fact that every human possesses dignity is a moral fact. The basic shared intuition is that human dignity exists due to something positive about human that can be labelled "human nature". In turn, evolutionary psychology claims that human nature is constituted by the tendency to cooperate, which consists of altruism and collaboration[64] or in a different formulation, by a narrow form of altruism and imperfect prudence, upon which the tendency to cooperate emerges.[65] Following the requirements of methodological naturalism, any conception of human dignity should be based on relevant, scientific facts, although human dignity does not have to be reduced to these facts. Following the rather dominant view of contemporary analytic metaphysics, moral facts depend in their existence on more basic, natural facts. Under these philosophical assumptions, my hypothesis is that human dignity ontologically depends on human nature. Human dignity cannot be reduced to human nature and, while it is true that human dignity supervenes on human nature, supervenience is too weak to express and explain the ontological dependence between human dignity and human nature. Let me scrutinise whether this dependence can be characterised as metaphysical grounding.

With respect to the logical properties, human dignity does not ground itself—it is not the case that human dignity holds because of human dignity (irreflexivity). If human dignity is grounded in human nature, it is required that human nature is not grounded in human dignity (asymmetricality). This seems right—evolutionary understood human nature does not exist because of human dignity. Evolutionary

[63] Załuski (2009), p. 14.
[64] Tomasello (2009).
[65] Załuski (2009).

understood human nature exists due to the genetic shape of our species. The logical properties of metaphysical grounding are satisfied.

The key issue is whether human dignity exists due to human nature. For evolutionary psychology human nature is constituted by the tendency to cooperate, formed by altruism and collaboration,[66] or in Załuski's conception narrow altruism and imperfect prudence, upon which the tendency to cooperate emerges.[67] Załuski explicitly draws moral conclusions from his conception of evolutionary seen human nature and claims that it is moderately optimistic.[68] Let me recall Załuski's framework (presented in detail in Sect. 3.3.3.1) on the moral conclusions drawn from human nature. Załuski argues that on the basis of possible answers concerning the dominant moral motive and the dominant mode of acting in human behaviour these are the following qualifications of human nature:

- *Extremely optimistic (1): human beings are genuinely moral and perfectly prudent.*
- *Extremely optimistic (2): human beings are genuinely moral and imperfectly prudent.*
- *Moderately optimistic (1): human beings are narrowly altruistic and perfectly prudent.*
- *Moderately optimistic (2): human beings are narrowly altruistic and imperfectly prudent.*
- *Moderately pessimistic (1): human beings are egoistic and imperfectly prudent.*
- *Moderately pessimistic (2): human beings are egoistic and perfectly prudent.*
- *Extremely pessimistic (1): human beings are malicious (immoral) and imperfectly prudent.*
- *Extremely pessimistic (2): human beings are malicious (immoral) and perfectly prudent.*[69]

Notice how moral conclusion changes on the basis of the hypothetical natural state of affairs about the dominant moral motive and the dominant mode of acting in human behaviour. The moral conclusions are different moral states of affairs; the one particular conclusion that describes the one particular state that actually obtains in our world is the moral fact (recall that facts are *obtaining* states of affairs). In turn, various hypothetical answers to the questions about humans' dominant moral motive and dominant mode of acting constitute the states of affairs concerning the natural, empirical sphere. The one that is true is an obtaining state of affair, and, what follows, is a natural fact. If our dominant moral motive was egoism and the dominant mode of acting was perfect prudence, the vision of human would be moderately pessimistic. If we had a tendency to behave maliciously and were imperfectly prudent, the vision of human would be extremely pessimistic. In turn, if we were

66 Tomasello (2009).

67 Załuski (2009).

68 Załuski (2009), p. 50.

69 Załuski (2009), p. 14.

genuinely moral i.e. had a tendency to act purely altruistically, and were perfectly rational, i.e. we did not prefer a lesser good now over a greater good in the future, the vision of human would be extremely optimistic. It follows from these considerations that the moral state of affairs depends on the natural state of affairs.

Evolutionary psychology demonstrates that human beings are narrowly altruistic and imperfectly prudent. This leads to the moderately optimistic vision of human nature. Tomasello, unlike Załuski, does not draw moral conclusions from his discussion of the notion of human nature, however, his notion also leads to positive, moderately optimistic vision of humans and their behaviour.

My claim is that under the framework followed in this work, this positive, moderately optimistic moral conclusion drawn from the discussion of human nature *is best interpreted as referring to* human dignity. In other words, the described obtaining moral state of affairs (moral fact) dependent on human nature *is* human dignity. Human dignity is the inherent worth of every human being. If the inherent worth of every human being is not an arbitrary, self-standing, primitive property it must have a certain basis. Under the classical notion of human dignity this basis is a perfection of being, under the Christian notion of human dignity this is being created as an image of God. Under the Kantian notion of human dignity this is the capability to establish moral norms, while under the Kantian-analytic notion this basis is formed by higher cognitive functions and ability to choose one's path in life. In turn, under the naturalistic reading of the basis of human dignity, this basis must consist of some natural, descriptive, empirically established natural facts. The adoption of evolutionary psychology allows us to identify these facts with human nature. The moral conclusion drawn from discussing human nature as an objectively existing state of affairs (fact) is that this nature is positive, moderately optimistic or simply good. In this way we reach human dignity which now is perceived as the moral fact dependent on its existence on human nature.[70] Following Hage's notion of values as abstractions of valuable things,[71] human dignity as a value is the abstraction of human nature. The existence of the value of human dignity is possible because of human nature. It means that evolutionary understood human nature is the foundation of human dignity. In other words, the existence of human nature necessarily leads to the existence of human dignity. In other terms, human nature metaphysically entails human dignity.[72] Therefore, human nature brings human dignity to existence. Human dignity holds in virtue of human nature. Thus, human dignity is metaphysically grounded in human nature. In such a way the existence of human dignity is explained due to its being metaphysically grounded in human nature. If one insists that the prohibition of instrumental treatment is an essential

[70] Let me notice that similar claims with using quite similar reasonings are developed within the natural law tradition, wherein what directly follows from human dignity goes up to human rights (cf. Crowe 2017).

[71] Hage (2016).

[72] Remember that the idea of metaphysical entailment does not mean an entailment of linguistic propositions but denotes a situation when a fact leads to the existence of another fact.

property of human dignity and not e.g. the consequence of having human dignity, I believe such a prohibition is also explainable in terms of evolutionary human nature—as human nature is positive, good and every human has a natural inclination to altruism and cooperation with others, no one can treat someone possessing such a nature in a purely instrumental way as an object. If someone is good in an innate way, I think it gives grounds for the way one should be treated.

Someone may wonder how it is possible that human dignity, which is a moral, normative fact is metaphysically grounded in human nature, which is a natural, descriptive fact.[73] In other words, how normative human dignity can exist in virtue of human nature. This problem does not occur in respect to the relation between particular human rights, universal human rights and human dignity. Particular human rights have among their grounds universal human rights and universal human rights are grounded solely in human dignity. Let me analyse this issue, which can be labelled the "possibility of normative grounding".[74]

6.5.1 How Human Dignity Can Be Grounded in Human Nature?

Pekka Vayrynen notices the problem of metaphysical grounding where the grounding fact is a descriptive fact and the grounded fact is a normative facts. He argues that in order for a descriptive fact to ground a normative fact, the descriptive fact must be of normative relevance. In other words, in order for a descriptive fact to be the foundation of a normative fact, the descriptive fact must have certain normative characteristics allowing it. But, as Vayrynen argues, this certain normative characteristics is actually a normative fact—if a fact has a normative relevance, it is simply a normative fact.[75] Consequently, no normative fact can be grounded solely (or using the theory of grounding language—fully) in descriptive fact. What is, however, possible is that a normative fact is grounded partly in a descriptive fact and fully in both a descriptive and a normative fact.

Fine seems to oppose Vayrynen's argumentation claiming that the normative relevance of a fact makes it a normative fact. Although Fine does not analyse the possibility of normative grounding, he explicitly enumerates certain following grounding relations:

(1) *The fact that the ball is red and round obtains in virtue of the fact that it is red and the fact that it is round;*

[73] Vayrynen (2013).

[74] Of course, no one denies that normative fact can ground another normative fact, this is out of the scope of this debate and the term "normative grounding".

[75] Vayrynen (2013).

(2) *The fact that the particle is accelerating obtains in virtue of the fact that it is being acted upon by some net positive force;*
(3) *The fact that his action is wrong obtains in virtue of the fact that it was done with the sole intention of causing harm.*[76]

For Fine these are intuitive examples of grounding relations. Fine claims that there are different kinds, or sub-classes, of metaphysical grounding related to different kinds of necessity that back each of the above examples, namely: metaphysical necessity, natural necessity and normative necessity.[77] As for the third example, which is interesting for this work, Fine claims that "(3) Necessarily, if the action was done with the intention of causing harm then it is wrong".[78] This is normative necessity, which according to Fine cannot be reduced to any other form of necessity. Fine does not further argue in favour of the possibility of normative grounding. Notice however that the fact that an action was done with the sole intention of causing harm is a descriptive fact—its description makes use of solely descriptive language. Let me also notice that we do not talk here about an act of causing harm—here some could indeed wonder whether "harm" is a purely descriptive term. However, the fact we discuss is the fact that an action was done with the sole *intention* of causing harm. No actual harm has to follow from this act. This is actually a mental fact concerning agent's attitude. There are no reasons not to regard it as a descriptive fact. The fact that an action was done with the sole intention of causing harm grounds the fact that the action is wrong. As we see, according to Fine's intuitive example of grounding, a descriptive fact grounds a normative fact. It appears that Fine would argue against Vayrynen's normative relevance argument and claim that descriptive fact can ground normative fact.[79]

One can also try to reconcile these two positions by claiming that descriptive fact must have some normative relevance in order to ground normative fact, yet this normative relevance does not necessarily make this fact to be normative fact.[80] This is Gizbert-Studnicki's solution for the problem of grounding legal facts, which are normative, in social facts, which are descriptive.[81] Gizbert-Studnicki argues that social facts, which ground legal facts, have normative relevance, however, this

---

[76] Fine (2012a), p. 37.

[77] Fine (2012a), p. 38.

[78] Fine (2012a), p. 38.

[79] I do not follow here the debate between moral naturalism and moral non-naturalism as it seems to me that moral naturalists will reject the idea of normative grounding as for them moral facts, and by extension normative facts, are reduced to natural facts, so they are no distinct moral facts to be grounded in anything. It is rather non-naturalistic stance that can host such a debate.

[80] I think it depends on one's metaethical views. If one believes that normative facts, including of course moral facts, are very distinct from descriptive or natural facts, then Vayrynen's position would be convincing. However, if one believes that normative facts, including moral facts, depend on descriptive or natural facts, then intuitive Fine's example will raise no problems. I share the same intuition as Fine and believe that normative facts, including moral facts, depend on descriptive, often natural, facts.

[81] Gizbert-Studnicki (2021).

relevance does not mean that they are normative facts. Gizbert-Studnicki makes use of an example of the fact that a certain action causes harm.[82] This is a descriptive fact—we do not describe it by any normative language, or in other formulation of normativity, this fact does not encompass any reasons for action. However, no one would deny that the fact that a certain action causes harm is normatively relevant. Consequently, there are descriptive facts, which are normatively relevant, without making this fact normative fact. Gizbert-Studnicki argues that this happens for the social facts that ground legal facts. These social facts have normative relevance, which we know from both our individual intuitions and from platitudes (truisms) that form the folk theory of law. He argues that this does not fall into Hume's Guillotine:

> The claim that normative legal facts hold in virtue of non-normative social facts is not subject to Hume's Guillotine. The scheme of our reasoning about legal facts is as follows:
>
> (i) A social fact that S is the case obtains.
> (ii) Social facts of the type to which S belongs are normatively relevant and in particular ground a legal fact F.
> (iii) Therefore, a legal fact F obtains.[83]

As we can see, descriptive social facts are the only facts that ground legal facts, which are normative. Being normatively relevant does not automatically trigger being normative fact. The reasoning is correct as the relation between them has the form of metaphysical grounding and not of logical entailment.

Let me address the discussed among metaphysician issue of the unity of grounding. Fine's position is that there are rather generic grounding relations resp.: metaphysical, natural and normative grounding relations.[84] This is however not a widely shared view. Berker argues that grounding is a unitary explanatory relation that encompasses every kind of a relation wherein a fact that A holds in virtue of a fact

---

[82] Gizbert-Studnicki (2021), p. 436.

[83] Gizbert-Studnicki (2021), p. 437.

[84] Fine (2012a), pp. 39–40. Here is the exact citation, underlines are mine: *It is an interesting question whether each of these explanatory relations should be defined in terms of a single generic relation. Thus it might be thought that "metaphysical ground" should be defined by:*

> *the fact that A grounds the fact that B iff the fact that B obtains in*
>
> *virtue of the fact that A (in the generic sense) and it is a metaphysical*
>
> *necessity that if A then B,*
>
> *and similarly for the other cases, but with another modality in place of metaphysical necessity. It might, on the contrary, be thought that each basic modality should be associated with its "own" explanatory relation and that, rather than understanding the special explanatory relations in terms of the generic relation, we should understand the generic relation as some kind of "disjunction" of the special relations. If there is a generic notion here, it is that which connects the modality to the corresponding explanatory relationship and that has no status as an explanatory notion in its own right.*
>
> *I myself am inclined to favor the latter view.*

that B.[85] Berker that there is no specific, generic grounding in the normative domain and this relation is of the same kind as any other grounding relation. I think that Fine's distinction on three types of grounding relations is right only if one strongly distinguishes between metaphysical and normative domains. I agree that metaphysical and normative necessities can be of a different kind. Nonetheless, this does not mean that normative necessity and related normative grounding do not belong to metaphysics as the inquiry on what exists (and what are relations between that what exists according to the new approach on metaphysics called here "relational metaphysics"). Consequently, there is no reason not to regard normative grounding as a sub-class of metaphysical grounding relation (in the broad sense—in most general sense as discussed in this work), even if it is based on a different sort of necessity than metaphysical grounding (in the narrow sense—in Finean sense as in above citation) and natural grounding.

Coming back to the starting point of presenting the possibility of normative grounding, which is Fine's example on the action done with the sole intention of causing harm, someone may argue and wonder why it is that the fact that his action is wrong obtains in virtue of the fact that it was done with the sole intention of causing harm. In other words, why the fact that an action was done with the sole intention of causing harm can be and is the foundation of the fact that the action is wrong. If we put it in the form of an argument we have:

(1) The action was done with the sole intention of causing harm.
 Hence
(2) The action is wrong.

Someone may argue that there is a missing enthymematic premise and the argument should have a form:

(1) The action was done with the sole intention of causing harm.
 (1a) Any action done with the sole intention of causing harm is wrong.
 Hence
(2) The action is wrong.

Only then the conclusion (2) is entailed by the premises (1) and (1a) and the argument holds properly. In fact, this problem can be formulated as such: "why conducting an action with the sole intention of causing harm is wrong?". One response to this problem, based on the deontological position in ethics, is that it is self-evident why doing action with the sole intention of causing harm is wrong. Then, it is clear why there is no reason to uncover this premise—it is self-evident and, as such, the premise is omitted in order to guarantee informative and smooth communication. Yet, someone may still wonder about the justification of this premise. It can be said that an action done with the sole intention of causing harm is wrong because the intention to solely cause harm is wrong. Probably someone might wonder further about the justification of the claim that the intention to solely

[85] Berker (2018).

cause harm is wrong. One option is to claim that wonders are inconceivable—it is self-evident that the intention to solely cause harm is wrong. One cannot imagine concerns about why it is wrong, it simply is. Therefore, such a claim is self-evident. As it directly entails that an action done with the sole intention of causing harm is wrong, similarly, to maintain clarity and informativeness of one's claims it can be omitted in reasoning.[86]

Another way to argue in favour of premise (1a) is to provide a consequentialist justification. Perhaps it is that an action done with the sole intention of causing harm causes certain negative consequences, in particular someone's pain. Or perhaps (1a) is true as in general doing actions with the sole intention of causing harm leads to less good/less pleasure and/or more evil/more pain (this is rule utilitarianism). Obviously, this is not the place to discuss the debate between deontology and consequentialism or utilitarianism. What I wanted to present are different possibilities of maintaining the validity of reasoning.

However, a problem occurs. It appears that it is no longer true that simply:

(1) The action was done with the sole intention of causing harm.
Hence
(2) The action is wrong.

[86] Such a solution might be understood as not compliant with my general framework where I regard normative facts to have foundations in descriptive, natural facts. First of all, let me say that I do not intend this work to provide a full-fledge framework for meta-ethics or ethics. I follow methodological naturalism but reject ontological naturalism claiming that moral facts simply are natural facts. I do not argue against any kind of usage of conceptual analysis and do not oppose arguments that rely on it, like the above one concerning an intention of causing harm being self-evidently wrong. My position is that we should rely on discoveries of natural science in philosophical inquiries, but this of course can be done when it is possible, and it does not mean that we should never make use of other methods of thinking. Consequently, in general, I do not oppose arguments based on conceptual analysis. And notice that I consider in this chapter, including the above issue of why an act causing harm is wrong, different arguments for possible objections. My personal position is in line with the framework I propose – I think that the fact that the action is wrong is metaphysically grounded in the fact that it causes harm (actually, it is the same as in the third Fine's example). For me, the normative fact that the action is wrong has foundations in the descriptive fact that it causes harm. What I wanted to present, is the possible further clarification for someone who might oppose it. Moreover, I do not think that an argument saying that the intention to solely cause harm is wrong triggers the problem of inferring from the identical class to the same attribute mentioned by White (1956) while analysing Moore's argumentation for the naturalistic fallacy (1903). White noticed a problem with Moore's argumentation that goodness cannot be identified with any natural property. We remember White's objection (discussed in Sect. 4.2), for instance terms "man" and "featherless biped" denote the very same objects, however it is not that man is a featherless biped. But I do not claim that the term "(intent of) doing harm" is equivalent to the term "(being) wrong". There are other things than doing harm that are wrong, e.g. lying. Lying without an intention of doing harm is still wrong. The term "(being) wrong" is broader than the term "(intent of) doing harm". Moreover, I do not form a conclusion that (intent of) doing harm is wrong solely because what the first term denotes is always equivalent to what the second term denotes. My proposal for a hypothetical argument is that (intent of) doing harm makes an action wrong, which is more to say than a claim about the relation between the scopes of what these claims denote.

By enumerating final premises (I skip mediate premises from deontological example and follow rule utilitarianism from the consequentialist example, of course it could be done similarly as for act utilitarianism), it is either that:

(1) The action was done with the sole intention of causing harm.
AND
(1a*) Any action done with the sole intention of causing harm is wrong.
Hence
(2) The action is wrong.

Or it is that:

(1) The action was done with the sole intention of causing harm.
AND
(1a**) Doing actions with the sole intention of causing harm leads to less good/less pleasure and/or more evil/more pain (which is wrong).
Hence
(2) The action is wrong.

Each of these forms of reasoning can be formulated in terms of metaphysical grounding (of course provided one accepts that the premises and conclusions describe facts, including moral facts, providing one accepts the theory of metaphysical grounding, etc.):

(1) The fact that the action was done with the sole intention of causing harm.
AND
(1a*) The fact that any action done with the sole intention of causing harm is wrong.
metaphysically ground
(2) The fact that the action is wrong.
Or it is that:
(1) The fact that the action was done with the sole intention of causing harm.

AND
(1a**) The fact that doing any actions with the sole intention of causing harm leads to less good/less pleasure and/or more evil/more pain (which is wrong).
metaphysically ground

(2) The fact that the action is wrong.

Let me just notice that both (1a*) and (1a**) are normative facts—they are described by the usage of normative language. What happened is that it was revealed that actually it is not true that it is only the descriptive fact that the action was done with the sole intention of causing harm grounds the moral fact that the action is wrong. There is also a normative fact, either (1a*) or (1a**) that is necessary to ground (2). (1) partly grounds (2) while along with (1a*) or (1a**) it fully grounds (2).

This analysis was needed to illuminate the problem of normative grounding that is visible for the grounding relation between human dignity and human nature. What I argue for is that human dignity is metaphysically grounded in human nature (to be technically precise facts about human dignity are grounded in facts about human nature, e.g. the fact that every human being has human dignity is grounded in the fact that every human being has human nature, etc.). It is so because human nature consists of the tendency to cooperate or in Załuski's formulation of narrow altruism and imperfect prudence. Załuski explicitly claims that evolutionary account leads to a moderately optimistic vision of human nature. In other words, it leads to a positive, or simply good, vision of human. As such, it means that there is an inherent worth of human being. And since human dignity is an inherent worth of human being, human dignity has foundations in human nature. Looking from the metaphysical perspective: human dignity is metaphysically grounded in human nature. Nonetheless, I claim that the evolutionary account of human nature is descriptive. It is despite the fact that, taking Załuski's formulation, it makes use of terms like "altruism" or "prudence". Yet, as I presented in Sect. 3.3.3.1, these terms are understood in a purely descriptive way. So, the question is similar to the one on why the action done with the sole intention of causing harm is wrong: why altruism (although narrow) and prudence (although imperfect) as well as cooperation (following Tomasello's formulation) are actually good. Let me clarify it in the form of reasoning (for brevity I make use of Załuski's formulation):

(1) Human nature consists of narrow altruism and imperfect prudence.
(2) Human nature leads to the morally good vision of human being, which means there is an inherent worth of human being.
(3) Human dignity is an inherent worth of human being.
Hence
(4) Human dignity holds in virtue of human nature (i.e. human dignity is metaphysically grounded in human nature).

For someone it can be valid reasoning with no gaps. Yet, others can object by arguing why (2) holds. Let me discuss here this matter.

One possible answer is that it is obvious and self-evident that altruism, prudence or cooperation are good. Take altruism, which for kin altruism means that "an agent sustains high costs for the good of a relative without expecting the return of these costs in the future".[87] I believe that it is good to sustain high costs for someone (although a relative) without expecting to get a return. As Załuski argues, concerning non-relatives we have the tendency to behave altruistically if we expect that someone may reciprocate our help (reciprocal altruism). The reciprocal altruism is best illuminated in the reverse way: if we know someone will not reciprocate our help (i.e. will take advantage of our action), we have the tendency not to help him.[88] It is also rather not that we have the tendency to help those who may reciprocate our help *because* they may reciprocate our help. Yet, it is true that we do not have a tendency to help those who will not reciprocate our help *because* they will not reciprocate our

[87] Załuski (2009), p. 3.

[88] The question is to what extent this is a natural tendency and to what it is learnt during the process of socialisation, cf. Tomasello (2009), pp. 29–30, pp. 82–84.

help. As Załuski argues this is both rational in the game theory sense and explicable in terms of human evolution. Notice also the discussion here is about altruistic defined as helping someone when the helping agent sustains some costs of the help. We are not talking here about helping if we do not bear any costs—in such cases we have a natural propensity to help others. Not helping in such cases would be egoistic or even malicious but we do not have tendency to behave in such a way.

The question is whether reciprocal altruism is good. I think it boils down to the question on the motive of acting with reciprocal altruism—if someone helps someone else who may reciprocate the help *because of* the fact that person may reciprocate the help, I see nothing morally good in such action. But I also don't see anything morally wrong—it is perhaps prudent and morally neutral. However, this motivation of acting with altruism *because of* the fact that another person may reciprocate the help is not the case with reciprocal altruism discovered by evolutionary psychology—as it is a natural tendency we just tend to behave like this without conscience decision making. Notice also that it most very likely that reciprocal altruism is best understood in a slightly different way—we have a tendency not to help those that may take advantage of our help or conscientiously not help others with the tendency to help anyone else. I think such a tendency is good—being naturally inclined to help others is good.

Moreover, there is kin altruism, which is (moderately) good. One might object claiming that kin altruism is instrumental as it only aims to enhance one's genes. Indeed, such is the function of the kin altruism on the biological level, however whether something is good is the subject of the discussion on ethical level. In my view there are no reasons not to regard e.g. mother's love as not being good. Parental care or taking care for one's siblings or parents would be instrumental if performed for some certain goals (for instance I take care of my parents because I hope to receive their assets in inheritance). Such actions are indeed controversial to assess them as good. However, we are talking about care performed with no such goals, i.e. care for done as a goal in itself. In my view, this is clearly good. Consequently, our altruistic tendency can be considered as good.

Concerning (imperfect) prudence and from the deontological perspective, I do not see reasons to assess it in moral terms. Whether human beings discount utility over time can be viewed as wise or not, but not moral or immoral. In fact, Załuski himself seems to regard it in the same way as he puts emphasis on the level of altruism in classifying different possible forms of human nature. For instance malice (acting against others' interests with no benefit for oneself) and perfect prudence is regarded as extremely pessimistic, while genuine morality and imperfect prudence is considered extremely optimistic.[89] So, it is the level of altruism that leads to a certain classification of human nature. Evolutionary psychology proves that the tendencies that human beings have are narrow altruism and imperfect prudence. Since there is altruism, although narrow, the evolutionary vision of human being is moderately optimistic because of the fact that altruism is good.

---

[89] Załuski (2009), p. 14.

There is no need to repeat such considerations for Tomasello's account. To remind, by cooperation Tomasello means altruism, which consists of "one individual sacrificing in some way for another" and collaboration, which holds when "multiple individuals working together for mutual benefit".[90] My above considerations about altruism hold here as well. I also believe that collaboration seems to be able to be assessed as morally good. The fact that multiple individuals have the tendency to work together for mutual benefit is in my view a positive thing.[91] Therefore, this is why also Tomasello's account of evolutionary human nature leads to the positive vision of human being.

Another possible way of justifying that (2) holds could be presented in light of consequentialism. It seems to be true that narrow altruism and imperfect prudence lead to pleasure/good, or that in general behaving altruistically and prudently maximises pleasure/good. It is more evident for Tomasello's cooperation, especially collaboration: if multiple individuals work together for mutual benefit, by far this produces more pleasure/good for all of them. However, I have serious doubts about employing consequential justification to the claim that human nature is good. Notice that (2) must be of inherent worth, so that it can then be the foundation of human dignity, which is an inherent worth of every human being. The problem is whether consequential justification is not contradictory with the feature of worth being inherent. If the foundation of human dignity, which is human nature, is not good per se, but because of some consequences, it is rather not of inherent worth. Instead, its worth is triggered by certain consequences it leads to. It is not the aim of this work to debate various ethical theories or to deeply elaborate on a possible justification of human dignity on consequential grounds. Nonetheless, if someone argues that (2) requires justification, in my view it is rather deontological justification that can be properly employed.

Coming back to the reasoning presenting that human nature grounds human dignity, responding to the objection that (2) needs justification, the premise (2*) can be added:

(1) Human nature consists of narrow altruism and imperfect prudence.
(2) Human nature leads to the morally good vision of human being, which means there is an inherent worth of human being.
    (2*) Human nature is good.
(3) Human dignity is an inherent worth of human being.

Hence

[90] Tomasello (2009), p. XVII.

[91] Of course, this is not to say that every collaborative action is good and requires protection by human rights. My argument is that evolutionary understood human nature is good, thus it can be the foundation of human dignity. And then, human dignity has certain normative consequences, which are human rights. It is a general framework and I take perspective from metaphysical rather than ethical point of view. I don't claim that for instance having a natural tendency to cooperate entails the human right to protect this tendency—that would be an invalid derivation of a normative statement from a descriptive one.

(4) Human dignity holds in virtue of human nature (i.e. human dignity is metaphysically grounded in human nature).

Now, the reasoning is correct. However, irrespective of the character of (2), by far (2*) denotes a moral fact, namely the fact that human nature is good. Thus, it is no longer true that human dignity is grounded solely in human nature. Human dignity is grounded also in the fact that human nature is good. A key point is to what extent this is an argument against normative grounding, i.e. grounding relation holding between a descriptive and a normative fact. One can counter-argue that it is obvious and self-evident that altruism is good (which is the core of the argumentation in favour of (2*)) and as such does not really play an independent role in the facts that ground human dignity. Analogically, it is simply the fact that the action was done with the sole intention of causing harm that grounds the fact that the action is wrong. One can wonder why the action that was done with the sole intention of causing is wrong, but only to illuminate it further. However, the further analysis of why the action that was done with the sole intention of causing is wrong will not reveal any new facts that ground the fact that the action is wrong. Similarly, as for human nature and human dignity, one can further illuminate why human nature is good but no new facts that ground human dignity will be revealed.

Another possible objection might be that even if we state that human nature is good it is still too little to establish the key consequence of human dignity, namely the prohibition of solely instrumental treatment. I don't think such an objection is sound—my argumentation is of metaphysical, not ethical, kind and there is no gap between subsequent steps. However, some additional arguments may be given. For instance, it can be claimed that a being with good natural tendencies must have the possibility to be able to realise these tendencies in practice. Hence, this being cannot be treated only as a means, which is precisely the prohibition of solely instrumental treatment. Looking in a slightly different way: a being with good natural tendencies have the right to act according to these tendencies. What is necessary for such ability to act is the lack of instrumental treatment. A consequential argument can also be given: human nature constituted by the tendency to cooperate and altruism can lead to positive, good actions of cooperation and helping others, therefore a being having such nature cannot be treated solely as a means because such a treatment would diminish the level of goodness that may happen. In such a way we can pass from good natural tendencies (human nature) to the prohibition of solely instrumental treatment.

If one still maintains that it is also the fact that human nature is good that grounds human dignity along with human nature, there is another way of looking at the problem of normative grounding between human nature and human dignity. Then, it can be said that indeed human dignity is grounded both in human nature and in the fact that human nature is good. One of the facts that ground human dignity is a normative fact, so the problem of normative grounding disappears. However, it would follow that it is not solely human nature that is the foundation of human dignity, as it is also the fact that human nature is good that grounds human dignity. Is it really so problematic to the philosophy of human rights? I do not think so. It comes as a consequence of philosophical analysis but does not oppose any core intuition about the foundations of human rights, nor any wording of human rights law that reveals them. Notice also that it is still that human nature alone partly grounds human dignity. Only if one operates on the level of full grounding, one must claim that both human nature and the fact that human nature is good fully ground human dignity. Notice also that it is not the case that human nature ceases to be the foundation of human dignity. Human nature is still the foundation of human dignity, as it grounds it, only it is not the full foundation as the fact that human nature is good is another fact among the grounding facts.

Whether one needs more justification for (2) is in my view the matter of one's ethical and meta-ethical beliefs. For Fine, it is clear that it is only the fact that the action was done with the sole intention of causing harm that grounds the fact that the action is wrong. For others, it can demand much more clarification. The same applies to human nature grounding human dignity. My personal view is that (2) is obvious and thus, it is only human nature that grounds human dignity. However, I am aware of the possible disagreement in this regard and I presented other routes for the claim that human dignity is grounded both in human nature and in the fact that human nature is good.

This is also why I presented the debate on the autonomy of ethics, which is very useful in the proper and clear understanding of what does it mean that a normative, moral fact derives from or depends on a descriptive, natural fact. The proposition including the concept of human dignity is not logically entailed by the proposition including human nature. This is cut by the logical autonomy of ethics, formulated firstly by Hume and known as Hume's Guillotine.[92] Human dignity cannot be defined in terms of human nature. This is the semantic autonomy of ethics, formulated firstly by Moore.[93] However, I do not claim that the proposition including the concept of human dignity logically follows from the proposition about human nature, neither I define human dignity in terms of human nature. The crucial question of the debate on the autonomy of ethics is whether there is ontological autonomy—i.e. whether moral facts actually are natural facts. Nonetheless, I do not claim that human dignity in fact is human nature. I claim that human dignity depends in its existence on human nature, holds in virtue of human nature, or most precisely, that human dignity is metaphysically grounded in human nature. I believe that such a framework on the "is-"ought" problem is the proper one. A colloquial and unnuanced notion of "no ought from is" claiming that there cannot be any connection between normative and descriptive spheres is flawed. When we come back to the original Hume's paragraph after the discovery of the "is-"ought" problem, there is an often omitted part: "and at the same time that a reason should be given, for what seems altogether inconceivable, how this new relation can be a deduction from

[92] Hume (1739).

[93] Moore (1903). This is formulated within the framework of the debate on the autonomy of ethics. As I mentioned previously, Moore would rather say that it is also ontological autonomy, or more precisely, that semantic autonomy entails ontological autonomy.

others, which are entirely different from it".[94] Hume himself does not claim that there is an unbridgeable gap between the descriptive and the normative. He claims, and this is the first, most known, part of this famous paragraph, that descriptive propositions do not logically entail normative propositions. But then, in the above citation, he focuses on the fact that if someone argues on the normative issues on the basis of the descriptive ones, there should be a clear explanation of the relation connecting these two spheres.[95] And this is exactly what I attempt to do in this work—I argue that the relation between human nature and human dignity has the form of metaphysical grounding.

My position is thus methodologically naturalistic but ontologically non-naturalistic—I make use of the relevant scientific knowledge in trying to identify the foundations of human rights, however, I don't claim that human rights and human dignity are natural facts.

To sum up, human dignity is grounded in human nature, which is of descriptive character. Human nature is constituted by the tendency to cooperate under Tomasello's account or by narrow altruism and imperfect prudence under Załuski's account. These tendencies lead to the positive vision of human. They provide the basis for the claim that there is something inherently good in each of us, that humans have some worth. This "something inherently good" or "worth" is human dignity since human dignity is an inherent worth of every human being. The existence of human dignity has been explained by reference to its foundations—human nature. Human dignity is metaphysically entailed by human nature—human nature leads to the existence of human dignity. It means that human dignity is metaphysically grounded in human nature. We can look on this issue also from another "direction". Human dignity holds in virtue of human nature since human nature leads to the positive vision of human. The grounding of human dignity in human nature is objective—it is not a human evaluation, understood as a cognitive act of human mind. In turn, the grounding relation exists objectively, what remains up to human is to recognise it. Thus, human dignity is not merely an evaluation of human nature, it is an objectively existing moral fact.

6.6 Consequences of the Grounding Account

I have argued that the following grounding relations hold: particular human rights are grounded in universal human rights and environmental and social facts; universal human rights are grounded in human dignity; human dignity is grounded in human

[94] Hume (1739), p. 335.

[95] Notice that the claim on the total separation of the normative and descriptive spheres is the child of logical positivism, 200 years younger than Hume and rather widely rejected due to its strongest claims (Putnam, 2002). As Jerzy Stelmach argues, we should not schizophrenically firstly assume the total separation of "is" and "ought" and later try to overcome it (2013).

nature. Grounding has transitive character, but there are difficulties with transitivity of partial grounding. These difficulties have been solved by Schaffer who proposed the contrastive treatment.[96]

Up to universal human rights there is no problem with transitivity since all grounding relations are the relations of full grounding. Thus, universal human rights are metaphysically grounded in human nature, since universal human rights are grounded in human dignity and human dignity is grounded in human nature. It means that universal human rights hold in virtue of human nature. Thus, the reference to human nature can explain the existence of universal human rights. I believe it is a profound conclusion, which is drawn solely by means of the logical property—transitivity—of the relation of metaphysical grounding. No further proof is required to form the claim that universal human rights are grounded in human nature. Yet, some remarks can be given here: if human nature leads to the positive vision of human, human nature demands some rights for its protection. These rights are (universal) human rights. The optimistic notion of human, concluded from evolutionary theory, justifies the existence of inherent rights of every human being. These arguments are consistent with my approach. Nonetheless, the claim that universal human rights are metaphysically grounded in human nature can be formulated solely by means of the transitivity of metaphysical grounding.

I shall add, however, that the issue of grounding particular human rights in human nature raises difficulties. Particular human rights are grounded both in universal human rights and in environmental and social facts. Each of these categories of the grounding facts ground particular human rights only partly, only if taken together they ground them fully. The problem is that while universal human rights are grounded in human dignity and further in human nature, environmental and social facts are grounded neither in human dignity, nor in human nature. There is the problem with the transition from particular human rights to human dignity, and consequently, to human nature, by means of grounding. In fact, among metaphysicians the transitivity of partial grounding is debatable. Let me now briefly discuss this problem and then provide a solution.

Schaffer notices partial grounding is problematic as for its transitivity.[97] I have referred to Schaffer's remarks while analysing the problem of transitivity of supervenience between particular human rights and human dignity. However, Schaffer analysed the issue of transitivity for metaphysical grounding. According to Schaffer, since grounding is analogous to causation, counter-examples against transitivity of partial causation can be transformed into counter-examples against transitivity of partial grounding. If A is caused by B and C, and C is caused by D, it is not true that A is caused by D.[98] The same goes for grounding: if A is grounded in B and C, and C is grounded in D, it is not necessarily true that A is grounded in D.

[96] Schaffer (2012).

[97] Schaffer (2012); Bliss and Trogdon (2016).

[98] Schaffer (2012).

Nonetheless, Schaffer proposes a solution to maintain the transitive character of partial grounding. He argues in favour of the contrastive treatment of metaphysical grounding, similarly to the contrastive treatment of causation.[99] This contrastive treatment means that actually any grounding claim implicitly has a form: "The fact that φ rather than φ* grounds the fact that ψ rather than ψ*".[100] Consider an analogy to causation and assume that we explain why Bob was late for a train. Bob was late both because he left his home too late and because the train left the station earlier. He left his home too late because he slept too long. Under the non-contrastive notion of causality, the fact that he slept too long does not solely cause the fact that he was late for the train. But under the contrastive one, it does: it is the fact that he slept too long rather than the fact that he watched TV that caused the fact that left his home too late. It is the fact that he left his home too late rather than the fact that there were traffic jams that caused the fact that he was late on the train. As a result, it is the fact that he slept too long rather than other fact that caused the fact that he was late for the train. Schaffer's contrastive treatment of grounding is as follows:

> If the fact that φ rather than φ* grounds the fact that ψ rather than ψ*, and the fact that ψ rather than ψ* grounds the fact that ρ rather than ρ*, then the fact that φ rather than φ* grounds the fact that ρ rather than ρ*.[101]

In such a way, partial grounding remains transitive after a deeper exploration of the character of this relation. In my view, contrastive treatment cannot be applied to the problem of transitivity of supervenience between particular human rights and human dignity because supervenience has no explanatory force, unlike causality in the natural world and grounding in the metaphysical world. Thus, no contrastive treatment could be applied in supervenience.

Let me now move back to the transitivity in the foundations of human rights. The first option is to agree that partial grounding is not transitive. When A is grounded in B and C, and C is grounded in D, it is not the case that A is grounded in D. It is because of the fact that D cannot fully explain the existence of A. A cannot be metaphysically entailed solely by D, since B is also necessary as the ground of A. In our case, particular human rights are not grounded in human dignity, and further in human nature, since neither human dignity, nor human nature can solely explain the existence of particular human rights. The metaphysical explanation of particular human rights cannot refer solely to human dignity and human nature in terms of transitive metaphysical grounding. Yet, these problems emerging from the logical properties of the metaphysical relation are fully consistent with the analyses conducted in the philosophy of human rights. For instance, Tasioulas claims that human rights hold because of human dignity and human interests.[102] Human interests are highly similar to what I call environmental and social facts. Other

---

[99] Schaffer (2012), p. 130.

[100] Schaffer (2012), p. 130.

[101] Schaffer (2012), p. 132.

[102] Tasioulas (2011, 2013, 2015).

philosophers of human rights distinguish universal and concrete human rights.[103] While the first are fully universal in terms of time and space, the latter are their instantiations in more specific conditions. The contemporary philosophy of human rights agrees that particular, specific human rights cannot be fully justified or explained solely in terms of "human dignity", "moral autonomy", etc. Some other contingent circumstances must be added as the basis for concrete human rights. The lack of transitivity of partial grounding is compatible with it. The fact that particular human rights are not fully grounded in human dignity, and further in human nature, is compatible with the fact that particular human rights cannot have foundations only in human dignity, moral autonomy, human nature or any other entity that is the "main" fundament for human rights in one's theory. The consequences of the logical properties of metaphysical grounding is compatible with the analyses of the philosophy of human rights. This demonstrates the properness and usefulness of employing metaphysical tools in philosophy of human rights. Moreover, I believe that the properties of metaphysical grounding can provide a deeper, metaphysical explanation for the claims of philosophy of human rights about the lack of possibility of justifying particular human rights solely by human dignity, or other abstract entity. This justificatory impossibility holds because of the fact that these various abstract entities only partly ground particular human rights. And when these entities (e.g. universal human rights) are grounded in some other entities (e.g. human dignity, human nature), due to the fact that partial grounding is not transitive, these other entities do not ground particular human rights. These other entities cannot explain the existence of particular human rights.

Yet, I have mentioned Schaffer's proposal to resolve the problem of the lack of transitivity of partial grounding.[104] He argues that since grounding, as metaphysical explanation, is similar to causality, which is an explanation characteristic to empirical sciences, contrastive treatment developed in causality theories can be employed in grounding as well. Under contrastive treatment, it is claimed that it is rather A than A* that is grounded in B rather than in B*.[105] By extending it to the issue of transitivity, we reach the formula that if it is rather A than A* that is grounded in B rather than in B*, and C rather than C* is grounded in B rather than in B*, it is the case that A rather than A* is grounded in C rather than in C*.[106] The aim of contrastive treatment is to present a comparison with some other entities and to demonstrate which one of them actually grounds the debated entity. In case of particular human rights, by following the contrastive treatment we reach the claim: particular human rights rather than e.g. social rights are grounded in universal human rights rather than in e.g. positive legal facts. The final claim, after following the whole chain of contrastive grounding relations, is that particular human rights, rather than some other entities, are grounded in human dignity and further in human nature,

[103] Griffin (2008).

[104] Schaffer (2012).

[105] Schaffer (2012), p. 130.

[106] Schaffer (2012), p. 132.

rather than in some other entities. In this way, the transitivity of partial grounding is maintained and particular human rights can be grounded in human dignity, and finally, in human nature. The price for these claims about the foundations of particular human rights is the weakened notion of grounding and its transitivity. It can only be claimed that particular human rights are grounded in human dignity and then in human nature if other entities are added in order to contrast these claims.

In my view, although contrastive treatment allows to maintain the transitive character of grounding, the traditional view on the lack of transitivity of partial grounding is much more intelligible. In the theory of causality, contrastive treatment seems to be a non-majoritarian and non-orthodox position[107] so its extrapolating into grounding theory may also be controversial.[108] Therefore, if one does not follow the contrastive treatment, the chain of grounding relations between the entities in the foundations of human rights is weakened by the fact that only one of the entities that ground particular human rights—universal human rights—is further grounded in human dignity and then in human nature. In turn, environmental and social facts are not. Consequently, particular human rights are not grounded in human dignity, neither in human nature. There is no "pure" metaphysical grounding relation between them, yet there is such a grounding relation under contrastive treatment of metaphysical grounding.

Nonetheless, the lack of transitivity of partial grounding means that it cannot be said that particular human rights are grounded in human dignity or in human nature. But what is here meant as grounding is full grounding. I believe that since particular human rights are grounded both in environmental and social facts and in universal human rights, there are no difficulties with claiming that particular human rights are grounded in environmental and social facts as well as in facts that ground universal human rights: human dignity and then in human nature. As a result, it is the case that particular human rights are grounded in environmental and social facts and in human dignity, and then in environmental and social facts and in human nature. Still, particular human rights are not grounded solely in human dignity, nor in human nature. This is the position that I adhere. As we see, it is compatible with the above-mentioned claims of philosophy of human rights about the necessary role of some contingent circumstances in determining particular human rights.

By making use of metaphysical grounding it becomes transparent which entities are ontologically prior—which are more fundamental in relation to others. As it appears, human nature is more fundamental than human dignity and both kinds of human rights. Human dignity is more fundamental than universal human rights and particular human rights, while universal human rights and environmental and social facts are fundamental in relation to particular human rights. However, the fundamentality of environmental social facts in relation to universal human rights, human dignity and human nature and *vice versa* cannot be determined.

---

[107] Beebee and Menzies (2019).

[108] cf. Javier-Castellanos (2014).

Recall also the way in which grounding is considered to be necessary. When a particular grounding relation holds and the grounding fact holds, it is necessary that the grounded fact holds as well.[109] There is the necessary link between the existence of discussed entities and their grounds. This form of necessity is clearly seen in the example of particular human rights and their grounds (other entities like universal human rights, human dignity and human nature are universal and cannot start or cease to exist in "our world" so the necessary link is quite obvious; they are able not to exist only in a different world wherein e.g. human nature would be different or there would be no humans at all). Particular human rights are grounded in environmental and social facts and universal human rights. If some environmental and social facts occur, then necessarily some particular human rights begin to exist (universal human rights do not matter here since they are universal and cannot start to hold as they are fully universal). For instance, if further development of technologies brings a threat to our decent level of life (environmental and social facts), then necessarily, certain corresponding particular human rights will begin to hold in virtue of these development and universal human rights.

Notice that the ultimate, yet partial, foundation of human rights is human nature, which is innate (we are all born with evolutionary human nature), equal (we all have the same human nature), inalienable (we cannot transfer or restrict our human nature) and universal (all people have the same human nature). In fact, these are the properties of human rights and of human dignity,[110] which are also present in truisms about human rights. It means that human nature can be understood as the basis of human dignity and human rights. The properties of human dignity and human rights are explicable in light of their foundation, which is human nature. Human dignity is innate since it holds for every human being solely in virtue of being human, which consists of possessing human nature. The same goes for universal human rights—if one has human nature, one has human dignity and consequently universal human rights. It means that we are indeed *born* with dignity and rights as art. 1 of UDHR claims.[111] Particular human rights require also some specific circumstances to be materialised. Human dignity and human rights have the property of being equal. Under my proposal, they are equal since they are grounded for everyone in the same fundament, i.e. human nature, which is equally the same for every human being. Human dignity and human rights are inalienable as no one can transfer or limit them. That is true as well. Human dignity and human rights are metaphysically grounded in human nature, which is a very strong, objectively existing relation of metaphysical explanation. It cannot be undone or restricted due to some contingent circumstances. Of course, human rights can be violated but this is a different issue than being inalienable. Human dignity and human rights are universal—since human nature is universal, the same goes for what it grounds. All

---

[109] Correia (2005), p. 61.

[110] Vienna Declaration (1993); Piechowiak (1999, 2012).

[111] Universal Declaration of Human Rights (1948), art. 1.

the properties of human rights and human dignity are explicable in terms of their grounds—human nature.

One can wonder whether in fact human dignity is necessary as an intermediary point between human rights and human nature. Perhaps, we could get rid of so unclear in its conceptualisation human dignity and claim that human rights (universal human rights, to be precise) are immediately grounded in human nature. I don't think such a route is plausible. First, there is a strong belief (truism), supported by claims found in international legal documents on human rights as well as in many domestic constitutions saying that human dignity is the foundation of human rights. Speaking from the point of view of legal philosophy, if we can philosophically make sense of this claim I believe there are no strong reasons to disregard it and say that it's only a fictional, legal provision that does not correspond to any extra-legal reality. There is also an argument from moral, social and political benefits of human rights—it's the belief that (1) human dignity exists and (2) that it's the basis of human rights that was the legal, moral and philosophical source of the promotion and respect of human rights that we witness since the second half of 20th century. One could say that deeply philosophically it's all a fiction and human rights have foundations in something different than human dignity. But I believe there must be very strong arguments in favour of such a view. Philosophy, especially legal philosophy, has its moral consequences that should be taken into consideration.

Up to this point a sceptic might say that I just keep to the legal text and am unwilling to approve any claim contrary to the literal meaning of law. But from the point of view of this book, metaphysical in its view on the foundations of human rights, there is one key argument against the claim that human rights are grounded directly in human nature—human nature is not able to determine human rights. Making use of the language used above, human nature cannot metaphysically entail human rights—altruistic and cooperative tendencies, which are good, are not enough to determine the scope and content of human rights. Bear in mind that my argument is not a straightforward derivation of the fact that e.g. altruistic behaviours should be protected from the fact that altruism is a natural human tendency. That would be an invalid derivation of "ought" from "is". How a right, even so abstract like one of three universal human rights, could be directly derived from a tendency, even though this tendency is good? Nonetheless, the tendency to cooperate and to altruism, due to being good and inherent, can be the basis of inherent worth of every human being, and that is human dignity. In turn, human dignity requires more practical realisation and protection by rights, and these are human rights. As we can see (it was discussed in much more details above, human dignity metaphysically entails universal human rights. It means that universal human rights are grounded in human dignity. We are not able to trace an analogical path from human nature to human rights, which means that there is no direct grounding relation between human nature and human rights (there is indirect or mediate grounding using analytic metaphysics terminology though as discussed above). This is the main reason from the metaphysical sphere why human dignity is in fact the direct foundation of human rights, while human nature is an the indirect one due to the transitive character of metaphysical grounding. As we can see, looking metaphysically, human dignity can be retained as a meaningful and not merely rhetorical or fictional foundation of human rights.[112]

Notice also that grounding is hyperintensional—grounding facts necessarily ground grounded facts but these two are not identical. In our case, human dignity is not identical to human nature, universal human rights are identical to human dignity and particular human rights are not identical to universal human rights and environmental and social facts. This is another argument to claim that human dignity and human rights are something different than natural facts, like human nature. So, even if someone would like to propose naturalistic, in its ontological variant, reading of the foundations of human rights, still, the distinction between human rights, human dignity and their natural facts basis can be maintained.

The most significant consequence of employing metaphysical grounding and determining the grounding relations between entities in the philosophy of human rights is that grounding has strong explanatory force. We can claim that particular human rights hold *because of* environmental and social facts and universal human rights, universal human rights hold *because of* human dignity and that human dignity holds *because of* human nature. The existence of human rights and human dignity is explained due to employing metaphysical grounding. Metaphysical grounding is able to express ontological dependences in the foundations of human rights. Moreover, it is able to explain them.

6.7 Conclusions

The relations between entities debated in this work have the form of metaphysical grounding. Particular human rights are grounded in environmental and social facts and universal human rights. Universal human rights are grounded in human dignity. Human dignity is grounded in human nature. Due to the transitive character of grounding, universal human rights are grounded in human nature. Similarly, transitivity makes the case that particular human rights are grounded in environmental and social facts and in human dignity, and further in human nature. The grounding entities constitute the foundations for the grounded entities: human nature is the foundation for human dignity, for universal human rights and partly for particular human rights. Similarly, human dignity is the foundation of universal human rights and partly of particular human rights. Ontological dependence between entities researched by the philosophy of human rights is expressed and explained in terms of metaphysical grounding. Since grounding involves a certain kind of explanation, the existence of human rights and human dignity is explained (in the metaphysical way). Therefore, the key claim of the naturalistic approach: "human rights are moral

[112]But bear in mind that I offer here a metaphysical perspective, if someone takes more ethical or political one, like Sangiovanni (2017), the conclusion may differ but I wouldn't regard it as a contradiction, rather a different perspective starting from different methods of analysis.

rights possessed by all humans simply in virtue of their humanity or being human"[113] can be understood in the following way: "human rights are moral rights that are metaphysically grounded in human nature". In turn, the claims from legal documents, like from the Preamble of the International Covenant on Civil and Political Rights claiming human rights *derive* from human dignity, or from the Polish Constitution claiming that human dignity is a *source of* human rights, should be read as saying that human rights are metaphysically grounded in human dignity.

References

Audi P (2012a) A clarification and defense of the notion of grounding. In: Correia F, Schnieder B (eds) Metaphysical grounding: understanding the structure of reality. CUP, Cambridge, pp 101–121

Audi P (2012b) Grounding: toward a theory of the in-virtue-of relation. J Philosophy 109:685–711

Beebee H, Menzies P (2019) Counterfactual theories of causation. The Stanford Encyclopedia of Philosophy (Winter 2019 Edition). https://plato.stanford.edu/archives/win2019/entries/causation-counterfactual/

Berker S (2018) The unity of grounding. Mind 127:729–777

Berto F, Nolan D (2021) Hyperintensionality. The Stanford Encyclopedia of Philosophy (Summer 2021 Edition). https://plato.stanford.edu/archives/sum2021/entries/hyperintensionality/

Bliss R, Trogdon K (2016) Metaphysical grounding. The Stanford Encyclopedia of Philosophy (Winter 2016 Edition). https://plato.stanford.edu/archives/win2016/entries/grounding/

Buchanan A (2015) Why international legal human rights. In: Cruft R, Renzo M, Liao SM (eds) Philosophical foundations of human rights. OUP, Oxford, pp 244–262

Chilovi S, Pavlakos G (2019) Law-determination as grounding: a common grounding framework for jurisprudence. Legal Theory 25:53–76

Correia F (2005) Existential dependence and cognate notions. Philosophia Verlag, Munich

Correia F, Schnieder B (2012) Grounding: an opinionated introduction. In: Correia F, Schnieder B (eds) Metaphysical grounding: understanding the structure of reality. Cambridge University Press, Cambridge, pp 1–36

Crowe J (2017) Metaphysical foundations of natural law theories. In: Duke G, George RP (eds) The Cambridge companion to natural law jurisprudence. Cambridge University Press, Cambridge, pp 76–102

Cruft R, Liao SM, Renzo M (2015) Philosophical foundations of human rights: an overview. In: Cruft R, Liao SM, Renzo M (eds) Philosophical foundations of human rights. OUP, Oxford, pp 1–44

Dasgupta S (2014) On the plurality of grounds. Philosophers' Imprint 14:1-28

Domaradzki S, Khvostova M, Pupovac D (2019) Karel Vasak's generations of right and the contemporary human rights discourse. Human Rights Rev 20:423–443

Fine K (1994a) Essence and modality. Philos Perspect 8:1–16

Fine K (1994b) Senses of essence. In: Sinnott-Armstrong W, Raffman D, Asher N (eds) Modality, morality and belief. Essays in Honor of Ruth Barcan Marcus. Cambridge University Press, Cambridge, pp 53–73

Fine K (2001) The question of realism. Philos Imprint 1:1–30

Fine K (2010) Some Puzzles of ground. Notre Dame J Formal Logic 51:97–118

[113] Griffin (2008), p. 2; Tasioulas (2011), p. 27.

Fine K (2012a) Guide to ground. In: Correia F, Schnieder B (eds) Metaphysical grounding: understanding the structure of reality. Cambridge University Press, Cambridge, pp 37–88

Fine K (2012b) The pure logic of ground. Rev Symbolic Logic 5:1–25

Gizbert-Studnicki T (2015) Metafizyka Pozytywizmu Prawniczego. Principia 61:19–40

Gizbert-Studnicki T (2016) The social sources thesis, metaphysics and metaphilosophy. In: Banaś P, Dyrda A, Gizbert Studnicki T (eds) Metaphilosophy of law. Hart Publishing, Oxford, pp 121–146

Gizbert-Studnicki T (2021) Social facts and legal facts: Perils of Hume's Guillotine. In: Spaak T, Mindus P (eds) The Cambridge companion to legal positivism. Cambridge University Press, Cambridge, pp 419–442

Gizbert-Studnicki T, Grabowski A (1997) Normy Programowe w Konstytucji. In: Trzciński J (ed) Charakter i Struktura Norm Konstytucji Wydawnictwo Sejmowe. Warszawa, pp 95–113

Gizbert-Studnicki T, Dyrda A, Grabowski A (2016) Metodologiczne Dychotomie: krytyka pozytywistycznych teorii prawa. Wolters Kluwer, Warszawa

Greenberg M (2014) How facts make law. Legal Theory 10:157–198

Griffin J (2008) On human rights. Oxford University Press, Oxford

Hage J (2016) Facts, values and norms. In: Taekema S, van Klink V, de Been W (eds) Facts and norms in law. Edward Elgar, Cheltenham, pp 23–49

Hume D (1739) A treatise of human nature. John Noon, London

Javier-Castellanos A (2014) Some challenges to a contrastive treatment of grounding thought. J Philosophy 3:184–192

Leary S (2017) Non-naturalism and normative necessities. In: Shaffer-Landau R (ed) Oxford studies in metaethics, vol 12. OUP, Oxford, pp 76–105

Luban D (2015) Human rights pragmatism and human dignity. In: Cruft R, Liao SM, Renzo M (eds) Philosophical foundations of human rights. OUP, Oxford, pp 263–278

Mazurkiewicz S (2019a) Review of Marek Piechowiak Plato's conception of justice and the question of human dignity Sophia. Int J Philos Tradit 59:177–179

Mazurkiewicz S (2019b) Legal positivism social source thesis and metaphysical grounding: employing metaphysical grounding based on metaphysical laws. Archiwum Filozofii Prawa i Filozofii Społecznej 20:5–19

McKeon M (2021) Logical consequence. The Internet Encyclopedia of Philosophy. https://iep.utm.edu/logcon/#SH2a

Miller D (2012) Grounding human rights. Crit Rev Int Soc Polit Philos 15:407–427

Moore GE (1903) Principia Ethica. Cambridge University Press, New York

Piechowiak M (1999) Filozofia Praw Człowieka. Prawa Człowieka w świetle ich Międzynarodowej Ochrony. Towarzystwo Naukowe KUL, Lublin

Piechowiak M (2012) Godność w Karcie Praw Podstawowych Unii Europejskiej: Destrukcja Uniwersalnego Paradygmatu Ujęcia Podstaw Praw Człowieka? Themis Polska Nova 2(1): 126–146

Plunkett D (2012) A positivist route for explaining how. Facts Make Law Legal Theory 18:139–207

Putnam H (2002) The collapse of fact/value dichotomy and other essays. Harvard University Press, Harvard-London

Raz J (1987) On the nature of rights. Mind 93:194–214

Rodriguez-Pereyra G (2015) Grounding is not a strict order. J Am Philos Assoc 1:517–534

Rosen G (2010) Metaphysical dependence: grounding and reduction. In: Hale B, Hoffmann A (eds) Modality: metaphysics, logic, and epistemology. OUP, Oxford, pp 109–135

Rosen G (2015) Real definition. Anal Philos 56:189–209

Rosen G (2017a) Metaphysical relations in metaethics. In: McPherson T, Plunkett D (eds) The Routledge handbook of metaethics. Talyor and Francis, New York, pp 151–169

Rosen G (2017b) What is a moral law? In: Schaffer-Landau R (ed) Oxford studies in metaethics, vol 12. OUP, Oxford, pp 135–159

Sangiovanni A (2017) Humanity without dignity: moral equality, respect and human rights. Harvard University Press, Harvard

Schaffer J (2009) On what grounds what. In: Manley D, Chalmers D, Wassrerman R (eds) Metametaphysics: new essays on the foundations of ontology. OUP, Oxford, pp 347–383
Schaffer J (2010) Monism: the priority of the whole. Philos Rev 119:31–76
Schaffer J (2012) Grounding, transitivity, and contrastivity. In: Correia F, Schnieder B (eds) Metaphysical grounding: understanding the structure of reality. Cambridge University Press, Cambridge, pp 122–138
Schaffer J (2017) Laws for metaphysical explanation. Philos Iss 27:302–321
Shapiro S (2011) Legality. Harvard University Press, Cambridge
Smet S (2017) Resolving conflicts between human rights: the Judge's Dilemma. Routledge, London, New York
Soh C, Connolly D, Nam S (2018) Time for a Fourth Generation of Human Rights? From Disruption to Transformation? Linking Technology and Human Rights for Sustainable Development, United Nations Research Institute for Social Development. https://www.unrisd.org/TechAndHumanRights-Soh-et-al
Stelmach J (2013) Błąd Naturalistyczny i Antynaruralistyczny w Dyskursie Normatywnym. In: Brożek A, Brożek B, Stelmach J (eds) Fenomen Normatywności. Copernicus Centre Press, Kraków
Stępniak K (2019) Koncepcja Jurydyzacji Czwartej Generacji Praw Człowieka w Międzynarodowym Systemie Ochrony. Przegląd Sejmowy 151:97–121
Tarski A (1936) O Pojęciu Wynikania Logicznego Przegląd Filozoficzny 39:58–68
Tasioulas J (2011) On the nature of human rights. In: Ernst G, Heilinger JC (eds) The philosophy of human rights: contemporary controversies. De Gruyter, Berlin, pp 17–59
Tasioulas J (2013) Human dignity and the foundations of human rights. In: McCrdudden C (ed) Understanding human dignity. OUP, Oxford, pp 291–312
Tasioulas J (2015) On the foundations of human rights. In: Cruft R, Liao SM, Renzo M (eds) Philosophical foundations of human rights. OUP, Oxford, pp 45–70
Tomasello M (2009) Why we cooperate? A Boston Review Book, Cambridge, London
Vašák K (1977) Human rights: a thirty-year struggle: the sustained efforts to give force of law to the universal declaration of human rights I UNESCO. Courier 11:29–32
Vayrynen P (2013) Grounding and normative explanation. Proc Aristot Soc 87:155–178
White M (1956) Towards Reunion in philosophy. Harvard University Press, Harvard
Załuski W (2009) Evolutionary theory and legal philosophy. Edward Elgar, Cheltenham

Chapter 7
Problems, Objections and Consequences

In this part, I would like to refer to potential problems and objections that can be posed to my proposal of explanation and justification of human rights. Some of them are already present in the philosophy of human rights and are posed against theories that may look similar to my proposal. Others are worth mentioning and referring to even they have not been so far formulated. Then, in this chapter, I would like to present theoretical and methodological consequences of my account of the foundations of human rights. Lastly, final conclusions will be formulated.

7.1 Explanation, Justification, Understanding

The employment of metaphysical grounding provides the explanation of entities researched by the philosophy of human rights, as well as the relations in which these entities stand to each other. Yet, someone may argue that the aim of the philosophy of human rights is not the explanation of human rights or human dignity in this sense, but rather its aim is their justification. Moreover, one may also point out that I have already criticised some theories of human rights that by far aimed to justify human rights and not to explain them.[1] If what I present in this work is only the explanation of human rights, and explanation and justification are two distinct kinds of things, such a critique would indeed be sound. Up to this moment, I deliberately used the terms "explanation" and "justification" interchangeably. In the following part of this work I will explore in greater detail what these terms mean, whether they are distinct, how are they related, and how it affects the explanation of foundations of human rights based on metaphysical grounding. Lastly, I will also introduce the concept of understanding and discuss whether my proposal for explaining or justifying human rights leads to their better understanding.

[1] Like Griffin (2008).

S. Mazurkiewicz, *Grounding Human Rights in Human Nature*, Law and Philosophy Library 141, https://doi.org/10.1007/978-3-031-30734-8_7

7.1.1 Explanation

The clear debate on the concept of explanation is to be found in the domain of philosophy of science, where the discussion on explanation emerged around mid-20th century. The Deductive-Nomological model described by Hempel and Oppenheim is the first elaborated idea on the explanation in science.[2] According to the Deductive-Nomological model, explanation in science consists of: (1) explanandum—a sentence about the phenomenon which is explained, (2) explanans—the class of sentences accounting for explaining the explanandum.[3] An explanation of a phenomenon has a form of deductive argument wherein the explanandum logically follows from the explanans.[4] The nomological part is that the explanans must contain some general "law of nature", which is the basis for the interference of the explanandum.[5] Since this model refers to explanation in empirical sciences, like physics, Hempel later formulated the Inductive-Statistical model wherein instead of general laws of nature, there are statistical regularities that form the explanans.[6] This model covers the explanation from social sciences.

The main problem of both Deductive-Nomological and Inductive-Statistical models is that they cover situations formally meeting the criteria of a given model, yet these situations are irrelevant from the point of view of a given law of nature. Consider the following example:

(L) All males who take birth control pills regularly fail to get pregnant;
(K) John Jones is a male who has been taking birth control pills regularly;
(E) John Jones fails to get pregnant.[7]

Even though the deduction is correct, the cause for the fact that John fails to be pregnant is not the fact that he regularly takes birth control pills. Rather, it is the fact that he is a male. So, the reference to such a fact does not provide explanation. As a result, other models of explanation has been proposed.[8] Salmon constructed the Causal-Mechanic model in which the emphasis is put on finding the cause of the phenomena that is going to be explained.[9] Another conception of explanation is Van Fraasen's development of the classical, Hempel's, account. Van Fraasen emphasises that the key issue of explanation is to answer the question "why"?[10] He argues that the view that explanation is the relation only between fact and theory is insufficient.

---

[2] Hempel (1942, 1965); Hempel (Oppenheim 1948).
[3] Hempel (Oppenheim 1948).
[4] Woodward (2019).
[5] Woodward (2019).
[6] Hempel (1965).
[7] Salmon (1971), p. 34.
[8] Janik (2019).
[9] Salmon (1984, 1998).
[10] Van Fraassen (1980).

Context is the third essential part of an adequate model of explanation.[11] Another conception of explanation is Kitcher's unificatory model focused on the need of providing unified image of the world on the basis of many premises.[12]

Bartosz Janik distinguishes two versions of explanation: the weak one and the strong one. Under the weak version, explanation consists of providing logical reasoning where the explanandum follows from a general law and initial conditions.[13] In turn, under the strong version, explanation consists of providing logical reasoning where the explanandum follows from a general law and initial conditions *and* of demonstrating that the given general law describes the mechanism generating the explanandum.[14] The general law is formulated as a conditional sentence. The weak version can be useful in some sense, after all, we know something more if we are able to present that a proposition describing a phenomenon logically follows from some law and initial conditions. Yet, the full explanation is given only if we also know why it happens.

To sum up, explanation according to the philosophy of science relates to explaining hypotheses about facts by providing general laws.

It seems, however, that the metaphysicians debating the relation of metaphysical grounding do not have in mind the concept of explanation as it is discussed by philosophers of science. Instead, they understand explanation in a much more basic way. Anne-Sofie Maurin claims that in case of the metaphysicians' notion of metaphysical explanation:

> Most seem to agree, it is an explanation which accounts for the nature and/or existence of something with reference to something else on which the first thing non-causally and synchronically depends. Something which somehow (again, non-causally and synchronically) determines or makes the second thing exist and be the way it is.[15]

As we see, there is neither reference to hypotheses, nor to general laws that are to be provided. Rather, in order to metaphysically explain something one needs to show what determines this thing, or makes that it exists. Maurin gives central examples of such explanations:

i. *Singleton-Socrates exists because Socrates exists.*
ii. *Socrates exists because a certain bundling of tropes exists.*
iii. *Wisdom exists because the class of all wise things exists.*[16]

Let me focus on the first example. Singleton-Socrates exists because Socrates exists. The explanation of the existence of Singleton-Socrates is provided by showing what is its foundation, here it is that Socrates exists. Notice there is neither reference to any hypotheses, nor to any general law as explanation according to philosophers of

[11] Van Fraassen (1980), p. 156.
[12] Kitcher (1989).
[13] Janik (2019), p. 22.
[14] Janik (2019), p. 22.
[15] Maurin (2019), p. 1574.
[16] Maurin (2019), p. 1575.

science would require. Metaphysical explanation is about showing why something holds. No other requirements are needed. Some could argue that this is because metaphysicians did not wonder about this issue and adopted a very intuitive and basic notion of explanation. Perhaps, before the beginning of the debate in the philosophy of science, scientists also did not have a very clarified notion of explanation. Next, someone could argue that there is a deeper structure in metaphysical explanation or perhaps that there are some general laws, e.g. metaphysical laws, that back metaphysical explanations.[17] Nonetheless, I believe that the current notion of metaphysical explanation is correct: it involves showing why something exists. If one tries to explain the existence of e.g. moral facts, one presents what makes that they exist, for instance, one argues that there are certain descriptive facts that make that moral facts exist. Or, in a slightly different formulation one may claim that the whole structure provides explanation.

One can wonder whether metaphysical explanation, and metaphysical grounding, can be regarded in terms of the same conditions as discussed in philosophy of science for scientific explanation, namely: to explain X one needs to demonstrate general laws and initial conditions (week version in Janik's terms) and the mechanism generating X in order to satisfy strong version of explanation in Janik's terms. Such a discussion is absent among metaphysicians discussing grounding and explanation who seem to believe but it can be here addressed. I think that the role of initial conditions is played by the grounding facts (i.e. the facts that ground certain grounded fact, let me call it here X)—they must be exist so that the fact that is grounded (i.e. X) can exist. As for the general law, some might argue that it is the relation of metaphysical grounding. Metaphysical grounding would be regarded as a general law, here in metaphysical domain, such that the sentence about the existence of X is entailed by the sentence describing general conditions and the sentence describing grounding as a general law. However, grounding is a general relation of metaphysics as a whole, while the model of explanation described by reference to work done in the philosophy of science refers to general laws, but in a given case. Such a general law is e.g. the first law of thermodynamics or Newton's second law—they are general as they refer to all particular cases within their fields, but not universal in the meaning they can explain every possible situation. If grounding was considered as a general law, it would mean that e.g. legal facts are explained by social facts (initial conditions) and metaphysical grounding as general law. But this is not sufficient explanation, grounding can be (and in my view it actually is) the relation between social facts and legal facts but it is not the general law holding between them. What gives explanation of why social facts ground legal facts is the elaboration on the Social Source Thesis, social practice, etc. but none of these is a general law as defined in philosophy of science. Another possibility for adopting in metaphysics the model of explanation based on the model from the philosophy of science would be to try to find some general laws. In fact, this is followed by already

[17] Cf. Leary (2017); Schaffer (2017).

mentioned works on metaphysical laws,[18] however its propositions are controversial. For instance, in some domains such laws perhaps could be found. But what would be the general law providing explanation for the claim that moral facts are grounded in natural facts (assuming this claim is correct)? The same can be said for the claim that mental facts are grounded in the facts about one's neuro-physical state of brain.

On the other hand, in spite of above mentioned difficulties, there remains the intuition that in metaphysics in order to explain a fact (let's say A), one must give its foundations (for instance the fact that grounds this fact (let's say B) and provide justification for the claim why its foundations explain the existence of B. I agree that a bare claim that "A is grounded in B" is not sufficient for explanation, but if it is accompanied with elaboration on why and how it happens, it meets the criteria of explanation in metaphysics. Probably, the model of explanation in metaphysics is different from the model of explanation in natural science discussed in the philosophy of science and an extrapolation of the latter to metaphysics is not adequate.

This is why it is widely believed by the proponents of metaphysical grounding, that metaphysical grounding involves metaphysical explanation as grounding is the relation that shows that a fact exists in virtue of another fact. Since metaphysical explanation involves showing what determines or makes that a thing exists, metaphysical grounding is a correct tool for such an exercise as its usage can demonstrate that a fact makes that another fact exists. Therefore, by presenting what facts ground a given fact, the existence of this fact is explained. As a result, metaphysical grounding involves or provides (metaphysical) explanation. Another, subsidiary argument for explanatory force of grounding is that it has the same logical properties as explanation.[19] Some grounding theorists claim rather that the grounding is a relation backing explanation, not that it itself provides explanation.[20] If we recall the problem of why the grounding holds, this is the reason for the position that rejects the majoritarian view on the primitive nature of grounding and argues that it is backed by metaphysical laws which are analogical to laws of nature.[21] These laws provide the explanation for the holding of metaphysical grounding, just like causal laws provide the explanation in the strong sense in scientific explanation in empirical sciences. I adhere to the majoritarian position in the primitive character of metaphysical grounding. In my view, grounding itself provides explanation (of course along with the justification that it holds between certain facts, I do not speak here about a bare claim that A is grounded in B). So, what is necessary is to demonstrate *how* and *why* a fact is grounded in another fact. If it is done, I believe that metaphysical grounding provides explanation.

Let me come back to the issue of the foundations of human rights. I argued that particular human rights are grounded in environmental and social facts and universal

[18] Leary (2017); Schaffer (2017).

[19] Fine (1995).

[20] Audi (2012); Bliss and Trogdon (2016).

[21] Leary (2017); Schaffer (2017).

human rights, universal human rights are grounded in human dignity and that human dignity is grounded in human nature. Each of these grounding relations provides explanation of the existence of each of the grounded facts.

If someone insists on following the model of explanation developed in the philosophy of science, I might try to formulate such general laws: "the level of inherent human worth depends on the level of moral assessment of human nature"—for instance, if human nature were evil, human dignity and an inherent worth of every human being would not exist. In turn, if human nature were perfect (i. a. fully altruistic, fully rational in game theory sense, etc.), human dignity would consist of an inherent *perfection* of every human being, not only inherent worth. Another one might be: "values require more concrete realisation"—such a general law could be formulated as a general law between human dignity and universal human rights. Another one could be: "concrete moral facts depend on more general moral facts and some specific circumstances"—such a general law could be formulated as a general law between particular human rights and universal human rights and social and environmental facts. I am sceptical for proposing such general laws. First, as mentioned a few paragraphs above, I do not think the extrapolation of the model of explanation developed in the philosophy of science for natural sciences to metaphysics is adequate. Second, I believe that each of the claims proposed above as general laws is true. But they are not true as general laws, they are true as arguments formulated in philosophical inquiry. Third, I do not think that proposing a category of general laws in metaphysics is correct if the same facts can be explained without postulating such a category (by showing why and how e.g. particular human rights are grounded in universal human rights and social and environmental facts). Fourth, general laws in metaphysics would require the same (or very similar) properties as general laws in science and I doubt that even if general laws in metaphysics can be formulated, they would have all these properties.

Therefore, I believe that referring to general laws is not required and my proposal of explanation of human rights and human dignity is methodologically correct. This happens because it was presented what makes that the grounded facts exist—these are grounding facts in each of these relations. In such a way, explanation follows the employment of metaphysical grounding. I believe that my claims on grounding relations holding between debated entities are covered by the claims on *why* and *how* these grounding relations occur. I do not provide a bare claim, e.g. that human dignity is grounded in human nature, rather I also present how it happens. Thus, under Janik's distinctions, the explanation of human rights presented here counts not only as their explanation in the weak sense but also in the strong sense, assuming explanation in metaphysics does not require providing general laws and instead of initial conditions there are mentioned the grounding facts.

7.1.2 *Justification*

While the concept of explanation is the matter of philosophy of science and metaphysics, the concept of justification is debated mostly in ethics and epistemology. Justification consists of giving reasons, either reasons for actions in ethics, or reasons for beliefs in epistemology (Alvarez 2017). Justification is of normative character, whereas explanation is of descriptive nature. What I mean is that justification consists of giving reasons for something, while explanation is about explaining why something happens with no moral adherence. The difference lies in the functions of justification and explanation. The difference between justification and explanation is clearly seen in an example concerning an immoral action. Imagine Bob walking down a street and scratching random cars with a knife. His action is explainable by his anger, frustration, lost job and hatred of society. Yet, there are no good reasons for him to scratch cars. His action is explainable but not justifiable.

However, my claim is that when we think of a concept or an entity which is good, there is no so strong distinction between justification and explanation. Take for instance Griffin's normative agency.[22] All human beings have normative agency because of being able to decide about one's lives, because of making choices and developing one's life. Is it more justification or rather explanation of normative agency? Of course, by explanation I do not mean a scientific explanation on the basis of causal laws, but rather metaphysical one on the basis of metaphysical inquiry. Is it more about giving reasons for normative agency or about finding grounds for it? The fact that we can truly wonder about it leads to the idea that in case of concepts or entities that are good, the distinction on justification and explanation is not so strong, or even collapses.

In my opinion, the strong distinction of justification and explanation has roots in the strong separation of natural and ethical spheres, which is a product of positivism and then of neo-positivism. If the method of thinking in empirical sciences and in other spheres, like ethics, is different, then explanation and justification are different too. If what truly exists are only natural facts, and metaphysics must be cut off, explanation as used in empirical science has nothing to do with ways of thinking in metaphysics or ethics. Yet, my view on the relation between natural sphere and metaphysics is totally different. I believe that the moral sphere depends on the natural sphere. In case of human rights and human dignity, which are moral entities, they are metaphysically grounded in human nature understood as a natural fact discovered by evolutionary psychology. There is the strong connection between the moral realm and the natural world. Methodological naturalisation, which I follow, is the framework presenting how to think about foundations of entities discussed by philosophy like e.g. human rights and human dignity. Therefore, explanation and justification are not so far from one another. My claim is that in case of foundations of human rights, the explanation of human rights can simultaneously serve as their justification.

---

[22] Griffin (2008).

7.1.3 Justification of Human Rights by Their Metaphysical Explanation

Particular human rights hold both in virtue of environmental and social facts, and in virtue of universal human rights. Universal human rights exist in virtue of human dignity and eventually in virtue of human nature. Thanks to that, particular human rights are finally (partly) grounded in human nature. This is the explanation of human rights. I believe that since human rights exist, no further reasons are needed in order to justify them. Human rights are objectively existing entities (moral facts). Therefore, no further reasons are required. If legal facts objectively exist, e.g. as institutional, artificial facts, I do not have to give reasons in order to persuade someone that they exist. The same goes for human rights. Or in another formulation: the explanation of human rights serves also as their justification. In my view, the grounds of human rights are also the reasons for human rights. The claim that particular human rights hold because of environmental and social facts and universal human rights gives reasons for particular human rights. These reasons are both on epistemic and ethical levels: we have reasons to believe in the existence of human rights as well as reasons to act on their basis. For instance, the particular right to free elementary education holds due to the fact that the basic knowledge about the world is necessary to live a decent life and due to the universal human right to liberty. This is the justification of the human right to free elementary education. Similarly, the claim that we all have universal human rights because of having human dignity, which demands its more practical realisation, is also the justification for universal human rights. No further, additional reasons need to be given in order to justify human rights. Therefore, I claim that the explanation of human rights proposed in this work constitutes also the justification for human rights.

7.1.4 Understanding

The dichotomy explanation/justification is absent in case of foundations of human rights. Another concept worth mentioning is the concept of understanding. While explanation involves an objective state of affairs wherein a phenomenon is explained, the concept of understanding denotes rather a subjective mental, cognitive state of an individual.[23] The concept of understanding is meant as a development of the problems concerning the concept of explanation. The main one is that even if a phenomenon is explained according to the Deductive-Nomological model, it may happen that no better understanding of the functioning of the world follows from this explanation for an individual.[24] In analytic epistemology, two positions about the

[23] Brożek (2016); Janik (2019), p. 26.

[24] Brożek (2016); Janik (2019).

concept of understanding are distinguished.[25] For the first one, understanding is defined by the reference to the concept of explanation.[26] For the second, understanding involves cognitive actions of an individual, mainly mental manipulations of a given phenomenon.[27] The main difference is that under the first notion, one needs to already know the explanation of a phenomenon, while for the second notion, one can understand some reality without having a prior (I do not mean here *a priori* knowledge) knowledge about its scientific explanation.[28] Similarly to the concept of explanation, Janik distinguishes between weak and strong versions of understanding. Under the weak version of understanding, "understanding of an issue P by X in the context K increases when there occurs a change of the epistemic situation of X, which is about an increase of the informational content of beliefs held by X as for P".[29] Under the strong version of understanding, all the properties of the weak notion are maintained, and additionally, "an increase of the informational content of beliefs held by X as for P leads to the fact that X can answer more question concerning P, which are generated by K, or can undertake actions in relation to P required by K".[30] Janik introduces also the concept of full understanding, in which X is able to answer all questions concerning P or undertake all the required actions in relation to P.[31] As we see, for him understanding is about the cognitive situation of an individual. I also believe that his notion of understanding, in any of his versions, fits not only to understanding of natural world phenomena, but also to those phenomena that cannot be explained by empirical sciences.

Janik demonstrates interesting connections between various versions of the concepts of explanation and understanding.[32] He claims that the strong notion of explanation entails the weak version of explanation and that the strong version of understanding entails the weak version of understanding. More interestingly, he argues that the weak notion of explanation entails the weak notion of understanding (the strong notion does so as well). Yet, it is not necessarily true that explanation of both kinds, entails understanding in the strong or full version.[33] It may happen, but it does not have to. It is the consequences of taking understanding to be a subjective act of an individual.

In the case of human rights, following Janik's claims, the explanation of human rights (no matter weak or strong—I believe it is strong explanation) entails understanding of human rights in the weak sense. It means that there is an increase in the informational content of beliefs about foundations of human rights. I believe it is

[25] Kelp (2015); Janik (2019), p. 32.
[26] Hempel (1965); Salmon (1984).
[27] De Regt (2009); Wilkenfeld (2013).
[28] Janik (2019), p. 33.
[29] Janik (2019), p. 36.
[30] Janik (2019), p. 36.
[31] Janik (2019), p. 36.
[32] Janik (2019), pp. 38–39.
[33] Janik (2019), pp. 38–39.

true, the informational content of beliefs about the grounds of human rights, about the relation between human rights and their foundations, increases along with accepting my explanation of human rights. I also believe that the explanation of human rights proposed in this work leads to understanding of human rights, and especially their foundations, in the strong sense. I think that more questions about the foundations of human rights can be answered on the basis of the increased informational content of beliefs of an individual. Some examples of such questions are: what are the foundations of human rights? What are the foundations of human dignity? Are there any relevant natural facts for human rights? What is the relation between human rights and their foundations? Therefore, in the case of the relation between the strong explanation of human rights (which serves also as their justification) and understanding of human rights, the strong explanation of human rights entails the strong understanding of human rights. Does it also entail the third among Janik's notions, which is the full understanding? Full understanding involves being able to answer all questions, in case of understanding of human rights, questions about human rights and their foundations. It is quite difficult to assess whether I have left any possible question unanswered, or unable to be answered consequently on the basis of my claims. I leave this matter to the reader's assessment.

7.2 Objection of Essentialism and Foundationalism

Human rights are explained, justified and their foundations are understandable. There are however some objections that I would like to refer to and assess to what extent they are sound. The first one is an objection that is often present in works on the philosophy of human rights. This is the objection of essentialism and foundationalism. Tasioulas, who agrees with this objection, characterises it in the following way:

> Foundationalism, which elaborates erroneously on the bare orthodox thesis that human rights have objective grounds, comes in both meta-ethical and normative versions. Meta-ethical foundationalists offer defective accounts of what objectivity is, how it is secured, or the nature of its implications. One example is the naturalist thesis that the objective grounding of human rights consists in their being logically derivable exclusively from an array of value-neutral facts about human nature or a metaphysical human essence.[34]

Tasioulas denies the plausibility of foundationalism in the normative version as he argues that human rights can have foundations in values common to every human.[35] Yet, he believes that the any justification of human rights that falls under meta-ethical version is not proper. His description of the objection of foundationalism is based on the "is"-"ought" problem. However, notice how he immediately regards that the only possible relation between human rights and facts about human nature or

[34] Tasioulas (2015), p. 45.

[35] Tasioulas (2015), p. 46.

metaphysical human essence is logical entailment (to be precise: relation between sentences about human rights and sentences about facts about human nature or metaphysical human essence). It seems to be aimed primarily against Gewirth's proposal for justification of human rights. I agree that these, descriptive concepts (or more precisely, sentences in which they are used) cannot logically entail the concept of human nature (more precisely, sentence using this concept). But on the basis of the framework known as the autonomy of ethics (Sect. 4.2), this is only the logical autonomy of ethics, or in this case, of human rights. I have argued that there can hold other, metaphysical, relations between human rights and their foundations, like supervenience and metaphysical grounding. They do not fall under the Hume's Guillotine and as for them, Tasioulas's objection of foundationalism is not sound.

Another part of the objection is that neither natural facts about human nature, nor metaphysically conceived essence of human, can constitute the fundament of human rights. It is also related to the "is"-"ought" problem in foundations of human rights as these are descriptive entities, yet it demands separate analysis since one of my key claims is that evolutionary understood human nature is the ultimate foundation of human rights. This objection can be called the objection of essentialism since it is based on a more general philosophical claim that there is nothing like "human essence". Tasioulas follows in this respect critical remarks to the way of justification of human rights formulated by Richard Rorty.[36] Rorty claims that there is no such entity as human essence or ahistorical, universal human nature and the proper question to ask is not "what is our nature" but "what can we make for ourselves?".[37] His idea is than essentialists projects in philosophy, like Plato's or Kant's have failed and since there is no human essence or human nature, no moral conclusions can be drawn from these non-existent entities. Moreover, essentialists' claims lead to utopian thinking and ascribing moral worth only to some part of human beings. Perhaps as for metaphysically understood essence of human, this objection is sound. This lies beyond the scope of this work. Nonetheless, claims of contemporary empirical sciences proved by scientific, experimental evidence, for instance of evolutionary psychology falsified the claim that there is no such thing as human nature. In fact, evolutionary psychology claims that there is a set of basic, innate tendencies that constitute our nature. These tendencies are different than basic, innate tendencies of other species. Evolutionary understood human nature is universal as every human being has the same basic, innate tendencies. Assuming that we mean the time of the existence of *homo sapiens sapiens* (circa 0.2 million years), it is also ahistorical. Notice that evolutionary understood human nature has been discovered by use of the scientific method and is backed by experiments. Following methodological naturalism, the claims of evolutionary psychology must be taken seriously and all philosophical claims must be consistent with them.

---

[36] Rorty (1993).

[37] Rorty (1993), p. 115.

However, the objection of foundationalism and essentialism can be also read in a different way: it may happen that there is human essence or human nature, yet nothing for human rights follows from it. This reading is based on the claim about the dichotomy on normative and descriptive spheres. Even though there is some human nature or human essence, normative human rights cannot be derived from it. It could be sound as for my proposal for foundations of human rights had I claimed that the propositions about human rights either are logically entailed by the propositions about human nature, or that human rights can be reduced to human nature, or lastly, that human nature causally triggers human rights. The first option—logical entailment as the relation between sentences about human rights and sentences about their descriptive fundament—is not what I claim. My argumentation is not that since human nature is constituted by the tendencies to collaborate and to behave altruistically, we *should* collaborate and behave altruistically. Next, a claim could be that the obligation that we should collaborate and behave altruistically can be transformed into obligations of human rights. Yet, this would be an example of an improper derivation of "ought" from "is". I do not also claim that human rights are reducible to human nature. Moreover, my proposition of regarding the foundations of human rights is about *metaphysical grounding* of human rights, not *causing* of human rights by human nature. My argumentations is not that in fact human rights *are* the tendency to collaborate and to behave altruistically, or that these tendencies causally trigger (I mean here causality) human rights. All of these hypothetical ways of justification of human rights fall under improper derivation of "ought" from "is". In turn, my argumentation is of a different kind. I claim that human nature metaphysically grounds human dignity and then, due to the transitive character of grounding, human nature metaphysically grounds universal human rights, and partly grounds particular human rights. Human rights are not natural facts and they are other entities that both human dignity and human nature. Notice also that I do not claim that particular human rights are fully grounded in human nature, which would mean that every single specific human rights could be explained by its being grounded in the basic, evolutionary tendencies we have. I believe that some other contingent facts—environmental and social facts—are required to explain them, so my proposal is not a "bare orthodox thesis" as in Tasioulas's formulation of the objection of foundationalism (2015, p. 45).

Let me also compare my proposal with Daniel Dennett's naturalistic views and his drawing of conclusions from (biological) evolution in wider spheres of thought than just biology.[38] Dennett is an adherent of the so-called universal Darwinism, which is the claim that evolution occurs in many others spheres than just the biological one. Evolution in biology is understood as the change in the proportions of biological characteristics in a population over time that is a result of variations.[39] Dennett believes that the analogical mechanism occurs beyond biology, in widely understood culture, giving rise to cultural evolution. It should be clearly noted that

[38]Dennett (2017).

[39]Millstein (2019).

evolution is not merely a change, it is a change based on the specific mechanism of natural selection, which by definition has no concrete aim. The existence of cultural evolution is controversial, and Dennett is the proponent of the controversial claim even among the adherents of the cultural evolution, which is that the basic unit of cultural selection is meme.[40] Meme is meant to be an analogue of gene in biology and it is the most basic unit that includes information. Memes are different from those who transmit them, which are humans.[41] These are very controversial claims, and in my view they have little or even no empirical justification.[42] Someone might argue that actually evolutionary psychology itself falls into the category of universal Darwinism as it tries to explain something different from biology in evolutionary terms, namely the human mental sphere. First, I do not think that the mental sphere is so distinct from the biological sphere that the extension of evolutionary methods is implausible. Second, it should be noted that evolutionary psychology is a wide current of thinking and there may be found claims that have little or no empirical evidence and the so-called objection of "just so stories" can be sound.[43] According to this objection, in evolutionary psychology, claims about what we are now (e.g. what mental capabilities we have) are tried to be given *post hoc* via some stories on how our ancestors lived or could live, but there is no clear (empirical) evidence for that.[44] We can dig bones from the grounds but we cannot dig the way our ancestors lived and thought 0.5 million years ago. Consequently, what is meant as explanation does not have a form of proper explanation according to natural science, but has a form of looking for some sort of making sense of some mental phenomena that exists now in terms of some peculiar circumstances that are hypothesised to exist in the long past. As such, it has a form of reasoning from the conclusion on the existence of some human mental phenomena to premises on some social circumstances that are proposed to have existed many years ago. From logical point of view, such a reasoning can be invalid, as there can be many premises justifying the same conclusion, for instance, there can be many types of hypothetical social conditions that could give rise to the same mental phenomena that we all have now.

Notice however that I do not refer to any such works. I refer to Tomasello's empirical comparative studies on young human infants and young chimpanzees and to Załuski's studies based on others' empirical studies and evolutionary game theory. This is what I mean by evolutionary psychology and I believe that its claims are methodologically correct as there is given empirical evidence that can be falsified (Załuski's game theory has nothing to do with "just so stories" as well). This is the difference from the works where the objection of "just so stories" can be sound as

[40] Żywiczyński (2019), p. 180.

[41] Dennett (2017).

[42] Perhaps, they even cannot be proved or falsified, which triggers concerns about their methodological status.

[43] Lewontin (1976a, b); Gould (1978); Richardson (2007); cf. Hubalek (2020).

[44] Lewontin (1976a, b); Gould (1978); Richardson (2007); cf. Hubalek (2020).

such works rather do not give empirical evidence for the claims that are aimed to explain some human mental characteristics but only propose some scenarios on how humans could live in the long past. Moreover, the methodological validity of what I refer to in this work as evolutionary psychology is also seen by the limitations of its claims. It is stated the evolution to modern man stopped circa 0.2 million years ago and our mental capabilities did not change from that time. The change that we can observe in human history comes from cultural factors (but not in the meaning of cultural evolution) and not from evolutionary factors. However, the cultural change is possible due to certain human innate mental capabilities that evolved during the course of evolution to the modern man, namely due to the tendency to cooperate (altruism and collaboration) or in Załuski's formulation narrow altruism and imperfect prudence. So, for instance, the building of irrigation systems in ancient Egypt and Babylon was enabled by our capability to cooperate to achieve common bigger goals, but someone made a rational decision to start irrigation works in the valleys of big rivers. Dennett would rather claim that there was a specific irrigation meme that spread by some means of natural selection, but this is by far now what is proposed in the works on evolutionary psychology that I refer to.

If human rights are concerned, Dennett's-like argument would be that human rights exist because they are passed through memes as societies that believe in them thrive, prosper and unintentionally spread them.[45] This is a totally different claim than mine, which is that, looking from the perspective of methodological naturalism and by adopting contemporary relational metaphysics, human rights are metaphysically grounded in human dignity, which in turn, is metaphysically grounded in human nature.

Therefore, my approach does not require adopting such radical and controversial claims as Dennett's ones but is based on much more moderate and acceptable views. Moreover, what I argue in this work does not presuppose any view on the existence of cultural evolution.

To conclude, I believe that the objection of foundationalism and essentialism is not sound in relation to my proposal of regarding the foundations of human rights. I have presented how relevant scientific knowledge, which consists of the evolutionary notion of human nature, can be helpful in understanding the foundations of human rights. I have also demonstrated that the "is"-"ought" problem in the grounds of human rights requires much more nuanced reading. There are some relations (supervenience, metaphysical grounding) that hold between human rights and their descriptive foundations that do not fall under Hume's Guillotine. One of them, metaphysical grounding, has explanatory force and is able to explanatorily connect human rights and their grounds, partly constituted also by human nature.

---

[45] Interestingly, the contemporary rise of China can challenge such a Dennett's-like claim, but this is not the place to discuss modern geopolitics.

7.3 A Worse Part of Our Nature

I have argued that human nature according to evolutionary psychology leads to a positive (optimistic) vision of human, which consequently gives grounds for human dignity. The evolutionary positive vision of human is explicitly claimed in Załuski's conception of human natureand as I think it also follows from Tomasello's notion.[46] Yet, we all know that humans sometimes do not collaborate and do not behave altruistically. Human beings can do and sometimes do immoral things. If these wrong deeds are not related to our evolutionary nature, no challenge to my claims arises. Notwithstanding, some evolutionary thinkers claim that some of the immoral acts have roots in the natural tendencies that constitute human nature.[47] For instance, racism seems to have roots in narrow altruism.[48] We have the natural tendency to help only our close relatives and those that may reciprocate our help if we must sustain costs of the altruistic help (if however no costs are sustained, the tendency is to help everyone, cf. Tomasello's and others experiments discussed in Sect. 3.3.3.1). Other groups, with whom one do not feel connection, are "naturally" likely to be excluded from such an altruistic help.[49] Załuski's second book on evolutionary theory is aimed to cover this, "wrong", part of human and explore how it affects the general claim on the positive evolutionary vision of human.[50]

Załuski analyses various forms of wrong, immoral tendencies and behaviour and wonders on their evolutionary sources, as well as on how they affect his earlier claims on the optimistic evolutionary vision of human.[51]

The first among the analysed tendencies is egoism. Załuski does not follow a common idea that egoism is a primitive feeling. He distinguishes three kinds of egoism, based on different sources. The first one is cognitively based egoism, which means that an individual overestimates one's "reality" over the "reality" of others.[52] This sort of egoism is close to the term of egocentrism. The second kind of egoism is instinct-based egoism. It consists of "excessive manifestation of biological instincts of self-preservation and reproduction".[53] It leads to evolutionary motivated hedonistic actions at the price of higher values.[54] The third kind of egoism is *hybris*, which is "the belief in one's own superiority over other persons and in one's special

[46]Załuski (2009a); Tomasello (2009).

[47]Załuski (2009a, 2018).

[48]Załuski (2009a, 2018).

[49]This issue shows why „ought" cannot be derived from "is": the fact that we have a tendency to narrow altruism does not mean that we should help only our relatives and those that may reciprocate our help.

[50]Załuski (2018).

[51]Załuski (2009a, b, 2018).

[52]Załuski (2018), p. 9.

[53]Załuski (2018), p. 12.

[54]Załuski (2018), p. 12.

rights and privileges flowing from this purported superiority".[55] According to Załuski, not all forms of egoism deserve the same negative moral assessment. Only *hybris* is genuinely immoral. Two first forms enable to preserve one's biological life. They also do not immediately lead to other people's harm. In turn, *hybris* is morally wrong and immediately leads to immoral behaviour. Interestingly, looking only at the biological level, while cognitively based egoism and instinct-based egoism are adaptive, *hybris* is not adaptive at all – it does not help in preserving one's genes as we, as a species, have a tendency not to help people who do not help others. They used to be removed from ancestral hunter-gatherer societies.[56] Thus, Załuski argues that *hybris* does not follow from our evolutionary "default" mode of being and is a corruption of one's moral faculty: "therefore those who manifest *hybris* behave *below* their evolutionary nature".[57] As we see, not every form of egoism is evolutionary based.

The next explored issue is envy. Załuski distinguishes three types of envy: malicious, just and benign. Malicious envy contains: "(1) an unpleasant emotion felt by the subject at the thought that she does not possess the good and the rival does and (2) a desire that the rival loses the good".[58] Just envy maintains all the properties of malicious envy and adds the reason for these feelings, which is that a desire that the rival loses the good is because "in the envier's view, it is unjust that the rival possesses this good".[59] In turn, benign envy is constituted only by the first condition of malicious envy—it is only an unpleasant emotion that someone has some good, yet with no desire that this good is lost.[60] Załuski argues that malicious envy cannot have biological, evolutionary roots—it is not adaptive and evolutionary models shows that such people, just like those with *hybris*, were removed from early communities. Malicious envy is an immoral pathology of human spirit—it does not have evolutionary sources.[61] According to Załuski, two other forms of envy have sources in our evolutionary shaped nature. Interestingly, the emotion of just envy is claimed to be the primitive foundation for the sense of justice.[62]

Załuski investigates also several tendencies, which are neutral *per se*, yet can constitute propensities for both moral and immoral actions. The first one consists of hierarchical propensities.[63] Christopher Boehm claims that we do not have a tendency to egalitarianism, instead, natural selection built hierarchical propensities into our default mindset: we want to dominate and do not want to be dominated.[64]

[55]Załuski (2018), p. 13.
[56]Załuski (2018), p. 14.
[57]Załuski (2018), p. 14.
[58]Załuski (2018), p. 15.
[59]Załuski (2018), p. 15.
[60]Załuski (2018), p. 16.
[61]Załuski (2018), pp. 18–19.
[62]Załuski (2018), p. 16.
[63]Załuski (2018), p. 25.
[64]Boehm (2001).

Hierarchical structure of our societies, with all its benefits, like social safety is able to exist because of this tendency. However, wrong domination, tyranny etc. are also "naturally" based on our hierarchical propensities. Another neutral on its own tendency is the desire for self-transcendence: we are inclined to want to be a part of a larger whole.[65] It can manifest in a creative way, as science, philosophy or art, nonetheless, Załuski follows Koestler's view that for the majority it takes a degenerated form of identification with a larger group like tribe, party, nation or church.[66] While the creative form of self-transcendence generally leads to morally proper actions, its form as identification with a larger group can lead to losing one's beliefs and committing serious evil in name of the group.

Notwithstanding, Załuski explores also tendencies that he calls "moral tendencies". The first one is empathy, but its various types can be distinguished as well. The first type is perfect empathy, which consists of "cognitive empathy, affective empathy and the tendency to take empathic actions".[67] Next, cognitive empathy involves "the capacity for a comprehensive and ethically proper understanding of other people's emotions". In turn, affective empathy is "the tendency to emotionally respond to other people's emotions in an ethically proper way".[68] The last component of empathy is the tendency to undertake emphatic actions towards others. Besides perfect empathy, there are also truncated empathy and contaminated empathy. Truncated empathy lacks one of the above-mentioned components of perfect empathy or consists of them, yet only in truncated form.[69] In turn, contaminated empathy adds to perfect empathy a self-regarding feeling of relief, anxiety, superiority or distress concerning one's situation in comparison to the situation of the subject of empathic emotion.[70] The key question is which form of empathy can be regarded as our natural, evolutionary-built tendency. Załuski claims that the natural form of empathy is very far from perfect empathy, yet empathy is evolutionary built into our mindset.[71] Evolutionary cause for that is quite simple: individuals with the propensity towards perfect empathy would not be able to care for their own interests enough.[72]

Other moral tendencies are various forms of altruism: kin altruism, group altruism and reciprocal altruism.[73] Altruism consists of helping others even if a sacrifice of some goods of the helper is required. The explanation of kin altruism has been provided as a development of the theory of natural selection: reproductive success is not only about measuring one's offspring but also about offspring of one's

---

[65] Załuski (2018), p. 27.
[66] Załuski (2018), p. 27; Koestler (1975), p. 240.
[67] Załuski (2018), p. 30.
[68] Załuski (2018), p. 30.
[69] Załuski (2018), p. 30.
[70] Załuski (2018), p. 31.
[71] Załuski (2018), p. 35.
[72] Załuski (2018), p. 35.
[73] Załuski (2018), pp. 39–44.

relatives.[74] We are naturally inclined to help not only our children, but also our relatives as e.g. nephews. Nonetheless, nepotism has its roots in kin altruism. The next form of altruism is group altruism (tribalism): the tendency to help members of one's group over others. The evolutionary development of this kind of altruism is very interesting and still debated. Under the first theory of group altruism, it is a development of kin altruism: the scope of those we naturally tend to help has been extended to a larger group.[75] It may be related to the fact that in early communities actually everyone was to some extent related to anyone else, or it might have evolved as a side-effect or mistake of our mental development.[76] The second theory of group altruism is based on the theory of group selection: whole groups, not individuals, compete. Groups where group altruism was present had an advantage over groups of egoists towards random members of the group. As a result, now, we all have a tendency for group altruism.[77] Altruistic inclination towards others is morally positive, however, racism and chauvinism seem to be the second side of group altruism. Reciprocal altruism, is the third form of altruism that forms our natural propensities: we tend to help those who help or may help us. It is explained as the best strategy in game theory sense: cooperate first and then imitate opponent's last move.[78] It enabled early human communities to remove those who took advantage of others' help but not reciprocated it.

Załuski's conclusion on the basis of the above-presented research is of two kinds. First, he claims that the genuine ethics cannot be built on the basis of our evolutionary tendencies. They are not fully moral, for instance, the propensity to reciprocal altruism is based on rather a prudential, not a moral, rule.[79] They also have many negative sides, which can easily lead to immoral actions. Genuine ethics must have (also) other foundations. Nonetheless, his second claim is that the most immoral, evil actions do not have sources in our evolutionary nature: both *hybris* and malicious envy have been determined to be founded upon the corruption of human moral faculty, not upon human natural tendencies. Załuski therefore upholds his main claim from his first book on evolutionary psychology, which is that evolutionary understood human nature leads to moderately optimistic vision of human.[80] His aim was to examine also a more negative side of our natural inclinations, yet even though we have both morally neutral tendencies that may lead to immoral acts, and immoral tendencies (although not in their biggest forms), still, positive tendencies prevail. Human nature is constituted by narrow altruism and imperfect prudence because these are the *dominant* tendencies in human way of thinking and human behaviour.

---

[74] Hamilton (1964); Załuski (2018), p. 39.

[75] Załuski (2018), p. 41.

[76] Załuski (2018), p. 41.

[77] Załuski (2018), p. 41.

[78] Załuski (2018), pp. 42–43.

[79] Załuski (2018), p. 43.

[80] Załuski (2009a).

Załuski's research from his second book[81] present another side of human, nonetheless, it does not undermines his first general claim on human nature being constituted by narrow altruism and imperfect prudence.[82] Tomasello's experimental research may give other, interesting insights into immoral human actions. His claim that the tendency to cooperate constitutes the evolutionary understood human nature is based on comparative experiments on human infants and very young children (in order to exclude any traits learnt in socialisation) and on young chimpanzees. His research shows that in fact children learn not to help on the basis of interaction with other children from around age of three years old: "children of this age more often help those who have been helpful to others".[83] If an inductive generalisation of Tomasello's experimental researches is correct (it needs by far much more experimental evidence), it can be claimed that we are naturally, innately, inclined to collaborate and to help others, even on our cost (altruism), and that these natural propensities are weakened in the process of socialisation. Consequently, it may be claimed that non-moral, or even immoral, behaviour is rather learnt while living in society and interacting with others, than is innately built into our evolutionary mindset. The non-altruistic behaviour is learnt, not naturally given.

This section has the title "wrong part of our nature". We can do immoral things, and some of them may have some sources in our natural tendencies (envy, egoism, etc.). However, immoral or even neutral tendencies do not constitute human nature understood as a set of *dominant* tendencies in human thinking and human behaviour. Positive tendencies prevail and they constitute human nature. Tomasello's research gives here more insights: it is likely that many non-altruistic and non-collaborative acts and further inclinations is the product of society, not nature. Thus, it turns out the "wrong part of our nature" does not constitute human nature as it is understood in this work. It is rather a wrong part of our tendencies, which however are not dominant. Since human nature is the set of dominant tendencies, immoral and non-moral tendencies do not form human nature.

7.4 The Problem of Psychopaths and Sociopaths

The last possibly problematic issue is the problem of psychopaths and sociopaths who seem not to have the tendency to altruistic behaviours, and most probably also to collaboration. Sometimes psychopathy and sociopathy are equated, but usually these two terms mean different things. Psychopathy is defined as a personality disorder that involves antisocial behaviour, impaired empathy and remorse as well as disinhibited and egoistic traits.[84] Since it is a personality disorder, it is often

[81] Załuski (2018).

[82] Załuski (2009a).

[83] Tomasello (2009), p. 29; cf. Vaish et al. (2010).

[84] Patrick et al. (2009).

thought to be biologically, genetically predisposed or caused. Sociopathy is a colloquial term, the closest proper psychological term is antisocial personality disorder, which is a personality disorder characterised by long term disregarding and violating others' rights.[85] Sociopathy, unlike psychopathy, is considered to be caused by environmental factors, like e.g. child abuse. Therefore, sociopathy does not undermine the claim on altruism and collaboration as forming human nature. Sociopaths have this nature but it was impaired and diminished by environment and is no longer visible in their lives. However, biologically they still have it, and it was present at the beginning of their lives.

Nonetheless, psychopathy is much more problematic. There are three theories on the sources of psychopathy. Under the first one, it is genetically caused or predisposed. A series of experimental psychological studies presents more than 60% heritability of patterns involving disregard for others and lack of empathy.[86] Empathy is a factor for inclination towards altruism and thus, it can be stated that they do not have a tendency to altruism. The same goes for collaboration as it requires the ability to join larger actions on mutual benefit, with possible zero benefit for a joining individual. Nonetheless, the slightly more than 60% heritability cannot explain all instantiations of psychopathy. Another theory proposes environmental causes, similarly to sociopathy, mostly related to family life. The last theory focuses on brain injuries, mostly those of prefrontal cortex. The widely known example for this theory is the case of Phineas Gage, a mid-19th century men who survived an accident when an iron rod passed through his head and his behaviour completely changed after the accident. Two last theories do not undermine the claim on altruism and collaboration as human nature—environmental or mechanical factors cause that certain humans (psychopaths) cease to possess the natural inclination towards altruism and collaboration.

However, the first theory raises more serious problems. If it is true, what requires much more experimental research, which of course cannot be conducted by me, it can undermine the view on innate, natural tendency to altruism and collaboration we all share. Moreover, it has implications for the proposed here justification of human rights—if psychopaths do not have the tendencies that constitute human nature, they do not have human dignity that is grounded in human nature as well. Consequently, they do not have universal human rights, which are grounded by human dignity. As a result, the necessary part of the foundations of particular human rights collapses. As a consequence, a part of humans does not have human rights. For me, such a conclusion would be a serious threat to the adequateness of my proposal for looking on the foundations of human rights. Notwithstanding, from the point of view of some theories of human rights, which were however criticised by me in this regard, it may not be so problematic. Griffin claims that some categories of humans, like people in coma, suffering from dementia and infants, do not have human rights.[87] Instead, they

---

[85] Berger (2016).

[86] Skeem et al. (2011); Neumann and Hare (2008); Glenn et al. (2011).

[87] Griffin (2008).

have some other rights and we have duties towards them. It would be therefore possible to follow Griffin's way of solving the problem of a category of human that does not possess an essential trait for justification of human rights—normative agency in Griffin's conception—the tendency to altruism and collaboration in mine. Consequently, psychopaths would not possess human rights, yet they would possess another category of rights. However, in my view, this is a wrong way to solve this problem. Psychopaths are still humans, they must possess human rights and human dignity as every human.

I propose another way of solving this problematic theoretical issue. The psychopath's genetic lack of the tendency to altruism and collaboration can be considered as a biological anomaly and pathology. It is a genetic deficient like some kinds of brain damage that also diminish e.g. joint, collaborative actions. Yet, people with this pathology—psychopaths—still possess evolutionary defined human nature since the proper human nature, which they *should* possess, is constituted by the tendency to altruism and collaboration. Notice that under the notion of nature as the set of dominant tendencies, not every individual X must have a given tendency in order to state that this is the dominant tendency, and consequently, the nature of X. In case of human nature, some humans may not possess this tendency, and still it will form human nature if it is generally dominant in humans.[88] I think that psychopaths have the same human rights as all humans.

Therefore, the case of psychopaths does not undermine the claim that evolutionary understood human nature is the foundation of human dignity and human rights. I have given these remarks assuming that psychopathy has genetic sources. It is however not yet exactly known. If its roots are of a different kind, e.g. environmental, the problem of psychopaths and evolutionary human nature vanishes. If the psychopath's lack of altruistic and collaborative tendencies is a genetic pathology, it does not undermine the claim on the tendency to cooperate (which consists of altruism and collaboration) as evolutionary conceived human nature.

7.5 How Does My Approach Help to Reject the Objection of Western Ethnocentrism?

The strongest objection against the idea of human rights is the objection of Western ethnocentrism.[89] The objection is that the whole conception of human rights is a Western idea, based on a Western way of thinking and the promotion of human rights is another manifestation of Western imperialism, this time in the sphere of broadly understood culture. It is very closely related to the issue of cultural relativism and its impact on human rights. If the objection of Western ethnocentrism is

[88] Obviously, psychopaths constitute a very small minority of the human population.

[89] Griffin (2008), pp. 129–148.

sound, it can truly undermine the whole idea of universal human rights. I believe that my approach is one of few that does not fall into this objection. Moreover, I believe that my way of the explanation and justification of human rights is able to reject the objection of Western ethnocentrism.

Piechowiak notices that the problem of the relativity of justification of human rights can be seen even in the legal document of a legal organisation, for which human rights are the most important fundament, and which aims to promote them globally.[90] In the Preamble to the Treaty on European Union (2007), the second paragraph goes as following:

> DRAWING INSPIRATION from the cultural, religious and humanist inheritance of Europe, from which have developed the universal values of the inviolable and inalienable rights of the human person, freedom, democracy, equality and the rule of law;[91]

Piechowiak criticises such a wording by stating that the foundations of human rights are claimed to be constituted by inheritance of Europe and not by e.g. universal human dignity.[92] If the fundament of human rights lies only in cultural, religious and humanist inheritance of Europe, which a contingent social phenomenon, how human rights can be universal and their justification not be ethnocentric? To give the full context, in the Explanations Relative to the Charter of Fundamental Rights, a legal document explaining what is meant by the Charter of Fundamental Rights, it is claimed that: "The dignity of the human person is not only a fundamental right in itself but constitutes the real basis of fundamental rights".[93] Let me just notice how confusing is the statement that human dignity is both a fundamental right and the basis of fundamental rights. Two notions of human dignity are confused here. Nonetheless, the Explanations restore the claim on human dignity as the foundation of human rights. Still, in comparison to the Preamble of the Treaty on European Union, it is a minor document. And according to the Preamble, the roots of human rights lie only in European, Western culture, not in any objective entity. The objection of Western ethnocentrism can be seen as manifested even in such a document.[94]

Coming back to the core of the objection, in my view, two variants of the objection of Western ethnocentrism can be distinguished. In the strong form, it is directed against the idea of human rights itself. In the weak form, its aim is the current, dominant way of justification of human rights that is based on Western philosophy. Let me start from the weaker variant.

The weak version of the objection of Western Ethnocentrism can be expressed in the following way: the dominant, contemporary way of justifying human rights is

---

[90] Piechowiak (2012), p. 143.

[91] Treaty on European Union (2007), Preamble.

[92] Piechowiak (2012).

[93] Explanations Relative to the Charter of Fundamental Rights (2007), Title I.

[94] By the way, it seems that European Union lives in a sort of intellectual schizophrenia—on the one hand, it believes in only culturally grounded human rights, on the other, it promotes them all over the world. It gives grounds for the strong version of the objection.

based on philosophical ideas developed by Western-world thinkers, which are based on Western culture. The ideas that are used in the philosophy of human rights consist of concepts like "moral autonomy", "normative agency", "value of person", etc. Their understanding is based on a highly individualistic notion of human being. Consider Griffin's normative agency. It enables us to decide about one's life, make choices, including those in the moral domain, and built one's conception of a good life. But is this really so universally acceptable and self-evident as Griffin assumes? I do not think so, there are many non-Western cultures that do not ascribe such a high value to concepts like normative agency or even disregard them as a threat to social cohesion, tradition and other important aspects of a given society. There are many cultures, especially Eastern cultures, that do not value individuality as much as Western culture, but rather see values in more social aspects of human being. Therefore, even the idea of a "good life"[95] developed on one's own may not be acceptable for them. I believe that the part of the philosophy of human rights that is based on contemporary liberal political philosophy and ethics, e.g. on what I called Kantian-analytic notion of person, faces the very serious threat of falling into the objection of Western ethnocentrism. Even the Kantian justification of human dignity, which further helps justify human rights, where human is "an end in itself" can be seen as problematic. Philosophy wants to be universal, notwithstanding it encompasses some cultural, often subconscious, assumptions about the world and the basic vision of human. I believe that conceptions of human rights based on ethics[96] are much more vulnerable to the objection of Western ethnocentrism than conceptions based on metaphysics.[97] The least problematic are theories that do not take a lot of advantage of philosophy, like the basic human needs approach[98] or Tasioulas's notion of human dignity and human interests being the foundations of human rights,[99] although it is not clear what is Tasioulas's justification of human dignity.

I believe that the proper justification of human rights must be based on either (1) concepts existing in every culture, not limited only to contemporary Western highly individualistic way of thinking about human, or (2) using concepts that must be justified in such a way that members of other cultures will accept them. In my view, although Griffin is aware of the objection of Western ethnocentrism and believes that his normative agency is acceptable for every culture,[100] his justification of human rights in fact falls as a victim of this objection. Normative agency is an instantiation of highly individualistic thinking about human where all value is ascribed to one's autonomy and capability of making choices, including choices in the moral domain, with a possible disregard for society and its common morality. Compare it with Nussbaum's capabilities approach wherein capabilities are defined

[95] Griffin (2008).

[96] Griffin (2008).

[97] Piechowiak (1999, 2019).

[98] Miller (2007, 2012); Renzo (2015).

[99] Tasioulas (2011, 2013, 2015).

[100] Griffin (2008), pp. 129–148.

in a descriptive way as real opportunities that one can choose, act on and achieve functioning.[101] In my view, the capabilities basis for human rights is acceptable for everyone.

Nonetheless, even if some accounts of justification of human rights are immune to the weak version of the objection of Western ethnocentrism, it does not entail that the strong version is also rejected. Under the strong version, not only the justification of human rights, but human rights themselves are argued against. It is claimed that the very idea of human rights is the product of Western culture and irrespective of its justification, its promotion is imposing Western culture on other societies, which is just another form of Western imperialism. To my best knowledge, the first instantiation of the strong version of this objection, and the first theoretically established example of the objection of Western ethnocentrism as such, occurred in 1947, at the time of drafting of the Universal Declaration of Human rights, even before its official establishment in 1948. It was provided by the American Anthropological Association (AAA) as a remark given in the process of drafting the Universal Declaration of Human Rights.[102] The AAA asked the following question:

> How can the proposed Declaration be applicable to all human beings, and not be a statement of rights conceived only in terms of the values prevalent in the countries of Western Europe and America?[103]

This point alone can be simply understood as a remark of an anthropologist organisation. We also cannot conclude whether AAA argues against weak, or strong version of the objection. Yet, the AAA proposed three principles for the drafting committee to avoid Western ethnocentrism. The third principle states that:

> Standards and values are relative to the culture from which they derive so that any attempt to formulate postulates that grow out of the beliefs or moral codes of one culture must to that extent detract from the applicability of any Declaration of Human Rights to mankind as a whole.[104]

These words clearly demonstrate that AAA argues against universal human rights themselves, as being born in Western culture, not only against some forms of their justification. Moreover, the whole context of its report presents that the question from the first citation of the AAA report is merely a rhetorical question. AAA firmly claimed that no universally acceptable justification of human rights is possible since morality is always relative to some culture. As human rights belong to the moral domain, and their justification has sources in moral standards and values, the objection of Wester ethnocentrism is inevitable. As for the objection of AAA and the process of drafting of the Declaration, it is worth mentioning that Universal Declaration of Human Rights was agreed by 48 countries from all world cultures

[101] Nussbaum (2000, 2006, 2011).

[102] Morsink (1999), p. IX.

[103] AAA (1947), p. 539.

[104] AAA (1947), p. 539.

with no against votes and eight abstaining.[105] Countries that abstained did it because of some concrete objections against some specific provisions. None of them abstained on the basis of rejecting the idea of human rights as a whole. For instance, six communist countries abstained because of no condemnation of Nazism,[106] Saudi Arabia because of the meaning of the right to freedom of religion and right to equal marriage[107] and the Union of South Africa because of the right to freedom of movement.[108] The agreement in favour of human rights *per se* was present all over the world.

I believe that the explanation and justification of human rights proposed in this work can serve as a serious argument against the objection of Western ethnocentrism, both in the weak and in the strong version. There is nothing solely Western in my proposal for foundations of human rights. Empirical science and its method are universal and widely accepted all over the world. A great part of evolutionary psychology, including Tomasello's conception of human nature, is based on empirical data. Załuski's notion is more based on game theory than experiments but he also highly relies on the interpretation of experimental data. Evolutionary understood human nature has nothing to do with Western view of human being. In fact, it presents a collective, rather than a highly individualistic, vision of human. Human nature contains both the tendency to collaborate with others in order to achieve some common good and the tendency to altruism. These are social, collective aspects of our basic, innate, natural propensities. Human nature does not contain ultra-egoistic, self-sufficient tendencies to pursue just one's happiness. Thus, actually, evolutionary defined human nature is much closer to non-Western, especially Eastern cultures and their cultural vision of human. Evolutionary understood human nature falsifies rather ultra-liberal, highly individualistic vision of human. Therefore, as for the vision of human, my proposition that makes use of human nature so understood, is consistent with the vision of human of non-Western cultures. Making use of evolutionary psychology in seeking the foundations of human rights is free of Western ethnocentrism since evolutionary psychology is (mainly) a natural empirical science (its other parts rely on game theory, which is also not solely Western). An interesting point is that evolutionary understood human nature is consistent with more collective vision of human of non-Western cultures. It leads to the claim that the naturalisation of the question on the foundations of human rights results in escaping Western ethnocentrism.

Another interesting issue, which I would like to mention here, is the question on human rights and Confucianism, noticed by Mateusz Stępień.[109] Stępień wonders why the idea of human rights was not discovered in China, where the most dominant

[105] Morsink (1999), p. 12.

[106] Morsink (1999), p. 23.

[107] Morsink (1999), p. 24.

[108] Morsink (1999), p. 26.

[109] Stępień (2014).

Confucianism philosophy have had a very positive vision of human.[110] Stępień argues that Confucianism views on human nature are highly consistent with recent discoveries of evolutionary psychology and cognitive sciences.[111] Stępień's explanation of the lack of development of an idea of natural rights in Chinese, especially Confucianism, philosophy is that the Confucian positive vision of human paradoxically blocked the thoughts on some natural rights that may serve as protection against other human actions.[112] Another point is more process-oriented, rather than essence-oriented, vision of human and its nature.[113] Yet, the idea of human rights is not contradictory to Confucian philosophy.

Another issue is the contemporary analytic metaphysics and the relation of metaphysical grounding. Analytic philosophy in general, and analytic metaphysics in particular, has been started and developed mostly in the Western world. However, in my view, it does not trigger the problem of being related to a specific vision of the world of only one culture. Nowadays, analytic philosophy seems to be the dominant school of philosophical thought all over the world. But most importantly, analytic philosophy focuses on logic, clear arguments and in the part that I follow, also on natural, empirical sciences (naturalisation project). None of these aspects is thoroughly Western. Notice also that I do not refer to analytic ethics or political philosophy in justification of human rights. I follow metaphysics, which, in my view, is much less culturally related than ethics or political philosophy. Metaphysical grounding is a universal explanatory relation that holds between various facts. I see nothing significantly Western in it. Since metaphysical grounding is thought to be analogous to causation and the general idea of causation is not based on particularly Western views or intuitions, I believe the same can be said about metaphysical grounding. It is nothing Western in trying to see the explanatory relations between various entities.

To conclude, the justification of human rights proposed in this work is free of the objection of Western ethnocentrism. Moreover, it can serve as the rejection of this objection. It is possible to justify human rights not on the basis of Western vision of human or Western ethics and political philosophy, but on empirical science and austere metaphysics. It means that human rights can be justified in non-Western terms (the weak version of the objection) and that human rights are not thoroughly Western idea (the strong version of the objection). Consequently, the objection of Western ethnocentrism must be rejected.[114]

---

[110] Stępień (2014).

[111] Stępień (2014), pp. 84–87.

[112] Stępień (2014), pp. 84–87.

[113] Stępień (2014), p. 88.

[114] For a postmodernist, it would not be so clear as she might claim that science serves to obtain power, or that analytic philosophy is ultra-rationalistic in its rigour and logic. This work is not aimed to provide the refutation of postmodernism, however, let me give just a few counterarguments. First, science simply works—it is able to explain the world. Second, if argumentative rigour and logic are rejected, we slide into no basis for any debate. Last, if for postmodernism, everything is meant as a

7.6 Theoretical and Methodological Consequences

The rejection of the objection of Western ethnocentrism is one of the key consequences of my account of the foundations of human rights. For this reason, I have decided to formulate it in a separate part of this work. There are however other theoretical and methodological consequences, which I will discuss on the following pages.

The first consequence refers to the project of naturalisation. It turns out that the question on the foundations of human rights can be naturalised in the mode of methodological naturalisation. Philosophy of human rights can be researched and developed in accordance with the knowledge generated in empirical sciences, in this case, in evolutionary psychology. Yet, human rights cannot be reduced to some natural facts, which excludes the possibility of ontological naturalisation of the question on what is the fundament of human rights. This works makes the naturalistic approach to human rights truly naturalised.

Second, my conception allows to define the relation between human rights and their foundations. It is supervenience in the following way: (1) particular human rights supervene on universal human rights and environmental and social facts, (2) universal human rights supervene on human dignity and (3) human dignity supervenes on human nature. However, it cannot be concluded that particular human rights supervene (even partly) on universal human rights, human dignity or on human nature (see Sect. 5.4). More importantly, supervenience is the relation of only a necessary covariance, with no explanatory force. Still, the determination of the precise nature of the relation holding between the above entities in philosophy of human rights is an important consequence. The relation between human rights and their foundations is the relation of metaphysical grounding:[115] (1) particular human rights are grounded in universal human rights and environmental and social facts, (2) universal human rights are grounded in human dignity and (3) human dignity is grounded in human nature. Due to the transitivity of grounding, universal human rights are grounded in human nature. Particular human rights are partly grounded in human dignity, and further, in human nature. Grounding provides explanatory force and allows us to acknowledge ontological priority. The consequence is that the relation between human rights and their foundations has been identified—it is metaphysical grounding. It is relation holding between facts themselves, not merely between concepts or ideas.

Consequently, following the approach presented in this work, the main claim of the naturalistic approach, which is that "human rights are moral rights possessed by all humans simply in virtue of their humanity or being human"[116] can be read as that

---

tool to obtain power, the same goes for postmodernism. Consequently, postmodernism is a self-defeating idea.

[115] It is nothing wrong to claim that more than one relation holds between A and B; cf. Chilovi (2018) who argues that grounding entails supervenience.

[116] Griffin (2008), p. 2; Tasioulas (2011), p. 27.

human rights are moral rights possessed by all humans that are metaphysically grounded in human dignity (partly as for particular human rights) and in human nature (partly as for particular human rights), as defined by evolutionary psychology. Similarly, the relation of derivation/being a source of/being the foundation of human rights that is mentioned in many legal texts about human rights is clarified—it is the relation of metaphysical grounding.

The successful reading of the question on fundaments of human rights in light of contemporary analytic metaphysics, more precisely, in light of the project of naturalisation and relational metaphysics leads to the third theoretical and methodological consequence. It is escaping the parochialism of the contemporary philosophy of human rights. With minor exceptions,[117] the contemporary philosophy of human rights is developed with no connections with other disciplines, except ethics and political philosophy. It makes the philosophy of human rights a parochial field of studies, wherein debates are conducted with no reference to other fields that may have already developed frameworks and conceptions useful for the philosophy of human rights. One such example is the prevalent claim, seen in Tasioulas's wording of the objection of foundationalism, which is that human rights cannot have foundations in natural facts.[118] It is based on a non-nuanced understanding of Hume's Guillotine. The reference to the framework of autonomy of ethics makes this issue much clearer and, in my view, enables to claim that metaphysical relations, like supervenience and grounding, can hold between human rights and their natural grounds. While in general jurisprudence the debate on metaphysical grounding has already drawn attention,[119] the philosophy of human rights seem not to take sufficient notice of this key debate of analytic philosophy, despite the fact that it researches what is the foundation of human rights and often makes use of the term "grounding".

I believe that my proposal for foundations of human rights is a significant step to open up the philosophy of human rights to other fields of knowledge, especially to analytic metaphysics and relevant empirical sciences, like evolutionary psychology.

I also think that my account of the foundations of human rights can be useful for analytic metaphysicians and their debate on metaphysical grounding. This debate is held on abstract level and various more concrete examples of employment of metaphysical grounding can be helpful for a deeper and better understanding of the relation of metaphysical grounding itself. One argument against metaphysical grounding is that it has no practical application or concrete explanatory role.[120] I believe that this work is able to falsify this critique of metaphysical grounding.

Another consequence is to be located in the philosophy of human rights. There is a debate that can be expressed by the question: "do we have human rights because of

[117] Piechowiak (1999, 2019); Mikhail (2012).

[118] Tasioulas (2015), p. 45.

[119] Plunkett (2012); Gizbert-Studnicki (2015, 2016, 2021); Chilovi and Pavlakos (2019); Chilovi (2019); Janik (2019).

[120] Hofweber (2009).

positive aspects of being human, or rather we have human rights because of negative things that we are able to do?" Mikhail gives a list of theoretical views that dismiss the idea that we have human rights due to some valuable aspect of human being.[121] One of such views is Michael Ignatieff's claim:

> The Universal Declaration set out to reestablish the idea of human rights at the precise historical moment in which they had been shown to have had no foundation whatever in natural human attributes. [. . .]We defend human rights as moral universals in full awareness that they must counteract rather than reflect natural human propensities. [. . .] For the idea that these propensities are natural implies that they are innate and universally distributed among individuals. The reality [. . .] is otherwise.[122]

Ignatieff claims that there is a deep problem in the justification of human rights, including the one from international legal documents. It is claimed that we have human rights due to something positive about us, like for instance human dignity, while in fact our natural tendencies are negative and human rights counter them, rather than manifest them. Rorty claims that the postmodern era blurred many widely established truths about the world and that:

> The result is to erase the picture of the self common to Greek metaphysics, Christian theology, and Enlightenment rationalism: the picture of an ahistorical natural center, the locus of human dignity, surrounded by an adventitious and inessential periphery.[123]

As there is nothing essential, also as for human, there can be nor human essence, neither human nature that can constitute the basis for human rights. Mikhail mentions also other philosophers who reject the idea of human rights as they claim there is no innate, natural morality: Gilbert Ryle, Kurt Baier, Alsdair MacIntyre.[124]

Mikhail provides very insightful argumentation against such views on the basis of recent development of empirical sciences. I have already argued against the view that there is nothing like human nature. Moreover, evolutionary psychology falsifies the view on the lack of some sort of natural tendencies related to human moral sphere. It is also falsified by cognitive sciences, which are used by Mikhail in order to argue for the natural foundations of human rights. My justification of human rights differs from Mikhail's. He claims that human rights follow from our natural, innate morality. He seems to propose a sort of a causal link between natural moral faculty and human rights. In turn, my proposal for the justification of human rights consists of metaphysical link. I also do not claim that human rights merely follow from human nature, rather they are practical realisations of human dignity, which holds due to the positive vision of human that follows from evolutionary understood human nature. Nonetheless, we see that the development of empirical sciences in around last two decades falsifies altogether the claim that there is no human nature, the negative vision of basic human aspects, and the conviction that there are no

[121] Mikhail (2012).

[122] Ignatieff (2003), pp. 78–80.

[123] Rorty (1993), p. 225.

[124] Ryle (1949); Baier (1958); MacIntyre (1981).

human natural propensities in the moral domain. Notice, however, that I do not argue that having human dignity holds on the level of whole human species as George Kateb claims.[125] Human dignity is held by every individual human being, not human species as a whole. Even though the altruistic tendencies I discussed earlier are identified as typical of human populations (and thus species), the nature identified through such investigation is characteristic of every human being.

Therefore, the question on whether we have human rights because we humans are so inherently good to have them, or rather because we are intrinsically bad, so we must have some protection against our natural tendencies, is to be answered in favour of the first option. This is what I argue in this work: we have human rights (partly in case of particular human rights—the other part are social and environmental facts) in virtue of human nature, since human nature grounds human dignity. Yet, I am aware of the negative, immoral side of humans, including the side that may have evolutionary roots, and I presented it over a dozen pages above, in Sect. 7.3. The conclusion I reached there was that neutral or even negative aspects of human thinking and behaviour do not undermine the general thesis about the positive evolutionary vision of human. The answer to the question on which side—positive or negative justifies human rights can be therefore more nuanced. Truly, we have human rights because of the positive side of being human. However, simultaneously, human rights protect us against things that may happen because of the negative side, which is, however, minor in comparison to the prevailing human nature. The negative side may sometimes have sources in our evolutionary propensities, but, as Załuski claims, the most immoral forms of egoism and envy do not have evolutionary roots, they are the products of the corruption of human moral faculty.

Although the book aims to present a new way of looking at the foundations of human rights and doesn't provide direct claims about the legal practice of human rights, some more practical views can be proposed in an indirect way. Of course, legal practice of human rights consists of interpretation of legal text that include provisions about human rights. As such, court or any official interpreting law that speaks about human rights doesn't need to refer to extra-legal (or simply metaphysical) foundations of human rights. Such a person needs mainly legal interpretation tools to interpret legal text and apply it in a practical case. On the other hand, I think the general framework that I propose may be useful in determination whether a certain subject has a certain human right in a given context. Practically, in order to establish that one has a certain human right some conditions must be met: (1) this right must protect a decent level of life, (2) this right must be grounded in a universal human right and in some environmental and social facts—in other words, there must be a clear link between this particular human right and its foundations and an official should think about such a link and clearly justify that it holds. Another postulate can be proposed: never refer to a violation or breach of human dignity but always justify violation of a particular human right. Human dignity as inviolable cannot be violated and for both theoretical and communicational clarity it is better to refer to a violation

[125] Kateb (2011).

of a given concrete human right than to make a short-cut and make a claim on violation of human dignity. One of the problems seen in the philosophy of human rights is over-inflation of claims that something is a human right—I think following the framework proposed in my work in legal practice may address this problem.

References

Alvarez M (2017) Reasons for action: justification, motivation, explanation. The Stanford Encyclopedia of Philosophy (Winter 2017 Edition). https://plato.stanford.edu/archives/win2017/entries/reasons-just-vs-expl/

American Anthropological Association (1947) Statement on human rights. Am Anthropol 48:539–543

Audi P (2012) Grounding: toward a theory of the in-virtue-of relation. J Philosophy 109:685–711

Baier K (1958) The moral point of view: a rational basis of ethics. Random House, New York

Berger F (2016) Antisocial personality disorder Medline plus. https://medlineplus.gov/ency/article/000921.htm

Bliss R, Trogdon K (2016) Metaphysical grounding. The Stanford Encyclopedia of Philosophy (Winter 2016 Edition). https://plato.stanford.edu/archives/win2016/entries/grounding/

Boehm C (2001) Hierarchy in the forest: the evolution of egalitarian behaviour. Harvard University Press, Cambridge

Brożek B (2016) Explanation and understanding. In: Brożek B, Heller M, Hohol M (eds) The concept of explanation. Copernicus Centre Press, Kraków, pp 11–43

Chilovi S (2018) Grounding entails supervenience. Synthese 8:1–18

Chilovi S (2019) Grounding legal reality. Doctoral Thesis. University of Barcelona, Barcelona, https://www.tdx.cat/bitstream/handle/10803/667056/SAMUELE%20CHILOVI_PhD_THESIS.pdf?sequence=1&isAllowed=y

Chilovi S, Pavlakos G (2019) Law-determination as grounding: a common grounding framework for jurisprudence. Legal Theory 25:53–76

De Regt H (2009) The epistemic value of understanding. Philos Sci 76:585–597

Dennett D (2017) From Bacteria to Bach and back: the evolution of minds. W.W. Norton & Company, New York

Fine K (1995) Ontological dependence. Proceedings of the Aristotelian Society 95:269–290

Gizbert-Studnicki T (2015) Metafizyka Pozytywizmu Prawniczego. Principia 61:19–40

Gizbert-Studnicki T (2016) The social sources thesis, metaphysics and metaphilosophy. In: Banaś P, Dyrda A, Gizbert Studnicki T (eds) Metaphilosophy of law. Hart Publishing, Oxford, pp 121–146

Gizbert-Studnicki T (2021) Social facts and legal facts: Perils of Hume's Guillotine. In: Spaak T, Mindus P (eds) The Cambridge companion to legal positivism. Cambridge University Press, Cambridge, pp 419–442

Glenn A, Kurzban R, Raine A (2011) Evolutionary theory and psychopathy. Aggress Violent Behav 16:371–380

Gould SJ (1978) Sociobiology: the art of storytelling. New Sci 80:530–533

Griffin J (2008) On human rights. Oxford University Press, Oxford

Hamilton W (1964) The genetical evolution of social behavior. Parts I and II. J Theoret Biol 7:1–16, 17–32

Hempel C (1942) The function of general laws in history. J Philos 39:35–48; reprinted in Hempel (1965):231–244

Hempel C (1965) Aspects of scientific explanation and other essays in the philosophy of science. Free Press, New York

Hempel C, Oppenheim P (1948) Studies in the logic of explanation. Philos Sci 15:135–175

Hofweber T (2009) Ambitious, yet modest, metaphysics. In: Manley D, Chalmers D, Wassrerman R (eds) Meta metaphysics: new essays on the foundations of ontology. OUP, Oxford, pp 260–289

Hubalek M (2020) A Brief (Hi)story of Just-So Stories in Evolutionary Science Philosophy of Social Sciences (forthcoming) https://doi.org/10.1177/0048393120944223

Ignatieff M (2003) Human rights as politics and idolatry. Princeton University Press, Princeton

Janik B (2019) Superweniencja i Ugruntowanie Norm Prawnych – Analiza Filozoficznoprawna. Doctoral Thesis. Kraków; Jagiellonian University. https://ruj.uj.edu.pl/xmlui/bitstream/handle/item/87118/janik_superweniencja_i_ugruntowanie_norm_prawnych_2019.pdf?sequence=1&isAllowed=y

Kateb G (2011) Human dignity. Harvard University Press, Harvard

Kelp C (2015) Understanding phenomena. Synthese 192:3799–3816

Kitcher P (1989) Explanatory unification and the causal structure of the world. In: Kitcher P, Salmon W (eds) Scientific explanation. University of Minnesota Press, Minneapolis, pp 410–505

Koestler A (1975) The Ghost in the machine. Picador, London

Leary S (2017) Non-naturalism and normative necessities. In: Shaffer-Landau R (ed) Oxford studies in metaethics, vol 12. OUP, Oxford, pp 76–105

Lewontin RC (1976a) Sociobiology – a Caricature of Darwinism PSA. In: Suppe F, Asquith PD (eds) Proceedings of the Biennial Meeting of the Philosophy of Science Association vol. 2. East Lansing: Philosophy of Science Association, pp 22–31

Lewontin RC (1976b) Sociobiology – a Caricature of Selection Theory PSA. Proceedings of the Biennial Meeting of the Philosophy of Science Association. Philosophy of Science Association. https://www.matierevolution.fr/spip.php?article286

MacIntyre A (1981) After virtue. University of Notre Dame Press, Notre Dame

Maurin AS (2019) Grounding and metaphysical explanation: it's complicated. Philos Stud 176: 1573–1584

Mikhail J (2012) Moral grammar and human rights: some reflections on cognitive science and enlightenment rationalism. In: Goodman R, Jinks D, Woods AK (eds) Understanding social action, promoting human rights. OUP, Oxford, pp 160–202

Miller D (2007) National responsibility and global justice. OUP, Oxford

Miller D (2012) Grounding human rights. Crit Rev Int Soc Polit Philos 15:407–427

Millstein R (2019) Evolution. The Stanford Encyclopedia of Philosophy (Summer 2019 Edition). https://plato.stanford.edu/archives/sum2019/entries/evolution/

Morsink J (1999) The universal declaration of human rights. Origins, drafting and intent. University of Pennsylvania Press, Philadelphia

Neumann C, Hare R (2008) Psychopathic traits in a large community sample: Links to violence, alcohol use, and intelligence. J Consult Clin Psychol *76*:893–899

Nussbaum M (2000) Women and human development: the capabilities approach. Cambridge University Press, Cambridge

Nussbaum M (2006) Frontiers of justice: disability, nationality, species membership. The Belknap Press Harvard University Press, Cambridge

Nussbaum M (2011) Creating capabilities, the human development approach. The Belknap Press of Harvard University Press, Cambridge/London

Patrick C, Fowles D, Krueger R (2009) Triarchic conceptualization of psychopathy: developmental origins of disinhibition, boldness, and meanness. Dev Psychopathol 21:913–938

Piechowiak M (1999) Filozofia Praw Człowieka. Prawa Człowieka w świetle ich Międzynarodowej Ochrony. Towarzystwo Naukowe KUL, Lublin

Piechowiak M (2012) Godność w Karcie Praw Podstawowych Unii Europejskiej: Destrukcja Uniwersalnego Paradygmatu Ujęcia Podstaw Praw Człowieka? Themis Polska Nova 2(1): 126–146

Piechowiak M (2019) Plato's conception of justice and the question of human dignity. Peter Lang, Berlin

Plunkett D (2012) A positivist route for explaining how. Facts Make Law Legal Theory 18:139–207
Renzo M (2015) Human needs, human rights. In: Cruft R, Liao SM, Renzo M (eds) Philosophical foundations of human rights. OUP, Oxford, pp 570–587
Richardson R (2007) Evolutionary psychology as maladapted psychology. MIT Press, Cambridge, MA
Rorty R (1993) Human rights, rationality and sentimentality. In: Shute S, Hurley S (eds) On human rights: the Oxford amnesty lectures. Basic Books, New York, pp 111–134
Ryle G (1949) The concept of mind. OUP, Oxford
Salmon W (1971) Statistical explanation & statistical relevance. University of Pittsburgh Press, Pittsburgh
Salmon W (1984) Scientific explanation and the causal structure of the world. Princeton, Princeton University Press
Salmon W (1998) Causality and explanation. OUP, Oxford
Schaffer J (2017) Laws for metaphysical explanation. Philos Iss 27:302–321
Skeem J, Polaschek D, Patrick C, Lilienfeld S (2011) Psychopathic Personality: bridging the gap between scientific evidence and public policy. Psychol Sci Public Interest 12:95–162
Stępień M (2014) The relationship between human nature and human rights. The Confucian example. In: Albers M, Hoffmann T, Reinhardt J (eds) Human rights and human nature. Springer, Dordrecht, pp 79–94
Tasioulas J (2011) On the nature of human rights. In: Ernst G, Heilinger JC (eds) The philosophy of human rights: contemporary controversies. De Gruyter, Berlin, pp 17–59
Tasioulas J (2013) Human dignity and the foundations of human rights. In: McCrdudden C (ed) Understanding human dignity. OUP, Oxford, pp 291–312
Tasioulas J (2015) On the foundations of human rights. In: Cruft R, Liao SM, Renzo M (eds) Philosophical foundations of human rights. OUP, Oxford, pp 45–70
Tomasello M (2009) Why we cooperate? A Boston Review Book, Cambridge, London
Vaish A, Carpenter M, Tomasello M (2010) Young children selectively avoid helping people with harmful intentions. Child Dev 8:1661–1669
Van Fraassen B (1980) The scientific image. OUP, Oxford
Wilkenfeld DA (2013) Understanding as representation manipulability. Synthese 190:997–1016
Woodward J (2019) Scientific explanation. The Stanford Encyclopedia of Philosophy (Winter 2019 Edition). https://plato.stanford.edu/archives/win2019/entries/scientific-explanation/
Załuski W (2009a) Evolutionary theory and legal philosophy. Edward Elgar, Cheltenham
Załuski W (2009b) Ewolucyjna Filozofia Prawa. Wolters Kluwer, Warszawa
Załuski W (2018) Law and evil. The evolutionary perspective. Edward Elgar, Cheltenham
Żywiczyński P (2019) Biological evolution, cultural evolution and the evolution of language. Review of Daniel Dennett's From Bacteria to Bach and Back Theoria et Historia Scientarum XVI:169–171

Chapter 8
Summary

Human rights are grounded in human nature—this is the main claim of this book. It follows from the claim that human rights are grounded in human dignity and that human dignity is grounded in human nature as it is accounted by recent discoveries of evolutionary psychology. More precisely, particular human rights (so those human rights that are related to some particular time and place) are grounded both in universal human rights (which are the right to liberty, the right to autonomy and the right to security) and in environmental and social facts. Universal human rights are grounded in human dignity, while human dignity is grounded in human nature. In such a way, due to transitivity, human rights are grounded in human nature (with reservation that it is partial grounding for particular human rights). As grounding involves explanation, the holding of human rights is explained by referring to their foundations—human nature.

Of course, such a reading of the foundations of human rights comes from adopting philosophical views that are the basis of this book—the project of naturalisation and the relational metaphysics. Notwithstanding, I argue that there are good reasons to adopt these projects of the contemporary analytic metaphysics. These projects have not yet been adopted in the philosophy of human rights so novelty of thought is one reason. The second reason is that applying these frameworks is helpful for the problems faced by the philosophy of human rights—the lack of clarity as for the relation holding between human rights and their foundations, whatever these foundations are according to one's notion, and the lack of references to natural sciences that are relevant for the discussion on human rights and their fundament. Therefore, as there are deficiencies in the dominant notions of human dignity—the Christian one assumes strong theological beliefs that are not universally acceptable, the classical one is based on philosophy that has strong metaphysical assumptions and is not widely endorsed, Kantian notion makes use of highly rationalistic way of thinking while its Kantian-analytic continuation is rather contradictory with the main claims of legally understood human rights.

Thus, I propose to regard human dignity as a value that must have foundations in some natural facts and I claim that evolutionary understood human nature is such a

S. Mazurkiewicz, *Grounding Human Rights in Human Nature*, Law and Philosophy Library 141, https://doi.org/10.1007/978-3-031-30734-8_8

fact. Evolutionary psychology by the use of scientific method claims that human nature is constituted by the tendency to cooperate (imperfect prudence and limited altruism in a slightly different notion). It can be claimed that such nature is good and as it is natural, innate, it can form the basis for inherent worth, which is human dignity. In such a way human dignity is grounded in human nature.

The route from human dignity to human rights is not difficult—human dignity as a value raises claim to its more concrete realisation and this realisation consists of universal human rights (the right to liberty, the right to autonomy and the right to security), which hold irrespective of time and space. Then, universal human rights along with concrete environmental and social facts give rise to particular human rights—rights that are universal but in relation to specific time and space. Most of the human rights mentioned in international documents on human rights are in this category—the right to free of charge elementary education, the right to healthcare, etc. So, universal human rights are grounded in human dignity while particular human rights are grounded both in universal human rights and in environmental and social facts. As grounding is transitive, universal human rights are grounded in human nature, and particular human rights are also, yet partly, grounded in human nature.

This way of looking at the foundations of human rights has several consequences. Grounding involves explanation so we can say that holding of human rights and of human dignity is explained by referring to what they are grounded in. I argue that in this case explanation involves also justification, therefore, human rights become justified by showing their natural-facts fundament. One of the objections raised against similar approaches to the foundations of human rights is the objection of essentialism and foundationalism. But they turned out to be misplaced as for my notion—the view that there is no such a thing like human essence perhaps may be true as for purely philosophical accounts of human nature, but is falsified by the recent discoveries of natural sciences, like evolutionary psychology, concerning human nature conceived as dominant tendencies in human behaviour. Then, foundationalism suggest that we cannot derive statements about human rights from any set of descriptive statements. But this view is based on a reading of the "is"-"-ought" gap that suggest that there can be only the relation of logical entailment between the relata of statement about human rights and their foundations. This is a very simplistic reading and more nuanced view based on the debate on the autonomy of ethics makes the case that the relation of grounding doesn't fall into the "is"-"ought" gap.

I also claim that it is my approach that not only doesn't fall to the objection of Western ethnocentrism, but moreover is able to dismiss it. Regarding evolutionary understood human nature as the foundation of human rights has nothing to do with solely Western thought and in fact claims of evolutionary psychology about human nature are compatible with the vision of human seen in Eastern cultures. Lastly, my account endorses the view that we have human rights due to positive aspects that we share, rather than we have them because of atrocities we are capable of doing.

Griffin proposed a method of assessing his approach, it was "by deciding whether it gives us human rights that fit into the best ethics overall".[1] I can rephrase this statement and say that the value of the account proposed in this book is by deciding whether it gives us the foundations of human rights that fit into the best metaphysics overall. Of course, the best metaphysics overall is a highly controversial matter (probably not even possible) and I don't claim that metaphysical background of my work is the best. But by far, these two projects that form the philosophical framework—the project of naturalisation and the relational metaphysics—are popular and *per se* rather not controversial so looking by their perspective at the foundations of human rights gives us the foundations of human rights that fit into contemporary notions of analytic metaphysics. And by referring to evolutionary psychology account of human nature it gives us the foundations of human rights that fit into recent discoveries of natural sciences.

Lastly, let me also present a summary of the book in points that form one conclusive line of argumentation. Each of these points is justified in the book.

1. International human rights documents and domestic constitutions claim that human rights derive from human dignity, or that human dignity is the source of human rights.
2. The key claim of the dominant, naturalistic approach is that "human rights are moral rights possessed by all humans simply in virtue of their humanity or being human".[2]
3. It is not clear what is the exact relation between human rights and their foundations, nor what is the foundation of human dignity.
4. Human dignity, as an inherent worth of every human being, exists due to something positive, more fundamentally valuable, or in general more fundamental about human.
5. This "something positive, valuable, more fundamental about human" can be named "human nature" and equates "humanity/being human" from the key claim of the naturalistic approach.
6. Following the requirements of methodological naturalism, human nature should be conceived of as it is understood in the relevant empirical science.
7. The relevant empirical science that researches human nature is evolutionary psychology. It claims that human nature is constituted by the tendency to cooperate, which is formed by altruism and collaboration,[3] or by the tendency to narrow altruism and imperfect prudence.[4]
8. Evolutionary understood human nature is the basis of the positive, optimistic vision of human.
9. This positive, optimistic vision of human is human dignity.

[1] Griffin (2008), p. 4.

[2] Griffin (2008), p. 2; Tasioulas (2011), p. 27.

[3] Tomasello (2009).

[4] Załuski (2009).

10. In such a way, human nature is the foundation of human dignity.
11. Human dignity is inviolable, but it requires more practical realisation.
12. This more practical realisation consists of universal human rights, i.e. human rights that do not depend on specific contingent conditions.
13. Therefore, human dignity is the foundation of universal human rights.
14. Due to (10) and (13), human nature is the foundation of universal human rights.
15. Universal human rights alone cannot determine the scope of various particular rights.
16. Thus, concrete environmental and social facts must be counted as foundations of particular human rights.
17. It follows that both universal human rights and environmental and social facts are foundations of particular human rights.
18. In such a way, the problem of universality of particular human rights is solved.
19. Since (13) and (17), human dignity is partly the foundation of particular human rights.
20. Since (10), (13) and (17), human nature is partly the foundation of particular human rights.
21. A reduction of particular human rights to universal human rights, universal human rights to human dignity, and human dignity to human nature is impossible.
22. Hence, ontological naturalisation in the philosophy of human rights is impossible, and methodological naturalisation is the most promising path to follow.
23. Particular human rights supervene on environmental and social facts and on universal human rights, universal human rights supervene on human dignity, human dignity supervenes on human nature.
24. Yet, supervenience is only a relation of a necessary covariance and has no explanatory force. It cannot express and explain why and how (10), (13), and (17) occur.
25. Particular human rights are metaphysically grounded in environmental and social facts and in universal human rights, universal human rights are metaphysically grounded in human dignity, human dignity is metaphysically grounded in human nature.
26. Since grounding is transitive, universal human rights are grounded in human nature and particular human rights are partly grounded in human dignity, and further in human nature.
27. Since grounding involves explanation, it can properly express (10), (13), and (17).
28. In such a way, the foundations of human rights are explained.
29. The explanation of existence of morally good entities means simultaneously their justification.
30. Hence, human rights are justified on the basis of their foundations.
31. The strongest objection against human rights is the objection of Western ethnocentrism.

32. Since this explanation/justification of human rights is not developed on the basis of solely Western ideas and is acceptable for members of any culture, the objection of Western ethnocentrism is rejected.

This is the way how human rights are grounded in human nature.

References

Griffin J (2008) On human rights. Oxford University Press, Oxford

Tasioulas J (2011) On the nature of human rights. In: Ernst G, Heilinger JC (eds) The philosophy of human rights: contemporary controversies. De Gruyter, Berlin, pp 17–59

Tomasello M (2009) Why we cooperate? A Boston Review Book, Cambridge, London

Załuski W (2009) Evolutionary theory and legal philosophy. Edward Elgar, Cheltenham